Powerful Voices

TRACKING POP

SERIES EDITORS: LORI BURNS, JOHN COVACH, AND ALBIN ZAK

In one form or another, the influence of popular music has permeated cultural activities and perception on a global scale. Interdisciplinary in nature, Tracking Pop is intended as a wide-ranging exploration of pop music and its cultural situation. In addition to providing resources for students and scholars working in the field of popular culture, the books in this series will appeal to general readers and music lovers, for whom pop has provided the soundtrack of their lives.

Listening to Popular Music: Or, How I Learned to Stop Worrying and Love Led Zeppelin
by Theodore Gracyk

Sounding Out Pop: Analytical Essays in Popular Music
edited by Mark Spicer and John Covach

I Don't Sound Like Nobody: Remaking Music in 1950s America
by Albin J. Zak III

Soul Music: Tracking the Spiritual Roots of Pop from Plato to Motown
by Joel Rudinow

Are We Not New Wave? Modern Pop at the Turn of the 1980s
by Theo Cateforis

Bytes and Backbeats: Repurposing Music in the Digital Age
by Steve Savage

Powerful Voices: The Musical and Social World of Collegiate A Cappella
by Joshua S. Duchan

Rhymin' and Stealin': Musical Borrowing in Hip-Hop
by Justin A. Williams

Sounds of the Underground: A Cultural, Political, and Aesthetic Mapping of Underground and Fringe Music
by Stephen Graham

Powerful Voices

THE MUSICAL AND SOCIAL WORLD
OF COLLEGIATE A CAPPELLA

Joshua S. Duchan

THE UNIVERSITY OF MICHIGAN PRESS

ANN ARBOR

First paperback edition 2016
Copyright © by the University of Michigan 2012
All rights reserved

Published in the United States of America by the
University of Michigan Press
Manufactured in the United States of America
⊛ Printed on acid-free paper

2019   2018   2017   2016   5   4   3   2

A CIP catalog record for this book is available from the British Library.

Library of Congress Cataloging-in-Publication Data

Duchan, Joshua S.
    Powerful voices : the musical and social world of collegiate a
cappella / Joshua S. Duchan.
        p.   cm. — (Tracking pop)
    Includes bibliographical references and index.
    ISBN 978-0-472-11825-0 (cloth : alk. paper) — ISBN 978-0-472-
02833-7 (e-book)
        1. Vocal groups—United States.   2. Music in universities and
colleges—United States.   I. Title.
    ML25.D83   2012
    782.5'08837873—dc23   2011043631

ISBN 978-0-472-03664-6 (pbk. : acid-free paper)

For Erin and Julia

Acknowledgments

Many people contributed to this book in a variety of ways, and to all of them I owe my sincerest thanks. First and foremost I must thank my wife, Erin, whose steadfast support has been a touchstone, and my daughter, Julia, whose infant smiles inspired me through the work's final stages. My parents, Lynn and Brian, and brothers, Peter and Evan, have also traveled this book's journey from its initial steps to its final form. Thank you for your unwavering confidence.

Of course, no work on collegiate a cappella would be complete without the assistance and perspective of the a cappella groups themselves. I thank the members, past and present, of the Boston University Dear Abbeys, Bowdoin College Ursus Verses, Bowling Green State University HeeBee BGs, Brandeis University Company B, Brandeis University Starving Artists, Brandeis University VoiceMale, Harvard University Fallen Angels, Michigan State University Capital Green, Northeastern University DownBeats, University of Michigan Amazin' Blue, University of Michigan Dicks and Janes, University of Michigan Gimble, University of Michigan Harmonettes, University of Pennsylvania Counterparts, University of Pennsylvania Off the Beat, Yale University Whiffenpoofs, and the three a cappella groups at Kalamazoo College: the Kalamadudes, Limelights, and Premium Orange. Esteemed members of the a cappella community have also been crucial in offering their seasoned views of the scene. I thank Katie Bank, Jaclyn Chisholm, Jim Diego, Don Gooding, Bill Hare, James Harrington, Mark Manley, Amanda Newman, Andrea Poole, Deke Sharon, Ben Stevens, and Sara Yood, as well as the many contributors to the discussion forums hosted by the Recorded A Cappella Review Board and the Contemporary A Cappella Society. I also thank Eric Wojahn at Solid Sound Studios, Ann Arbor, for his years of patience, advice, and hard work on several recording projects that inform my research.

The staffs at several libraries were helpful in locating various texts, images, and other items related contemporary and historical aspects of collegiate a cappella. In particular, I owe thanks to the Yale Music Library and Manuscripts and Archives (especially Remi Castonguay and Barry McMurtrey); the archival librarians at Boston, Brandeis, and Harvard Universities, as well as the University of Michigan; and the staff at the Upjohn Library at Kalamazoo College.

Much of the initial research for this book was undertaken as part of my doctoral dissertation at the University of Michigan. There I found a thriving community of musical scholars, whose feedback, criticism, and camaraderie have sustained me. I am particularly grateful to Kate Brucher, Christi-Anne Castro, Rebecca Fülöp, Charles Hiroshi Garrett, Sarah Gerk, Jesse Johnston, Alyson Jones, Amy Kimura, Fiona Linn, Nathan Platte, Colin Roust, Yona Stamatis, and Jim Wierzbicki for their feedback, over the course of many years, on ideas, conference papers, and early drafts of my work. Through professional societies and my faculty positions at Kalamazoo College, Bowling Green State University, and Wayne State University, I have been fortunate to meet others whose support and feedback have been especially helpful: Judah Cohen, Tom Evans, Rob Fallon, Sandra Graham, David Harnish, Andrew Koehler, Kathy Meizel, Mary Natvig, Leslie Tung, Jim Turner, Zaide Pixley, Kate Powe, Gillian Rodger, Kay Kaufman Shelemay, Marilyn Shrude, John Vander Weg, Denise Von Glahn, Amanda Villepastour, Elizabeth Wakefield, Jeremy Wallach, and Mary Wischusen. For the portions of this book that have appeared in earlier forms in other publications, I am especially thankful for the hard work and critical perspective of the anonymous readers of *American Music* and the *Journal of American Folklore* and their editors, Michael Hicks and Kati Szego, respectively. I'd also like to thank Chris Hebert, my editor at the University of Michigan Press, for his enduring confidence in my work and his efforts to help me shepherd this project from idea to publication.

Finally, the members of my dissertation committee at the University of Michigan deserve my heartfelt thanks for providing insight that helped to shape my thinking about the historical, analytical, anthropological, musicological, and ethnomusicological issues considered in these pages. Kelly Askew and Mark Clague offered critical perspectives that challenged my work and forced me to continually improve it. Albin Zak has been a valuable mentor through the dissertation and also as one of the editors of the University of Michigan Press's "Tracking Pop" series, whose ranks this book joins. And Judith Becker and Richard Crawford have been the foundation on which my scholarship rests—she for her intellectual rigor, vast ethnomusicological knowledge, and steadfast, no-nonsense support and he for his continual encouragement, enthusiastic engagement with my ideas, and the original suggestion that I "take that a cappella thing and run with it."

Copyright Permissions

Contents

Introduction

Sometimes it seems like one can visit any American college or university and collegiate a cappella groups are easy to find. In fact, a campus visit may not even be necessary, since many groups sing at community venues, travel the country on tour, upload their latest clips to YouTube, and even appear on the occasional television show. As self-directed ensembles of student singers, they arrange, perform, and record a repertory that draws heavily from pop/rock songs of the latter-twentieth and early-twenty-first centuries (though one hears the occasional jazz standard, Broadway show tune, novelty song, or non-Western piece), and they do so without instruments. Music faculties treat them variously as a good old college tradition, a mere curiosity, or a musical and curricular distraction.

College singing dates back at least to the fifteenth century at Oxford and Cambridge in England, and to the colonial era in the New World, but collegiate a cappella saw increased participation and growth in the twentieth century, most explosively in the 1980s and 1990s. A cappella groups usually consist of eight to sixteen singers and come in men's, women's, and mixed varieties. They are usually extracurricular activities; with few exceptions, students do not receive academic credit for their participation, and faculty leadership is nonexistent. Singing is as much a social activity as it is a musical pursuit, but most groups treat their musical efforts with some degree of seriousness.

A cappella is Italian for "in the style of the chapel" and today describes vocal music sung without instrumental accompaniment. In its broadest sense, it can describe genres from Gregorian chant (plainchant) to South African Zulu choral pieces to Islamic Koranic recitation to some Western choral works, barbershop quartets, doo-wop groups, and the ensembles examined here. I use the term *collegiate* (or *college*) to distinguish collegiate a cappella from other and earlier "classical," "light-classical," sacred, or vernacular *a cappella* choral genres. (Throughout this book, the term a cappella in a normal roman typeface indicates collegiate a cappella as a musical genre, practice, and community, while *a cappella* in italics indicates a more general sense of unaccompanied singing.) The term *collegiate* also separates collegiate a cappella groups from professional ones, which share a similar repertory but tend to be smaller in size, pay their members directly, travel more widely, and perform more frequently. Collegiate a cappella involves a significant number of people, as recent estimates place the number of a cappella groups in the United States, Canada, and the United Kingdom at around twelve hundred.[1] Meanwhile, for years the genre has received press coverage in major media outlets.

Singing *a cappella* is a musical technique that has been around for millennia, but collegiate a cappella may be distinguished musically by its repertory and the way it is translated into the voices-only medium. Vocal parts are conceived instrumentally. Emulation is balanced with originality as groups strive to sound like a song's original recording while offering their own interpretation of it. Recordings sometimes employ the technological tools of professional recording studios to create an idealized performance or alter vocal sounds to seem as close to a song's original recording as possible.

Socially, a cappella groups tend to be tight-knit ensembles in which close interpersonal relationships are formed. They are what Mark Slobin calls "affinity groups," "charmed circles of like-minded music-makers drawn magnetically to a certain genre that creates strong expressive bonding."[2] Most spend far more time rehearsing than giving live performances, and rehearsals are a site of socialization and the negotiation of a group's musical and social identity, a "microcosm of an idealized social system."[3] More broadly, a national (indeed, international) network has emerged through which individuals and groups encounter one another and share musical ideas through joint concerts, tours, competitions, recordings, and the Internet. An a cappella community can thus be found within any particular a cappella group, on any campus that includes a cappella groups among its student organizations, and can be felt by those who participate in this wider a cappella scene.

Culturally, a cappella enables young men and women to join together and share experience as they pass through the liminal space and time known as college, a delicate period during which identities are (re)formed on the path from adolescence toward adulthood. Singers offer each other emotional, social, and academic support while learning to lead and follow, manage time, and develop other skills through work toward shared goals. In rehearsals and performances, they not only reenact gestures and personae from popular culture but also embody and perform social roles to critique the world around them, from their campus to international politics.

A cappella is simultaneously an extension of a rather old way of making music and a product of historically situated newer ways of making music, which arose in the years following the advent of rock 'n' roll and rock music in the 1950s and 1960s. "The rock 'n' roll that emerged in the 1950s," writes Reebee Garofalo, "would define the broad parameters of popular music in the United States for at least the next forty years."[4] Moreover, with rock, as Theodore Gracyk and Albin Zak have shown, new creative avenues emerged that were technologically inspired.[5] Indeed, many aspects of a cappella are deeply informed by ideas embedded in rock music. On one level, rock's prominence of rhythm, gestures indicating an "authentic" performance, masculine character, and prominent use of technology all provided the foundation for a new way of thinking about music that a cappella singers embrace. On another level, a basic unit of rock music, the band, is largely replicated within a cappella groups as musicians learn cooperatively and forge social bonds—banding together—while their voices re-create the rock ensemble's sounds.

There are few publications on collegiate a cappella aside from the occasional newspaper or magazine article.[6] Anna Callahan wrote an instructional manual for collegiate a cappella arranging in 1995, and for years students have been writing academic papers on the topic in anthropology, folklore, linguistics, and music classes.[7] Mickey Rapkin's 2008 trade book, *Pitch Perfect: The Quest for Collegiate A Cappella Glory,* followed three groups during the 2006–7 academic year, weaving into their stories brief snapshots of other aspects of the a cappella world, from a nutshell version of its history to journalistic profiles of its major personalities.

As the first scholarly monograph on collegiate a cappella, this book sets out to delineate the practice, distinguish it from other vocal traditions, and explore its most important features and the social and cultural issues they raise. The mutual influence of musical and social forces is a theme that emerges repeatedly, from the discussion of how the music is made to the conditions under which the genre developed to the ways musicians use their group and its music to effect distinctions. The sometimes competing ideas of "purity," "authenticity," "naturalness," "artificiality," and "technology" reveal the ways in which a cappella is a mediated (and mediating) tradition, despite the discomfort this fact sometimes causes. Finally, musicians, the matters they attend to, and the benefits they receive from participating in the music—chiefly, the creation and maintenance of community—are crucial components of this research.

One idea to which this work returns again and again is power, a term the *New Oxford American Dictionary* defines as "the ability to do something" and, in a related sense, "the capacity or ability to direct or influence the behavior of others or the course of events." Power is at work in all facets of collegiate a cappella, from the minutest decisions regarding how to sing to the definition of "good a cappella" derived through direct or indirect interactions between groups of varying prestige and cultural capital. The basic questions "who controls or influences the way music sounds?", "who is empowered to make artistic decisions on the behalf of others?", "how do those decisions affect those of other musicians and musical groups?", and "how do the musicians and ensembles interact with their surrounding community?" are only sometimes posed by scholars and rarely asked by a cappella singers. Yet the answers shape the way the music is produced, experienced, and made meaningful.

This study joins a small but growing body of academic writing on choruses while adding to the broader field of music scholarship in several ways. It brings to the scholarly discourse on choral music a previously unexplored genre and a serious consideration of popular music, a topic historically fraught with discord and disagreement.[8] It also adds to the relatively sparse literature on amateur music making in the West, embracing those whom Ruth Finnegan calls "the hidden musicians" and their oftentimes ignored institutions.[9]

Importantly, this work pays attention to musical processes and group music making, which are sometimes lost in studies of popular music that focus on individuals and their products. Lately, some of the most promising ethnographic research on interaction between musicians may be found in genres such as jazz (e.g., Ingrid Monson's work) and Indonesian gamelan (Benjamin Brinner's).[10] Brinner's theories are particularly useful to the study of musical interaction in a broad sense, as his concept of musical "competence" is multifaceted and takes into account both musical and social contexts. Bringing these ideas to bear on a cappella not only shows their efficacy across genres but also brings vocal and popular musics into this scholarly domain.

Recent scholarship, such as the volume of essays *Chorus and Community*, has paid due attention to the formation and maintenance of communities through choral groups.[11] But whereas many studies have been circumscribed geographically, this one is multisited and defined by its practitioners, their repertory, and the ways they make music. Moreover, this work focuses its ethnographic methodologies on a context that is often marginalized in (ethno)musicological scholarship, the college or university campus—a place where much musical study happens but much musicking goes unnoticed. At the same time, due to its familiar locales, it resonates with the debates about "fieldwork" and "home-work" following anthropology's critical turn in the 1980s and 1990s, which problematized the (rhetorical) distance between sites of faraway ethnographic research and the closer-to-home production of ethnography.[12] Here, as in Ted Solis's *Performing Ethnomusicology*, that distance is collapsed.[13]

I began this project having already been an a cappella singer throughout college (with the University of Pennsylvania Counterparts) and graduate school (with the University of Michigan Amazin' Blue). While conducting fieldwork in Boston in 2004–5, I worked closely with groups from Boston, Brandeis, Harvard, and Northeastern Universities. I traveled to work with groups in Connecticut, Maine, elsewhere in Massachusetts, Michigan, New York, and Pennsylvania. And I conducted interviews and corresponded with a cappella musicians from Maine to California.

But most of my time in 2004–5 was spent with three groups: VoiceMale, a men's group at Brandeis founded in 1994; the Fallen Angels, a women's group at Harvard founded in 2000; and the Treblemakers, a mixed group at Boston University founded in 1996. I focused initially on the observation side of participant observation, attending at least one rehearsal per week with each group. Over time they began seeking feedback from me; I gladly offered my thoughts, as this reframed my presence there as an exchange of knowledge.[14] I also interviewed several members of each group. (Due to the number of direct quotations from interviews and personal communications throughout this book, they are not documented individually. Instead, please consult the bibliography.) When I returned to Michigan in the fall of 2005 to finish my dissertation, I continued to sing with and direct Amazin' Blue. When I joined the faculty at Kalamazoo College (Kalamazoo, Michigan), I helped start two a cappella groups there, and I remain an active participant in the a cappella community throughout the Midwest and elsewhere. All of this is to say that, like many ethnomusicologists, my writing is motivated both by a scholarly impulse—a desire to better understand the human condition—and by a dedication to and passion for the music I study and the musicians whose lives I have shared in the process. Ultimately, the research I present here reveals the close intersections between musical and social life by examining the ways in which musical and social processes shape each other and are shaped by human interaction in a historically situated, technologically mediated, and politically and culturally circumscribed context.

This book is organized in two parts. The first offers a brief historical sketch of the traditions and conditions from which collegiate a cappella developed. Providing a context for the analyses in part II, these chapters address nineteenth-century collegiate vocal ensembles, glee clubs, and barbershop harmony (chapter 1); the "first" a cappella group, the Yale University Whiffenpoofs (chapter 2), and several mid- and late-twentieth-century popular *a cappella* genres (chapter 3). The fourth chapter examines the a cappella "explosion" of the 1980s and 1990s, proposing several foundational developments that preceded this key event and exploring a few that resulted from it. While these chapters do not comprise a complete history of collegiate a cappella, the historical episodes they contain can hopefully be a first step.

Part II focuses on contemporary collegiate a cappella. It begins, in chapter 5, with a description of a cappella's musical components and the forces that shape them. This chapter may also serve as a primer for those who have never attended an a cappella concert or heard an a cappella recording, offering a sense of the music around which the rest of the practice centers. The remaining chapters proceed through the main activities in which a cappella musicians participate: rehearsals (chapter 6), performances (chapters 7 and 8), and recordings (chapters 8 and 9). Important issues are highlighted, including gender, sociability, and the politics in/of a cappella, as well as technology and the debates regarding the "naturalness" or "artificiality" of the music. Ethnographic and musical analyses support these arguments, but the aim is to explore how these issues—which recent scholarship has shown to be important in many musical traditions—play out in this musical practice.

While writing this book, I have been keenly aware that my audience includes at least two different sorts of readers: scholars, including musicologists, ethnomusicologists, and others interested in issues relevant to their disciplines, such as musical detail, cultural representation, and ethnographic nuance; and a cappella singers looking for a thorough and accurate account of their music along with the "objective" conclusions my academic perspective might yield (regardless of whether the scholarly readers believe such objectivity is actually attainable). Herein I attempt to satisfy both readerships while painting a broad, yet detailed, picture of a vibrant musical practice taken seriously by its participants and valued not only for its social and cultural functions but also because, when you get down to it, it's good fun.

PART I

Collegiate A Cappella's Predecessors, Inception, and Historical Moment

CHAPTER 1

From Nineteenth-Century Glee Clubs
to Barbershop Harmony

It might be tempting to look at recent pop culture and conclude that collegiate a cappella suddenly came out of nowhere. Or in 2009, to be exact. In its eighth season that year, the hit television show *American Idol* featured Anoop Desai, a member of the Clef Hangers, a men's a cappella group from the University of North Carolina, Chapel Hill. In April, piano-pop singer-songwriter Ben Folds released *Ben Folds Presents: University A Cappella!*, an album consisting entirely of a cappella renditions of his own compositions, with fourteen of the album's sixteen tracks recorded by collegiate groups.[1] After broadcasting the premier episode in May, the Fox television network aired the first season of its series, *Glee*, about a high school glee club; the second season featured the Warblers, an a cappella group from a rival school whose voices were provided by a collegiate group, the Tufts University Beelzebubs. And in December, NBC aired a four-episode singing contest featuring a cappella groups (three of which were current or former collegiate groups) entitled *The Sing-Off*, which was quickly renewed for additional seasons. In a newspaper article covering the competition, the president of the University of Virginia Hullabahoos, a men's group, is quoted saying, "[A] cappella was kind of dormant. Then, all of sudden, it's something everyone knows about."[2]

Collegiate a cappella did not suddenly appear in the early twenty-first century, however; it merely caught a good dose of the media spotlight. Instead, student vocal groups have been a central part of American college life since its inception. Although men and women have been singing without accompaniment for millennia, the roots of contemporary collegiate a cappella lay in three places: nineteenth-century choral singing on American college campuses, barbershop harmony of the late nineteenth and early twentieth centuries, and vocal popular music in the twentieth century. The first two are explored in this chapter, and the third will be discussed in chapter 3, a sequence that should not suggest the independence of each genre and practice. Rather, they often intersected and interacted, and each also shows traits both similar to and different from today's a cappella.

Choral Ensembles in Colonial, Federal, and Nineteenth-Century America

The church or meetinghouse was a common base for choirs in colonial and early federal America, especially among New England youth, where the teaching of collective singing to amateurs was institutionalized in a religious context.[3] The founding of secular societies dedicated to choral singing, such as the Handel and Haydn Society of Boston (1815), is also significant for the degree that they organized choral activity and invested it with prestige.[4] And choral singing grew as the nineteenth century continued. Old World glee clubs, particularly those in England and Germany, such as the Noblemen and Gentlemen's Catch Club in London (1761) and the Glee Club (1783), were models for American clubs such as the Deutsche Liederkranz (1847) and its rival, the Männergesangverein Arion (1854), both in New York City; the Mendelssohn Glee Club (New York City, 1866); the Apollo Club (Boston, 1871); the Apollo Club (Chicago, 1872); the Mendelssohn Club (Philadelphia, 1874); and other clubs in Midwestern cities.[5] Many were community efforts embracing the increasingly common rhetoric of edification and music as a moral force. For example, "rather than emphasizing stars, virtuosity, publicity, and the national stage, Chicago's choral music tradition [perpetuated] community ideals of participation, education, uplift, civic pride, and the local stage."[6] While many of these organizations, such as the Handel and Haydn Society of Boston, dedicated themselves to large-scale choral works with orchestral accompaniment, their European predecessors also performed short, smaller-scale secular pieces such as glees, catches, canons, and rounds. And although the glee repertory included pieces that called for women's voices, both the Old and New World clubs were largely men's domains.[7]

Students of the era followed suit. Published tune books and songsters present evidence of colonial choral groups at Yale and Harvard Universities whose repertory included psalms, fuging tunes, and drinking songs.[8] From the first commencement at Dartmouth College until the 1790s, the Musical Choir regularly sang anthems, including some composed by the school's graduates.[9] Marshall Bartholomew's unpublished history of the Yale Glee Club describes the Yale Musical Society as an ensemble of twelve chapel singers, founded in 1812. The singing of secular songs was first formally organized at Yale with the establishment, the same year, of the Beethoven Society, which also sang sacred works.[10] These ensembles sometimes formed the basis of what would become college or university musical societies and were significant for their cultivation of music as a pleasurable, and often religiously motivated, enterprise. They also provided instruction that was later taken up by music departments and singing clubs, disseminating musical know-how to members who later founded singing schools of their own.[11]

Student singing at Dartmouth thrived even before the founding of the Handel and Haydn Society or the ensembles at Yale. Although the Musical Choir had disbanded by 1805, a new singing club, the Handel Society, was formed in 1807 and soon performed at events closely associated with college life, such as commencement and prom. A precursor to the intercollegiate exchanges that would mark a cappella a century and a half later, the society also participated in instructional "conventions" and academic festivals in New England at a time when travel around the region, particularly during the winter, was no simple matter. The society's last recorded meeting was held in 1888, by which time the Dartmouth Glee Club had appeared.[12]

Student vocal ensembles of the nineteenth century not only preceded their twentieth- and twenty-first-century counterparts in their integration into college life but also in their sociability. In the early English glee associations and the later German-influenced clubs in American cities, club meetings were both musical and social affairs.[13] Likewise, drink and merriment abounded in college clubs. For example, in the Pierian Sodality, an early Harvard student instrumental group founded in 1808, meetings included brandy, punch, cigars, and convivial singing. Michael Broyles reports that the minutes of the group's meetings "make it absolutely clear that their principal purpose was to have a good time. Their activities and repertoires indicate a down-to-earth, high-spirited approach to music," which was viewed as "an indulgent amusement, simply one-third of the triad, wine, women, and song."[14]

College Glee Clubs

College glee clubs appeared in the mid-nineteenth century, with the first founded at Harvard in March 1858.[15] Pierian Sodality records indicate that the Glee Club was established by Benjamin William Crowninshield and shared rehearsal space with the sodality. Its first concert, on June 9 of that year, featured compositions by Europeans Mendelssohn, Donizetti, Cherubini, Lortzing, and Flotow, as well as Harvard alumnus Francis Boot. Mounted in Lyceum Hall, Cambridge, it drew an audience of six hundred.[16] Boston critic John Sullivan Dwight praised the group's vocal selections, drawing particular attention to its *a cappella* performance.

> The concert on Wednesday evening gave evidence of a higher musical culture among the students than past experience led us to expect. The vocal selections were mostly of a high order; and the instrumental pieces [performed by the Pierian Sodality], although belonging to the category of "light" music, were such as the occasion and materials required, and showed good skill and taste in treatment . . .
>
> Something in this right direction might be seen already in the performances of the "Glee Club," composed of sixteen voices, who sang the Mendelssohn part-songs, the Latin chorus, etc., wholly without accompaniment, with admirable blending, light and shade, etc.—quite up to the standard of our German "Orpheus," as we thought, and more uniformly in good tune.[17]

The following year, 1859, the University of Michigan Men's Glee Club was founded, followed by the Yale Glee Club in 1861 and others thereafter.[18]

College glee clubs were, and largely continue to be, single-sex ensembles. After all, most nineteenth-century institutions did not offer coeducational instruction. To perform a work for mixed choir, a men's glee club joined forces with a women's club. Harvard University drew on singers from nearby Radcliffe College, for example. The gender makeup also differentiates glee clubs from later university choruses, which were integrated ensembles likely to focus more exclusively on classical and sacred works.

Early college glee clubs usually operated without the direct involvement of faculty or university officials. The University of Michigan Men's Glee Club, for example, came under faculty leadership only in 1908, although the official history calls it merely an "advisory" role until the 1920s.[19] Music professor

Archibald T. Davison began leading the Harvard Glee Club in 1912, more than fifty years after its founding. The Yale Glee Club coalesced out of the tradition of extracurricular singing within each academic class, which was particularly strong at Yale in the 1840s and 1850s. Members of the Class of 1863 Glee Club, sitting on the fence around New Haven Green at Chapel and College Streets, recruited college organist Gustave Stoeckel, a German émigré, as their conductor. Student leadership was not completely absent, though, as assistant conductor Howard Kingsbury was a student member of the club.[20]

As with the Dartmouth Handel Society nearly sixty years earlier, early college glee clubs offered public performances in connection with university events. Unlike the earlier Dartmouth ensemble, however, their performances often featured both vocal and instrumental music. As Dwight notes in his review, early concerts by the Harvard Glee Club featured the Pierian Sodality. A performance on June 8, 1859, a year after the club's premier, featured the Haydn Flute Quintets, nos. VI and VII, as well as the overture to Verdi's *Ernani*.[21] Later, glee clubs shared the stage with banjo and mandolin clubs, which in the late nineteenth century enjoyed particular popularity.[22] At Michigan, for instance, such combined efforts began in the 1890s.[23]

The diversity of the glee club repertory varied by club. The Harvard Glee Club, for example, strongly emphasized European works. Its 1859 concert included pieces by Cherubini, Chwatal, Eisenhofer, Flotow, Härtel, Haydn, Kalliwoda, Kücken, Lorenz, Lumbye, Mendelssohn, Verdi, and Werner—all European art music composers or conductors.[24] Although Walter Spalding's 1935 history of music at Harvard notes that "even then the question between classical and so-called popular music was vigorously debated," the sample program he provides (from April 23, 1875) lists exclusively art music compositions, excepting only the final selection, "college songs," for which no named composer is credited.[25] When the club did mix in other genres, the reception was not always positive. Reviewing an 1874 concert in Portland, Maine, one critic observed a dissonance between the art music selections that comprised most of the program and the college songs that ended it: "The College songs were not as happily selected as they might have been, were not quite characteristic in fact. The students seemed a little afraid to unbend themselves, and one missed the old familiar choruses." The club, it seemed, was better suited to pieces like "Comrades In Arms," by Thomas Adams (an English composer and organist), than to Harvard college songs, for it was in the Adams piece that "the voices all showed evidence of careful culture."[26]

The repertories of other college ensembles were more wide ranging, however. The performances of the Pierian Sodality, founded decades before the Harvard Glee Club, were diverse from the start, including European classical pieces but also popular ballads, marches, and airs.[27] The Yale Glee Club's first tour, featuring sixteen concerts in Connecticut, Massachusetts, New Hampshire, and New York, included a Garibaldi Hymn and "Latin Songs" ("Interger Vitae," "Gaudeamus," and "Loriger Horatius"), "American Songs" ("Battle Prayer," "Springfield Mountain," "Nellie's Grave," and "Aunt Rhody"), "Madrigals and Airs" ("Ye Shepherds Tell Me," "Call John," "Play On," "Serenade," and "Barcarolle"), and "College Songs" ("Alma Mater," "Co-ca-che-luak," "Menagerie," "I-eel," and "Upidee").[28] The later combination of glee clubs with banjo and mandolin clubs indicates that this diverse repertory continued, even for the Harvard Glee Club. An 1891 concert included such pieces as "The Owl and the Pussy Cat," by Broadway composer Reginald DeKoven, and a double quartet titled simply "Drinking Song."[29] In the early twentieth century, folk songs were programmed as well. A 1923 promotional pamphlet for the Harvard Glee Club lists six pieces in its sample repertory, including three Russian songs ("Songs of the Lifeboat Men," "Fireflies," and "At Father's Door"), two Scottish songs ("The Hundred Pipers" and "Bonnie Dundee"), and one Irish song ("Lament for Owen Roe O'Neill").[30]

Glee clubs began as small choral groups, ranging from quartets to octets, and by the mid-1800s had become staples of college life and started to multiply. Yale student Carl Lohmann recalled, "Back in the eighteen-sixties and 'seventies, there were the Midnight Caterwaulers, the Beethoven Bummers, the Four Sharps, the Theologians, the Owls and probably others."[31] As faculty started to direct them, glee clubs sometimes grew. At the same time, however, they introduced smaller ensembles, drawn from within their ranks, as separate acts in their concerts to add variety to their program or to enable them to book more performances. Bartholomew writes, "Almost from the very beginning of its existence the [Yale Glee] Club had a quartet in its program. As a matter of fact, in the early days, graduates of the Glee Club and others organized small, informal singing groups (quartets) in addition to the Club."[32] By 1914, the University of Michigan Men's Glee Club boasted two such smaller groups, the Varsity Quartette and the Midnight Sons.[33] Such quartets or double quartets were well suited to barbershop harmony, particularly as that genre emerged toward the end of the century.

Why Sing in the Glee Club?

Why would nineteenth-century students organize themselves into glee clubs? What purposes did they serve? The most obvious answer is that they provided enjoyable experiences, musically and socially. In this way, nineteenth- and twenty-first-century collegiate singers share a basic goal. Another answer may be that singing in glee clubs helped students retain a sense of community and identity as they navigated their college experience. (This idea is explored in more detail in part II.) The early glee clubs at Yale, organized by academic class, would seem to have provided such social support. This would represent another similarity in the experience of collegiate singing spanning two centuries.

A third answer may be found in the concept of "college life," the world of extracurricular activities in which students participated. In her 1987 study of undergraduate culture during the nineteenth century, Helen Lefkowitz Horowitz shows how the school paper, athletic teams, fraternities, and music clubs were arenas in which certain young men sharpened their competitive teeth in preparation for life in business and society. Many students "perceived college as a field for combat . . . Each college man had something he could do. The codes of college life exempted no student from some form of extracurricular activity."[34] Participation was essentially mandatory since it developed the "proper taste" of a productive and cultured member of society. By contrast, according to Horowitz, it was the goal of the "outsiders" (Jews, immigrants, blacks, and farm boys aiming for the ministry) to raise their social standing and future prospects through college attendance. Participation in "college life" was not necessary to do so.

In women's colleges, similar extracurricular pursuits became central to the college experience. "Three areas dominated official campus life," Horowitz writes in a separate historical study of seven women's colleges: "organizations, athletics, and dramatics." The first area taught leadership, the second fostered teamwork, and the third enabled women to assume roles otherwise closed to them (including male/masculine ones). Dramatics in particular "saw almost universal participation" among students and gave rise to a competitive calendar of productions, some of which probably included music. Aside from socioeconomic status, it was partly through these areas of college life that students were sorted into a hierarchy of social groups.[35]

Thus, underlying the good times (and good drink) of college glee clubs were strong, implicit notions of the social purpose those clubs served: to affirm social distinctions. Indeed, as later chapters will show, distinction is also a prominent concept in contemporary collegiate a cappella.

Jubilee Choruses

Emerging parallel to the mostly white glee club tradition, jubilee choruses, found at historically black colleges, illustrate additional aspects of collegiate choral music in the nineteenth century. Perhaps most notable in this vein were the much-heralded Jubilee Singers from Fisk University, although other ensembles of a similar stripe, such as the Hampton Institute Choir, the Tuskegee Institute Choir, the Morehouse College Quartet (which performed for both Franklin D. Roosevelt and Herbert Hoover), the Wilberforce College Octette (composed of four women and four men), and the Howard University Glee Club, deserve mention.[36] They, and the imitators that followed, were significant for their pioneering efforts, which brought black music to the attention of a wide, northern, white audience.

Under the direction of a white teacher George L. White, the Jubilee Singers, an ensemble of nine singers plus a pianist, gave its first public performance (before even adopting its name) in Nashville in 1867, a year after Fisk opened its doors. Short trips to nearby towns followed, and in 1871 the group began touring nationally and internationally to raise funds for the university.[37] The Jubilee Singers was similar to the predominantly white a cappella groups that would emerge decades later in that it was a highly visible emblem of its institution. But while many of the vocal ensembles discussed earlier (as well as today's a cappella groups) performed at official functions on campus, the Jubilee Singers' fame derived from its performances off campus and for audiences unconnected with Fisk. Moreover, as a co-ed ensemble, the Jubilee Singers featured both men's and women's voices, a departure from the single-sex membership typical of college glee clubs.

The core of the jubilee chorus repertory was the "Negro spiritual," a genre of religious song associated with black church congregations in the South and derived from earlier, less formal black religious worship. Spirituals were often based on biblical verses or stories (such as the Jews' departure from Egypt, as described in Exodus, in the spiritual "Go Down, Moses"), but they were also reinterpreted in the context of black culture at the time. Based on a study of nineteenth-century anthologies, Sandra Graham shows that spirituals "not only penetrated, but were integral components of, white college song cultures" as early as the 1870s and were absorbed into the college glee club repertory by the 1890s.[38] Additionally, while maintaining the underlying principles of nineteenth-century black folk music (including syllabic singing, call-and-response, and dialect), the style of the black collegiate groups began shifting slightly toward a more Europeanized delivery. Recordings of the Fisk University quartet from 1909–11 reveal a vocal timbre "generally more reflective of European ideals" and a substitution of homophonic texture for a heterophonic one.[39]

American Barbershop and Close Harmony

Another type of small vocal ensemble arising in the nineteenth century that laid the foundation for today's collegiate a cappella is the barbershop quartet. A uniquely American genre, barbershop typically features four amateur singers in close *a cappella* harmony. Gage Averill traces the genre's roots to German and Austrian models, including the *Singverein* movement, German composer Franz Abt's many well-known part songs, and their presence on university campuses after having been transplanted by immigrants such as Stoeckel of the Yale Glee Club. European ensembles touring the United States in the mid–nineteenth century generated popular enthusiasm for vocal quartets, inspiring American versions such as the Euterpian Quartette, Boston Minstrels, and Hutchinson Family Singers, which performed ballads, comic songs, and airs of a patriotic or topical nature.[40]

Although sometimes perceived as a white tradition, like glee clubs, American barbershop harmony also has roots in African American vocal practices.[41] Indeed, in black vocal harmony in the late nineteenth century, singers whose notes were not part of a song's melody would change pitch while the melody note stayed constant, thus creating new chords in a technique called "snaking." The mixture of such chord progressions with their extemporization in practice "created new performative logics and chord vocabularies that flowered in black close harmony." Thus, while some distinguishing traits of barbershop musical practice have European precedents, they "also seem to respond to deeply traditional aspects of African American performance practice."[42]

As with collegiate a cappella, the barbershop repertory consisted largely of popular songs. During the genre's "golden era," from the 1890s through the first two decades of the next century, singers took enthusiastically to the songs of George M. Cohan and Irving Berlin but stayed away from the later styles of the

Gershwin brothers, Rogers and Hart, and Cole Porter. The harmonic proclivities of the earlier Tin Pan Alley generation, which included secondary dominant ("seventh") chords well suited to four-part vocal settings, faded with the later group, which favored extended chords like major sevenths, ninths, and elevenths, altered chords, and larger melodic leaps whose harmonies are more difficult to sing. By the 1930s and 1940s, the songs of the earlier generation had become canonized and reimagined, according to Averill, "not as commercial ephemera"—their original form—"but as a timeless heritage of American songs."[43]

Barbershop singing was institutionalized when O. C. Cash founded the Society for the Preservation and Encouragement of Barber Shop Quartet Singing in America (SPEBSQSA) in Kansas City in 1938. (It has since been renamed the Barbershop Harmony Society.) The new society formally organized the musical practice, emphasizing particular stylistic features, such as block chords, circle-of-fifths harmonic motion, and a relaxed approach to tempo.[44] Lyrics, which usually pertain to certain suitable topics (such as innocently cast courtship), should be uncomplicated, "clean," and delivered clearly. Competition and compositional rules specify a high level of homophony and low incidence of melisma. This texture enables as wide an audience as possible to appreciate the music and comprehend the lyrics, promoting "maximum inclusiveness" musically.[45] While many of these musical features, such as circle-of-fifths motion, relaxed tempo, and clean lyrics, did not leave a lasting impression on a cappella, the barbershop style did affect its earliest incarnation, as the next chapter will show.

The formalization of barbershop practice by SPEBSQSA also spurred the genre's ideological development, which focused on harmony as a metaphor for social cohesion and an egalitarian ideal.[46] Voices must cohere perfectly in the act of singing each chord, thus enabling each singer to embody social coherence. Meanwhile, the equal weight placed on each of the quartet's voices models an egalitarian outlook. Both effects are achieved at the intersection of musicality and sociability, but while the former continues into a cappella the latter does not.

An important aspect of barbershop's ideology is its emphasis on authenticity, its "discourse of the natural." Performers aim for the aural and visual appearance of "sing[ing] from the heart" even though the techniques used to achieve this goal during competitions, from the risers on which quartets and choruses stand to the costumes they wear and props they use to the carefully choreographed gestures they execute, reveal its constructedness. "Hence," Liz Garnett writes, "[T]he detailed schooling in technique instructs performers in the art of constructing an *illusion* of the natural, while the recourse to the discourse of the natural acts as a means to disguise this process of construction."[47] Good interpretation, then, "requires unanimity within the ensemble; the individuality of the performers is acknowledged, but is subordinated to the group."[48] Each performer must modify his or her presentation, vocal and gestural, to match that of fellow singers in the pursuit of a "unit" sound or perfect blend; the performance is ultimately a scrupulously mediated event, not a "natural" one. But barbershop's "discourse of the natural" generates an underlying aesthetic, what I call an "ideology of blend," which powerfully shapes the musical practice. Its force carries over into a cappella, where the concept of blend enjoys similar prominence and import.

Due to barbershop's compositional strictures, vertical considerations of harmony (such as chord quality) outweigh horizontal ones (such as voice leading). The emphasis on "ringing chords" over steady pulse runs counter to many styles of Western art and popular music, yet it is considered "natural," aesthetically pleasing, and essential. Its temporal elasticity implies that the performers and audience members have the leisure time to savor the ringing chords. In an empowering move, the singers stake their claim on that time. One can imagine how this implication might appeal to collegiate quartets whose members are reveling in the idea of controlling their own time in the face of competing academic and social pressures, whether in the nineteenth, twentieth, or twenty-first century.

As American society changed during the twentieth century, so, too, did barbershop. The efforts of SPEBSQSA cemented an image that was white and exclusively male, but in time, two additional societies devoted to American barbershop emerged: Sweet Adelines International (founded in 1945), devoted to women's barbershop; and Harmony, Inc., which split from the Sweet Adelines in 1959 following a disagreement over the admission of black singers. Institutionalized barbershop has also claimed its place on the collegiate music scene. The Barbershop Harmony Society's international Collegiate Barbershop Quartet Contest has been held annually since 1992, blossoming around the same time as the collegiate a cappella movement's explosion (see chapter 4).[49]

Amateur, unaccompanied singing has deep roots in American music, many of which bear a resemblance to today's collegiate a cappella. Glee clubs and their musical predecessors were thoroughly implicated in college life, whether singing in the college chapel, at commencement ceremonies in the 1780s, or in regional academic festivals or hanging out on the college green in the 1860s. They began as small groups, and as they grew in size they continued to field small quartets and octets, keeping the small ensemble (under about twenty members) a constant presence on American college campuses. And they were not strictly bound to campus but reflected a broader upswing in the founding of American choral societies in the mid-1800s.

Jubilee choruses differed from glee clubs racially, but in other aspects they continued the rise in nineteenth-century collegiate choral ensembles. As a consequence of their distinctive repertory entering the glee club tradition, the impact of the glee club on a cappella necessarily includes traces of black folk music and spirituals, even if, by the time the jubilee choruses were firmly established, some of their musical features had perhaps been slightly "Europeanized." Black improvised harmony also played an important role in the development of early barbershop, another a cappella predecessor. Moreover, jubilee choruses became musical ambassadors for their institutions, a role later a cappella groups would embrace.

Finally, the history of barbershop connects to a cappella in several ways. Bartholomew notes that the composition and style of early vocal groups associated with college glee clubs owe something to the influence of barbershop in their repertory, arrangements, and aesthetics. The repertory of barbershop quartets, unlike that of glee clubs, was almost exclusively secular, popular, and American in composition, a quality that largely carried over into a cappella practice. And barbershop's emphasis on an ideology of blend, as later chapters will show, remains an important aspect of how a cappella singers conceive of their music.

The practices of the glee club, jubilee chorus, and barbershop quartet converged in the Whiffenpoofs, the Yale University group often cited as the "first" a cappella group. Emerging from the Yale Glee Club in 1909, the group sang a repertory that was, in its beginning, based largely on barbershop-style arrangements and influenced by at least one local black barbershopper. The Whiffenpoofs, its history, and its role in the development of collegiate a cappella are the subject of the next chapter.

CHAPTER 2

The Whiffenpoofs:
The "First" A Cappella Group

Collegiate a cappella is often said to have begun at Yale University with the Whiffenpoofs.[1] Indeed, the men's ensemble holds a special place in a cappella's history. It is the oldest group still singing today, with a long and venerable tradition spanning over a century, and its music and performances have gone farther and reached broader audiences than those of other groups. Founded near the beginning of the twentieth century, the men have sung at the White House, Carnegie Hall, and the Rose Bowl and appeared on *The West Wing, Jeopardy!,* the *Today Show, Saturday Night Live, Gilmore Girls,* and *The Sing-Off.*[2] Cole Porter, among the group's oldest and most famous alumni, was a member of the 1913 lineup.

Given the history of vocal groups on college campuses, however, the claim that a cappella began with the Whiffenpoofs may be debatable. At the very least, the traditions discussed in the previous chapter suggest that the Whiffenpoofs were not unprecedented. Nonetheless, given its special status, it is worth exploring how this group came into existence, how it reflected the musical practices preceding it, how it grew and changed, and how contemporary incarnations of the Whiffenpoofs reflect and eschew broader trends in a cappella—the very idea of which was anathema when the group was founded.

The Formation of the Whiffenpoofs

The Whiffenpoofs emerged from the Varsity Quartet, a subset of the Yale Glee Club, in January 1909 and gave weekly performances at Mory's Temple Bar, a popular student pub in New Haven.[3] By the end of the semester its members had adopted their name, which refers to comedian Joseph Cawthorne's performance in the Broadway production of Victor Herbert's *Little Nemo* (1908). Cawthorne coined the term in 1891 while he and fellow actor, John D. Gilbert, were extemporizing nonsense verses: "A Drivaling Grilyal yandled its flail one day by a whiffenpoof's grave."[4] In *Little Nemo*, Cawthorne's nonsense was interpolated into a sketch about fishing; cheese was used as bait, which infuriated the whiffenpoof fish and caused it to come up to the surface, "squawk," and subsequently get caught. The Whiffenpoofs' version became, "If you infuriate us with food (and drink) we come up and squawk."[5] As founding member James M. Howard reports, "'Whiffenpoof' fitted in with our mood of free and exuberant fancy and it was adopted with enthusiasm."[6] Joining Howard that first year were Denton "Goat" Fowler, Carl "Caesar" Lohmann, Meade "Minnie" Minnigerode, and George "Doodle" Pomeroy (see fig. 2.1).

There were extracurricular student singing groups at Yale at least sixty years before the Whiffenpoofs, including the Cecilias (1856) and, later, the Beethoven Bummers, Owls, Four Sharps, Midnight Caterwaulers, and Theologians.[7] The group the Black Sheep was formed on Friday, February 7, 1902, over dinner at Mory's and held its last meeting in June of that year. The name may have been drawn from a musical setting of Rudyard Kipling's 1892 poem, "Gentlemen-Rankers," which refers to "little black sheep who've gone astray."[8] The Black Sheep was also known as "Six Little Lambs," since there were six members, and they would substitute their number (or the number of singers present) for "poor" in Kipling's line "poor little lambs who've lost our way." The Growlers, whose membership included singers who would later start the Whiffenpoofs, was active in 1907 but disbanded in the fall of the year following the graduation of its first tenor; it also sang regularly at Mory's. The group's founding members each had a nickname, a tradition that continued in the Whiffenpoofs.[9] Its repertory included Mae Auwerda Sloane's "My Evalyne," a setting of the 1861 George Wither poem "Shall I, Wasting in Despair," and the *Yale Song Book* arrangements of the traditional tunes "I Got Shoes," "And When the Leaves," the spiritual "The Moaning Lady," and the Joseph Warren Fabens poem "The Last Cigar."[10]

As the Black Sheep and the Growlers illustrate, groups usually did not last long. The Whiffenpoofs bucked this trend. As Howard's history explains, the drafting of a constitution was an important step in formalizing the group and ensuring its "perpetuity."[11] The original document limited the group to seven men, but others were soon included as "honorary members" or "perpetual

Fig. 2.1. The founding members of the Yale University Whiffenpoofs, 1909. *From left:* Denton "Goat" Fowler, James "Merry" Howard, Carl "Caesar" Lohmann, Meade "Minnie" Minnigerode, and George "Doodle" Pomeroy. (Photo courtesy of Yale University Libraries.)

guests." As members left for military service during World War II, numbers dwindled; in response, the membership was officially expanded. One year during the war, only one Whiffenpoof remained on campus, prompting an alumni effort to reconstitute the group. The group now admits fourteen senior men annually for terms of one year. I was told that the group's performance schedule is so demanding that some members take the year off from college to participate. Members are selected by audition during their junior year, judged by the outgoing singers. This system distinguishes the Whiffenpoofs from most other a cappella groups, whose ranks are not similarly restricted.[12]

Repertory and the "Whiffenpoof Song"

The Whiffenpoofs' repertory began with a small handful of tunes, including "Shall I, Wasting in Despair" and "Mavourneen," an adaptation of "Barney

O'Flynn," from the operetta *Babes in Toyland* (1903). Both are mentioned in the "Whiffenpoof Song," an adaptation of Kipling's "Gentlemen-Rankers," which quickly became the group's signature song. This poem depicts young nineteenth-century English soldiers with an endearing, sympathetic fatalism.

> To the legion of the lost ones, to the cohort of the damned,
> To my brethren in their sorrow overseas,
> Sings a gentleman of England cleanly bred, machinely crammed,
> And a trooper of the Empress, if you please.
> Yes, a trooper of the forces who has run his own six horses,
> And faith he went the pace and went it blind,
> And the world was more than kin while he held the ready tin,
> But to-day the Sergeant's something less than kind.
>
> We're poor little lambs who've lost our way,
> Baa! Baa! Baa!
> We're little black sheep who've gone astray,
> Baa—aa—aa!
> Gentlemen-rankers out on the spree,
> Damned from here to Eternity,
> God ha' mercy on such as we,
> Baa! Yah! Bah![13]

The term *gentlemen-rankers* derives from military classification, indicating "men who had risen from the ranks but were of noble birth" at a time when commissioned officer corps were drawn primarily from the aristocracy rather than enlisted men.[14] John Whitehead describes gentlemen-rankers as "the 'black sheep' of a good family who, having been disinherited for some misdemeanor, had been forced, though belonging to the 'officer class,' to join the army as private soldiers."[15] Thus, the term carries implications that apply to the gentlemen-songsters, who enjoyed a certain privileged status but had to work their way up the class ranks to achieve it.

The story of the "Whiffenpoof Song" is clouded and mercurial. "Gentlemen-Rankers" was in the air before the Whiffenpoofs adopted it. College students around the turn of the twentieth century studied English poetry as part of their curriculum, so Yale students were likely familiar with the poem. But there are conflicting accounts of Yale singers' encounters with it. Howard claims it was "known to have been sung at Yale as far back as 1902."[16] The Growlers is also reported to have sung a version of the song in 1907.[17] According to another story, Judge Tod B. Galloway (Amherst, Class of 1885), wrote the melody at an alumni "smoker" party in Columbus, Ohio, on January 1, 1908, and subsequently performed it for Yale Glee Club members on their Christmas tour. However, music historian Sigmund Spaeth reports that the melody was instead composed by Guy H. Scull (Harvard, Class of 1898).[18] By the time the "Whiffenpoof Song" was included in Marshall Bartholomew's 1935 edition of *Songs of Yale*, it was attributed to Minnigerode, Pomeroy, and Galloway, with no mention of Scull.[19]

The Whiffenpoofs' early assimilation of the song, as well as its importance, is shown by its inclusion in the group's constitution. Section II, article IV states, "The meetings shall open and close with the singing of the 'Whiffenpoof Anthem'; at the close, all standing," and continues by specifying that the anthem "shall under no consideration be sung at any other time or place."[20] This practice was dropped after a recording of the song by crooner Rudy Vallée (a 1927 Yale graduate who was never in the Whiffenpoofs) aired on the popular NBC radio show, *The Fleischmann Hour*. Vallée first recorded it in 1937, followed by Bing Crosby, Perry Como, Elvis Presley, Count Basie, and others.[21] Vallée's use of the song caused much controversy within the group, between the Whiffenpoofs and Vallée, and between Vallée's publisher (Miller Music) and Yale.

"Gentlemen-Rankers" experienced some changes when adapted as the "Whiffenpoof Song." Kipling's tone is serious, with his opening dedication to fallen comrades and a slow, downward spiral into despair and, eventually, death: "And the Curse of Reuben holds us till an alien turf enfolds us / And we die, and none can tell Them where we died." Minnigerode and Pomeroy's tone is more sarcastic, drawing on the close male social bonds of the gentlemen-rankers but recasting their plight into a less threatening environment, where "passing" may imply graduation rather than expiration: "We will serenade our Louis while life and voice shall last / Then we'll pass and be forgotten with the rest." The new chorus bears a similar tone.

> We're poor little lambs who have lost our way: Baa! Baa! Baa!
> We're little black sheep who have gone astray: Baa! Baa! Baa!
> Gentlemen songsters off on a spree
> Damned from here to eternity
> God have mercy on such as we: Baa! Baa! Baa!

In Howard's analysis, the changes in the lyrics "transmute the cynicism of an old barrack-room at some forsaken outpost of the British Empire to the genial atmosphere of Mory's." The "bitterness" of "a group of young aristocrats, disinherited perhaps, serving as enlisted men in Her Majesty's forces and drinking themselves to death" disappears in favor of good old-fashioned collegiality, as "gentlemen-rankers" become "gentlemen-songsters."[22] Moreover, Minnigerode and Pomeroy customized the song's lyrics to include a reference ("we will serenade our Louis") to Louis Linder, the first honorary Whiffenpoof and the proprietor of Mory's from 1908 until his death in 1913.

The lyrics of the "Whiffenpoof Song," like Kipling's text, are striking for their fatalistic tone, which binds men together in common experience and suggests a formidable adversary. Under such conditions, the characters are driven to drink (Kipling: "Can you blame us if we soak ourselves in beer?"; Minnigerode and Pomeroy: "assembled with their glasses raised on high"). In the male collegiate context of the late nineteenth and early twentieth centuries, it was common to portray college life as a war between students and their professors.[23] (One can imagine how the consumption of alcohol at Mory's could exaggerate this view.) Like Kipling's young officers, Yale's college men may have been far from home and were certainly in a competitive environment, albeit one of different stakes. In the eyes of the faculty, the Whiffenpoofs may have been "poor little lambs who have lost [their] way" or "little black sheep who have gone astray," but in singing those lines together the students seize their agency. They ask not for sympathy or pity, although their sarcasm might at first suggest it, but instead revel in their condition because it brings them together in musical fraternity to enjoy life before embracing the responsibility of the competitive postcollege world.

Musically, the "Whiffenpoof Song" emphasizes group unity and an overall harmonic consonance and balanced form (see example 2.1). Unity is suggested most directly through the song's homophonic, block chord texture, in which each of the four voice parts sings the same rhythm at the same time. There is little in the score to suggest room for improvisation, and no voice departs from the others in any significant fashion, a move that might suggest a measure of independence.[24] The harmonic structure reinforces the solidarity suggested by the vocal homophony. Tonic and dominant harmonies in G major comprise twenty-eight of the verse's thirty-two measures.[25] The chorus reveals more varied harmonies (vii^7/ii in mm. 33 and 41 and vi$^6_4$ in m. 48) and a few moments of chromatic voice leading (e.g., the baritone A–A$^\#$–B in mm. 37–38 and the chro-

Example 2.1. Excerpt from the "Whiffenpoof Song." (Used by permission of Alfred Music Publishing Co., Inc.)

matic descent in the bass, G–F#–F in m. 55). But even the ultimate cadential phrase, mm. 56–63, while featuring the heightened tension of a secondary dominant (V^7/ii in m. 56), reverts immediately to more conventional harmonic procedure. The result is an overall sense of stability, of the song departing little and at not too great a distance from the familiar confines of the G-major tonality.

Harmonic stability is reinforced as conventional forms balance the song with a thirty-two-bar ABAC verse and a thirty-two-bar AABA chorus. Of the verse's four eight-measure phrases in 2/4 time, the first three differ melodically only at the cadence (ending on a B, G, and B respectively), while the fourth takes the melody into a higher range, stops momentarily on a dissonant fermata, and then concludes with the melodic shape of the second phrase. The chorus, also comprising four eight-measure phrases, has a more regular feel to it, with steadier and predictable rhythms in 3/4 time as well as the repeated refrain, "Baa, baa, baa!" The melody is generally restricted to chord tones in the first, second, and fourth phrases. In the third, the tonic major-seventh chord, with the melody on the seventh (m. 54), adds a touch of interest by delaying the melodic resolution until the last measure of the phrase while simultaneously executing a *poco rit.*, as if to evoke "eternity."

Much of the song's social meaning is generated in the act of singing. Although the original score does not suggest it, in practice the Whiffenpoofs often treat the verse nonmetrically, as can be heard, for example, on the recording of the song from the album *The Whiffenpoofs of 1958* (1958). Without a strong sense of meter, the rhythms are less easily predicted. This temporal elasticity, reminiscent of barbershop practice, requires that the men spend time together, rehearsing the timing and dynamics of each phrase and ensuring that the chords lock and ring correctly. A successful performance is one in which the men coordinate their voices, an embodied discipline that reinforces a sense of unity. The stronger rhythmic pulse that arrives in the chorus invites a swaying motion that adds to the men's physical entrainment. Thus, the lived experience of singing the "Whiffenpoof Song" fosters a feeling of community. In this way, the "Whiffenpoof Song" acts not only as a musical emblem of the group but as a musical embodiment of their social relationships, a musical artifact found in many of the collegiate a cappella groups that would follow.

The Whiffenpoofs' Interracial Interactions

One of the more fascinating episodes in the Whiffenpoofs's early history involves the interaction between the founding members and black musical practice. Indeed, black music had long included *a cappella* harmony among its most distinctive aspects. And if, as Sandra Graham suggests, spirituals had entered the glee club repertory by the 1890s, it would not be surprising for the founding members of the Whiffenpoofs to have encountered such music as they sang with the Yale Glee Club or the Growlers.[26] But they also reportedly encountered it outside the Glee Club through Bill Hillman, a black itinerant barber and letter carrier from Tuscaloosa, Alabama, who arrived in New Haven in 1902 and

sang with a quartet there. According to Minnigerode's account, Hillman taught
songs "by ear" to more than one Yale quartet.

> My first contact with him was in Freshman Year when I was in the Apollo
> Glee Club, and was chosen for the Quartet. We went to Goat Fowler's room
> in the Hutch on Crown St. and there was Hillman to teach us some songs. He
> lined us up and then in each guy's ear, line by line of the song, he sang each
> part of the harmony with words. When we had one line of the song down pat
> he went on to the next. Naturally his rhythm and phrasing of the words were
> exactly the same for each part, which made for excellent timing by the quar-
> tets he instructed.[27]

The precision of Hillman's singing aligns his vocal style with that of barbershop
harmony, wherein finely coordinated phrasing is necessary for the lyrics to be
clearly understandable. Minnigerode's account illustrates the early Whiffenpoofs' connection not only to the barbershop style—much of the group's early
repertory was improvised in that tradition—but also to a specifically black
style.

Bartholomew insists that the "Negro influence" was felt rather strongly at
Yale before World War I, when many students came from the South by ship
(and later railroad) and when New Haven was a summer resort for southern-
ers. He points to the "Whiffenpoof Song," observing that the melody of the first
phrase of the verse and the chorus are borrowed note for note from the spiritual "Been a-Listinin' All the Night Long."[28] In fact, although written in different keys (G major and B-flat major respectively), those phrases are similarly
constructed. In each, the melody skips downward from the fifth scale degree to
the third, then from the fifth down stepwise to the fourth. (In the "Whiffenpoof Song," this takes us as far as "To the tables down at Mory's, to the place
where Louis dwells" in the verse and "We are poor little lambs who have lost
our way" in the chorus.) Moreover, both phrases move from tonic to dominant
harmonies. Beyond these opening passages, the melodies diverge and the resemblance is lost.[29] But the fact that the melodic and harmonic resemblance
exists strongly suggests that the spiritual influenced the melodic composition,
if not the character, of the "Whiffenpoof Song." The "Whiffenpoof Song" remains today the cornerstone of the Whiffenpoof repertory, still sung at every
performance.

The Stylistic Evolution of the Whiffenpoofs

In the years surrounding World War II, close harmony singing at Yale saw significant stylistic changes. Bartholomew observed:

> Even the traditional barbershop has long since given way to a more sophisti-cated kind of informal singing—we might call it educated barbershop—with any number from eight to twelve taking the place of the original four. It is a real discipline for these informal groups as they perform today. As the result of a better grounding in music and the advantages of a better musical education be-fore coming to Yale, the arrangements are not so stereotyped as in the old days. The harmonies, counterpoint and rhythms are involved and original, and per-haps the most important thing of all is the intensive rehearsing that the better of these groups undergo. Some of the organizations rehearse almost every day and even get together before college opens for a week or two of preliminary work. The songs they choose are still very much on the popular side but the performance is frequently expert, elaborate and difficult. The old four-part singing is more frequently than not eight or ten parts.[30]

This description of the new singing style on campus is remarkably prescient. Nearly all of the aspects identified here remained true throughout the twenti-eth century and continue in today's collegiate a cappella, from the number of singers per group to the quality of the arrangements to the fervor and intensity of rehearsals.

Dovetailing nicely with Bartholomew's observations, Richard Nash Gould breaks the Whiffenpoofs' style into three historical periods, beginning with the "barbershop style," 1909–49. Four-part arrangements predominated, although sometimes a fifth part (a "rover") was added. The melody line was most often in the second tenor part (typical of barbershop), and harmonies and rhythms were of rather simple and straightforward construction. Few songs featured so-los, and many were initially drawn from the *Yale Song Book*. Later selections came from vaudeville, burlesque, and popular Tin Pan Alley hits but also in-cluded spirituals, coon songs, and the occasional number from an operetta, such as Howard's arrangement of "Velia" from Franz Lehár's operetta, *The Merry Widow*.[31]

The second period was the "jazz style," 1950–69, which included arrange-ments of five or six parts, a high proportion of solos, and a repertory drawn from musical comedy and traditional songs. Barbershop songs remained but were frequently "upbeat novelty items, notably old chestnuts rendered almost tongue-in-cheek" or new songs composed purposefully in that style. New elements also emerged, including a richer harmonic vocabulary (such as ninths, added sixth chords, augmented triads, and diminished sevenths) and the introduction of more complex rhythms. The expanded harmonic palette drew inspiration from musical theater, specifically the works of George Gershwin, Jerome Kern, Richard Rogers, and Whiffenpoofs alumnus Cole Porter. Certain techniques were employed to support songs that featured soloists, such as parallel motion and elevation of the melody from the second tenor part to the first. The increasing frequency of arrangements for solo voice with vocal accompaniment may have resulted from the embrace of musical theater, but it also points to an evolving idea of the singing group as a band of individual solo-quality voices rather than a strictly equal-voiced collective. With the melody in the top voice, it no longer competed with the others and could be more easily recognized than in a typical barbershop setting, while giving the lower voices greater "freedom to assume different configurations—either closely spaced or widely separated."[32]

In the "diverse style," beginning in 1970, songs remained in five or six parts with a high proportion of solos, and musical sources included folk, rock, musical comedy, and soul. At times, the group included instrumental accompaniment in its performances, although *a cappella* singing remained the core of its practice. New arrangements featured songs by Burt Bacharach ("Raindrops Keep Falling on My Head"), Lennon and McCartney ("Let It Be"), and Joni Mitchell ("I Don't Know Where I Stand"). Facing a "crisis of relevance" in the 1970s, the group members made their live performances more spontaneous, talking more directly to the audience and putting on a more theatrical show than before; they became more of an "extroverted, versatile, and polished group of individual entertainers." Soloists more frequently personalized their songs, which had been "formerly sung with cool, reverent uniformity." In the 1980s, they also introduced choreography to their shows, enhancing their comedic aspects and overall theatricality.[33] This style would seem to bring the Whiffenpoofs closer to that of contemporary collegiate a cappella groups.

A Twenty-First-Century Whiffenpoofs Performance

The history of the Whiffenpoofs outlines a compelling narrative. A small group of good-natured, white Yale "college boys" establishes a singing group (with a good dose black barbershop technique) that quickly becomes an institution, not only within their university but within an entire musical genre. As the century progresses, their style continues to evolve and they remain an important force in the genre they established. The problem is, when I saw the Whiffenpoofs perform at Harvard University in November 2004, I witnessed a group that did not quite meet the expectations raised by this interracial encounter or Gould's stylistic history.

One of the remarkable aspects of black barbershop in its early days was its improvisatory nature. Indeed, Minnigerode's memory of learning songs from Hillman "by ear" leaves open the strong possibility that some of the Whiffenpoofs' early songs were improvisatory in nature. Gould's history makes a point of the fact that the group's early performances at Mory's were mostly improvised and much of the early repertory was not written down.[34] But today's Whiffenpoofs seem anything but improvisatory. My notes include references to several musical passages that *suggested* improvisation but were clearly not actually improvised. For example, at one point during "The Girl From Ipanema," the background singers (consisting of most of the group, behind a soloist) sang humorous phrases, such as "beggars can't be choosers!," poking fun at the song's protagonist. Because this lyric was sung in harmony by several voices, it was clearly part of the arrangement rather than an in-the-moment extemporization.

A lack of actual improvisation can perhaps be attributed to nearly a century of evolution of the Whiffenpoofs' style. However, other aspects of the performance were hardly characteristic of the group's so-called diverse style. In fact, the Whiffenpoofs' performance, featuring the men in their signature tuxedos with tails and white gloves, was generally rather subdued. Afterward, I wrote in my field notes:

> Even the more recent, "popular" numbers were delivered in a restrained manner. The guys didn't seem to interact with each other; they just stood there and sang. In most cases the soloists, too, were expressionless in their delivery (however impeccably in tune it was), leaving the lyrics and melody to carry the songs' emotion rather than any other aspect of their performance such as articulation, delivery, or gestural or other performance techniques. The Whiffs used no vocal percussion—the snapping on "Waiting In Vain" [the only time in the show when the men removed their white gloves] was the most percussive the group got the entire night—and their syllables were extremely smooth, focusing on open vowels, tight blend, and carefully placed breaths.[35]

Thus, I found little of the "personalized" solos and very limited choreography; a routine of humorous gestures delivered by three members standing near the soloists on "Midnight Train to Georgia" was the choreographic peak. On the other hand, the group's vocal style emphasized the same qualities found in barbershop practice.

So while it may be a stretch to say that the founding members' encounters with Hillman had a clear and lasting effect still evident today, it is clear that some aspects of barbershop (and, I would argue, choral) practice remain in force. And if the Whiffenpoofs' performance style in the first decade of the twenty-first century retreated somewhat from that of its last stylistic period, this merely demonstrates that the group's style, like any musical tradition, is constantly changing.

One conclusion to draw from the Whiffenpoofs' performance is that the group has different musical aspirations than most other contemporary collegiate a cappella groups (see chapter 5). Its style seems older, timeless, classic. Its members eschew the harsher-sounding syllables found in other groups' arrangements. They value entertaining the audience—albeit in their own way—over faithfully emulating an original recording. And their bodily movements are much more rigid and restrained than the fluid, bopping bodies one sees at other groups' concerts. Indeed, such individualized movements may be counter to the exceptionally unified image—and sound—the Whiffenpoofs aim for, in which opportunities for a single person to stand out (in a way perhaps reminiscent of a "rock star") are purposefully rare. Thus, the Whiffenpoofs' performance style may not be representative of today's a cappella, but the performers' sense of group unity and artistic excellence remains firmly rooted in the ensemble's history and continues to resonate in the music's wider contemporary practice.

CHAPTER 3

Doo-Wop and Late-Twentieth-Century Vocal Pop

The last two chapters outlined several forms *a cappella* harmony took in the United States in the nineteenth and early twentieth centuries and looked closely at one particular manifestation of it, the Yale University Whiffenpoofs. The kind of music the Whiffenpoofs made in their early years was both similar to and different from the kinds of vocal harmony that would develop and become popular in the mid- and late twentieth century. This chapter discusses three of those forms: vocal harmony in the swing era, doo-wop around midcentury, and vocal pop closer to its end. These brief glimpses reveal musics that achieved popular success in American musical culture and became predecessors of later collegiate a cappella.

Early Recorded Vocal Harmony and the Mills Brothers

Vocal harmony has long featured prominently in popular music, with black and white quartets among the first to record on phonograph and gramophone.[1] As the nascent recording industry entered the twentieth century, it continued to include vocal ensembles, one of which was the Mills Brothers. Although not the only well-known black vocal group of its time (others included the Ink Spots, for example), their recordings crossed racial lines. In 1932, for instance, they recorded with the popular Boswell Sisters.

Consisting of brothers Herbert, Harry, Donald, and John Mills Jr. from Piqua, Ohio, the Mills Brothers was one of the most successful vocal groups of the swing era, and the brothers' recording career included collaborations with Bing Crosby, Ella Fitzgerald, and Louis Armstrong.[2] Although secularized, their style drew on a long-standing tradition of black religious vocal music stretching at least as far back as the jubilee choruses of the mid–nineteenth century (like that of Fisk University) and later popular gospel quartets (such as the Golden Gate Quartet). They began singing together around 1922 and in 1929 became the first black ensemble to receive official commercial sponsorship by a major network, CBS.[3] Among their early hits was a version of the Original Dixieland Jazz Band's "Tiger Rag," which featured their smooth, jazz-influenced, and well-blended harmonies. They recorded it multiple times in October 1931 and again in 1932 for the soundtrack to the film *The Big Broadcast* (1932).

The Mills Brothers was distinctive because of its vocal imitation of instruments, which sounded more realistic than similar mimetic efforts like scat singing. For instance, "Tiger Rag" features a tubalike bass tone and a remarkably convincing vocalized muted trumpet. These imitations supposedly began when one day the singers forgot to bring their kazoos to a local concert. They cupped their hands over their mouths, attempting to re-create them vocally. The new sound was striking enough to land them a regular show on the radio station WLW and eventually to begin recording for the Brunswick label in 1931.[4] Their instrumental imitations were convincing enough, and important enough to their style, that their early records bore the disclaimer "no musical instruments or mechanical devices used on this recording other than one guitar."[5]

All of the Mills Brothers' 1931 and 1932 recordings of "Tiger Rag" include a chorus-length scat section followed by an equally long vocalized trumpet solo. These two improvisatory (or at least improvisatory-sounding) sections take up fully half of the song, sandwiched between the opening chorus, sung to harmonized lyrics, and a nearly identical closing chorus. The fact that this vocalized trumpet remained a feature of the piece over the course of several recordings suggests that the brothers themselves considered it central to their act. By contrast, at the time of "Tiger Rag" the Whiffenpoofs was in its "barbershop period," whose style did not feature instrumental imitation.[6] So while the Mills Brothers' vocal harmony was not influenced by collegiate a cappella at the time, one of its most distinctive techniques eventually became one of a cappella's central pillars.

Doo-Wop

A few decades later, black men's vocal groups carried on another *a cappella* tradition: doo-wop. This genre drew on the black vocal harmony groups of earlier decades, such as the Mills Brothers and the Ink Spots, and later successes like the Ravens and the Orioles. The term *doo-wop* was retrospectively applied in the early 1960s to vocal music from the previous decade, and even then it was familiar mainly to an African American audience.[7] It was a racially marked, vernacular, street-corner tradition of amateur quartets or quintets.[8] Five basic elements formed its stylistic core: vocal group harmony; a wide range of voices including the lead, first tenor (singing in falsetto), second tenor, baritone, and sometimes-independent bass; the use of nonsense syllables; a simple beat (and later the use of light instrumentation); and simple music and lyrics.[9] Like most of rock 'n' roll, doo-wop prominently featured a soloist, creating a lead-and-accompaniment texture that singers called "backgrounding," an aspect collegiate a cappella shares in practice if not in name.[10]

Doo-wop was primarily local music, found mostly in urban centers such as New York, Chicago, and Philadelphia. Successful groups performed at local clubs and earned contracts with local record companies. One example is the Five Satins, a black group from New Haven, which scored a hit with the song "In the Still of the Nite" (1956). Penned by Fred Parris and sung by Parris, Al Denby, Ed Martin, and Jim Freeman, the record reached number 3 on *Billboard*'s rhythm and blues (R&B) charts and number 24 on the pop charts that fall. It was originally released by the Connecticut-based Standard Records (and later on New York–based Ember) as the B-side to "The Jones Girl," a play on the 1954 Mills Brothers song "The Jones Boy."

In many ways, "In the Still of the Nite" is a classic doo-wop number: the lead soloist carries the melody and lyrics, which focus on young, innocent love; the other voices provide background chords on vocables (the well-known "shoo-doo, shoo-be-doo") in baritone, tenor, and bass ranges; and a piano and drums (and presumably bass) provide accompaniment. Harmonically, the song maintains a simple, diatonic I–vi–IV–V[7] pattern in F major for the chorus with little variation beyond a plagal (IV–I) cadence.[11] The bridge focuses on IV and allows the background singers lyrics ("I remember"). The recording itself, made in a New Haven church basement, captures a charming amateur quality. Parris's lead is earnest and seemingly untrained. Imperfections, such as ragged entrances and cutoffs and a baritone part that sounds louder than the others, did not seem of great concern. While the song may, half a century later, be emblematic of the 1950s, it has not been completely forgotten by a cappella groups—it was a staple of Brandeis University VoiceMale's repertory in 2004–5, which enabled the group to tap a well of nostalgia with older audiences.

Later Twentieth-Century Vocal Pop

As with many American popular music styles, genres that originally appeared in black communities were later taken up by white performers. "In the Still of the Nite" crossed over onto the white-oriented pop charts, becoming fodder for imitators, some of whom were not black.[12] And although they were not initially at the forefront of the movement, white and integrated doo-wop groups soon emerged. Indeed, the early successes of Frankie Valli and the Four Seasons, such as their 1962 hits "Big Girls Don't Cry" and "Sherry" (which topped both the pop and R&B charts but do not maintain a strong presence in the collegiate a cappella repertory today), may be seen as harbingers of things to come, as white singers continued to adopt black styles. Thus, by 1983 Billy Joel could draw on what was already a twenty-year-old, racially hybrid tradition of popular American vocal harmony in his *a cappella* hit "The Longest Time." It reached number 14 on the pop singles chart, topped the adult contemporary chart in early 1984, and remains an a cappella standard.

Billy Joel was born in 1949 in Hicksville, New York, which makes him too young to have understood doo-wop in its original (black) incarnation but well positioned to appreciate the genre as it became whiter in the 1960s. Purposefully composed to evoke the sounds of his youth, "The Longest Time" comes from *An Innocent Man,* an album comprising, according to critic Stephen Holden, "a collection of affectionate imitations of early '60s urban rock fashions."[13] With its *a cappella* setting, soaring falsetto, and deep bass, the "The Longest Time" effectively replicates some of doo-wop's defining characteristics. The background voices have a relaxed tone, and entrances and cutoffs are not always precise. Although the bass line could have easily been sung—and actually is when performed by a cappella groups—Joel uses an electric bass; there is no instrumental imitation.

The song embraces themes of love and courtship germane to doo-wop of the late 1950s and early 1960s. Although early doo-wop (ca. 1952–54) may have contained more explicit or suggestive lyrics (e.g., the sexual innuendo of the Dominoes' "Sixty Minute Man" [1951] and the Midnighters' "Work With Me Annie" [1953]), by the time of the "classical doo-wop era" (1955–59) the lyrical themes had been cleaned up and featured younger, more innocent voices.[14] But Joel's perspective is rooted in 1983: he sings "now I know the woman that you are" and constructs his first-person identity as one who is not a romantic novice ("I'll take my chances / I forgot how nice romance is / I haven't been there for the longest time"). These are the words not of an innocent, naive teenage boy of the mid-1950s but rather of a man in his midthirties whose worldly experience leads him at first to be cautious ("I had second thoughts at the start / I said to myself, 'hold on to your heart'") and then to recognize that, whether good or bad, his actions carry costs ("I don't care what consequence it brings / I have been a fool for lesser things"). This hint of maturity separates "The Longest Time" from the doo-wop it imitates.

The off-beat snapping and steady rhythmic pulse keep "The Longest Time" from sounding too much like barbershop. But the harmonic vocabulary of the song, with its secondary dominants (V^7/V, V^7/vi, and V^7/IV) and the chromatic alterations to the melody they entail (raised fourth, fifth, and lowered seventh scale degrees) recall barbershop's circle-of-fifths motion more than the diatonic harmonies of classic doo-wop. Thus, Joel draws on both traditions in a recording that closely predates the rise of a cappella in the following decade.

"The Longest Time" was not an isolated case. Rather, the 1980s saw several successful *a cappella* recordings. In 1982, the Manhattan Transfer, a vocal jazz outfit, won Grammy awards in three categories for its *a cappella* album *Mecca for Moderns*, which provided a Top 10 hit, "Boy From New York City."[15] Soon after, more *a cappella* hit the mainstream with Bobby McFerrin's *The Voice* (1984). His enormously successful single, "Don't Worry, Be Happy" (from his 1988 follow-up album, *Simple Pleasures*), once again brought *a cappella* singing, and this time instrumental imitation in particular, to the attention of the mainstream, pop audience.

One hears in "Don't Worry, Be Happy" a reggae sensibility, with chordal accompaniment occurring primarily on beats two and four, while the lead vocal line is delivered with a Jamaican accent. The song's lyrics, while lightheartedly encouraging listeners to relax and rid themselves of life's stresses, also evoke fantasies of island tranquility.[16] Using multitrack recording techniques, McFerrin performs all the voices himself, including the bass, chordal accompaniment, melodic interludes, lead vocal, and other effects. (In this way, technology has removed the requirement for a *group* of singers.) The off-beat chords are delivered using the vocable "coo-coo," often in syncopated variations, carrying percussive qualities. Otherwise, the song has little percussion.

"Don't Worry, Be Happy" is perhaps McFerrin's most successful musical venture and certainly his most widely recognized. It won Grammy awards in

1988 for Best Pop Vocal Performance (Male), Song of the Year, and Record of the Year. Yet it is significant not only for the awards it received but also for the fact that none came from jazz or R&B categories, which might suggest the continued currency for *a cappella* songs within the category of "pop." Not all *a cappella* had been deemed pop, however, as the R&B vocal group Boyz II Men's debut album on the Motown label, *Cooleyhighharmony* (1991), shows. It was a 1991 Grammy winner in the Best R&B Performance by a Duo or Group with Vocal category and topped the R&B charts in the year of its release, and although most tracks on the album included instrumental accompaniment, it also featured much close harmony. (The same album also included a rendition of "In the Still of the Nite.") "It's So Hard to Say Goodbye to Yesterday," the album's *a cappella* ballad, was popular enough to hit the top of the R&B singles chart, as well as number 2 on the Billboard Top 100 that same year, indicating considerable crossover appeal, though not enough to be recognized at the National Academy of Recording Arts and Sciences' Grammy Awards as something other than R&B.

The most significant difference between "Don't Worry, Be Happy" and "It's So Hard to Say Goodbye to Yesterday" is vocal styling: Boyz II Men's Nathan Morris, Wayne Morris, Shawn Stockman, and Michael McCary take their cue from Whitney Houston in their use of melodic embellishments, winding their way around melody pitches in long melismatic passages of virtuosic display. McFerrin avoids such ornamentation, partly due to stylistic differences between reggae and R&B. His delivery is more straightforward and speech-like, focusing more on the message in the lyrics than on vocal display. The same can be said of Joel's "The Longest Time."

"Don't Worry, Be Happy" and "It's So Hard to Say Goodbye to Yesterday" also differ dramatically in their use of background voices. Those on McFerrin's recording maintain an instrumental function, whereas Boyz II Men's arrangement features background voices that both sound like and function as voices. They sing conventional vocables such as "ooo" and support the lead melody, which is passed around among the quartet's members, by articulating words from the song's lyrics, especially during choruses. Their recording highlights the individual background voices by separating them temporally, through unique rhythmic entrances in certain passages, and spatially, across the stereo spectrum. Where McFerrin's recording illustrated the rhythmic possibilities of vocal music, Boyz II Men's demonstrated a lyrical, choral-pop approach. Both may be found in the a cappella music they inspired.

Beatboxing and/or/as Vocal Percussion

One thing that distinguishes collegiate a cappella from the forms of vocal harmony discussed earlier is vocal percussion, or beatboxing, the imitation of drum sounds with the voice. Scholars have located its invention in the late 1970s and early 1980s, as rappers and masters of ceremonies (MCs) sought to perform their music and rhymes to steady beats.[17] As an alternative to drum machines—devices that can be programmed to produce a regular, audible drum pattern—some hip-hop artists used their own voices instead.[18] Prominent early beatboxers included the Fat Boys and Doug E. Fresh. The first claim to fame for the Fat Boys (a Brooklyn, New York, trio consisting of Mark "Prince Markie Dee" Morales, Damon "Kool Rock-Ski" Wimbly, and Daren "Buff the Human Beat Box" Robinson) was when it won a 1983 talent contest at Radio City Music Hall with its vocalized percussion sounds. Buffy (Robinson) was known for his technique of breathing between kick and snare drum sounds. Although the group produced several albums, its recording career fizzled by the early 1990s. Doug E. Fresh claims to have invented beatboxing in 1980 and was featured in the 1985 hip-hop film *Beat Street*.[19] In "The Show" (1986), he even goes as far as to sing, about five and a half minutes in, "I am the *original* human beatbox!"

The terms *beatboxing* and *vocal percussion* (sometimes abbreviated as VP) are sometimes used interchangeably. There is some question within the a cappella community about the relationship between vocal percussion and beatboxing and other vocal techniques that aim to provide a nonpitched rhythm, such as "mouth drumming" and "multivocalism." When the question was posed on the Recorded A Cappella Review Board (RARB) online discussion forum, one respondent contrasted a cappella singing with rap, calling a cappella's vocal percussion the "imitation of existing drum sounds" and rap's beatboxing the "art of creating beats with one's voice" regardless of whether the sounds mimic extant drums (acoustic or synthesized).[20] Another contributor drew the distinction in terms of timbre, with vocal percussion "brighter" because, when amplified, the microphone is usually a short distance from the mouth (allowing some acoustic reflections to be picked up in addition to the primary source sound) and beatboxing "darker" because practitioners hold a microphone against their lips and cover the capsule with their hands (blocking such reflections).[21] A third contributor noted that beatboxing, while initially accompanying rap, has evolved into a solo or group art form, as opposed to vocal percussion, which always accompanies a group of singers.[22] Thus, the differences have been attributed to the sounds of the two practices and their function in the musical texture.

Beyond its use in a cappella, beatboxing has a community of its own, complete with its own version of its history, which describes vocal percussion as "the art form from which beatboxing spawns." Beatboxing, then, is "a form of vocal percussion in which the artist emulates the sounds of a 'beat box' or drum machine." By contrast, vocal percussion is defined as "making percussion sounds (including drum sounds) with the mouth," adding that "traditionally, vocal percussionists in a cappella groups have tried to emulate real drum sounds."[23] Authenticity thus plays a key role in these distinctions, as difference is located between the imitation of "real drums" and that of a "drum machine." Mimesis gains a new layer, since many of the sounds in drum machines were, themselves, imitations of "real drums."[24]

A historical account of beatboxing, authored by TyTe, Definicial, and White Noise, grounds the practice in a long historical arc whose reach includes scatting, African "over-breathing," barbershop, and the blues, as well as thirteenth-century French troubadours.[25] Considering that the same document defines *beatboxing* as the imitation of drum machines, this final historical claim may seem questionable. The overall narrative, however, does connect beatboxing to other genres previously discussed as precursors of and contributors to collegiate a cappella, such as scatting and black barbershop. Indeed, beatboxing may be traced largely to African-derived or black musical traditions, but it certainly has not remained solely in that milieu. Deborah Wong's ethnographic evidence, for example, points toward beatboxing as a staple of Asian American hip-hop.[26]

Given the appeal of hip-hop to young adult consumers in recent decades, particularly as its audience expanded demographically, it was probably only a matter of time before those listeners matriculated at colleges and universities, bringing their appreciation for the sounds and practice to a cappella groups. The evidence is unclear on the matter of when and who did it first, however. Jane McIntosh credits the Tufts University Beelzebubs, a men's group, with bringing vocal percussion to a cappella on its 1991 album, *Foster Street*.[27] The all-male University of North Carolina Clef Hangers' *Safari* (1992) also includes it, and recording engineer Bill Hare recalls the Stanford University Mendicants, also a men's group, recording vocal percussion around 1990. Most a cappella recordings are produced in limited quantities and not widely distributed, so conducting a comprehensive survey is difficult. Moreover, a group's recordings may sound quite different from its concerts. Thus, it cannot be assumed that recorded vocal percussion indicates its frequent use in live performance, although anecdotal evidence suggests that it was new to the co-ed University of Pennsylvania Counterparts when the group met the Beelzebubs for a joint performance in Boston in 1991.

Through these brief snapshots, a story emerges of vocal harmony in several genres, styles, and contexts within the history of American music. It is largely a male story, which perhaps helps to explain, along with other factors explored in the next chapter, why men's groups dominated collegiate a cappella for much of the twentieth century (and also some of a cappella's gender norms, discussed in chapter 7). As the number of groups, including women's and mixed ensembles, increased dramatically toward the century's end, their music was also inspired by and connected to these genres, styles, and contexts. A cappella's prominent instrumental imitation draws on the Mills Brothers from the twentieth century's first half and Bobby McFerrin and hip-hop–inspired beatboxing from its second half. Its homophonic, lead-and-accompaniment texture recalls doo-wop, and later Billy Joel. Meanwhile, throughout the century, vocal harmony remained a constant, if episodic, presence in American popular music and on its sales charts. Finally, the technology that contributes to some of today's a cappella recordings (see chapters 8 and 9), such as multitracking, can also be found in these earlier vocal genres. But a cappella practice took new and innovative turns in style and structure, giving it a sound distinctive from other and earlier forms of close harmony and choral singing on campus while drawing and exciting new participants. Those innovations, the development and institutionalization of a cappella, are the subject of the next chapter.

CHAPTER 4

The A Cappella Explosion

Although small, student-led vocal groups existed at certain American colleges and universities earlier, their numbers grew significantly during the twentieth century. The 1980s and 1990s, in particular, saw an explosion of collegiate a cappella groups. This dramatic rise built on a foundation laid by certain developments in music education, higher education, and popular culture. It also produced certain effects, including the institutionalization of the a cappella movement, complete with a society, newsletter, and competitions, all of which, when combined with the ease of communication over the Internet, enabled the creation of a larger community. This chapter suggests, then, some of the ways in which collegiate a cappella became a self-sustaining subculture.

Tracking the Movement's Growth

No complete directory or list of collegiate a cappella groups exists, although it has been suggested that the groups number about 1,200.[1] In 2006, I began surveying the collegiate a cappella landscape in order to gauge how many groups are active, their gender profile, their founding date, and whether they are affiliated with a larger ethnic or religious group (e.g., Christian, Jewish, African American, Asian American, multicultural).[2] My figures are based on the resulting database, which accounts for approximately 1,039 groups. Of those, I located founding dates for 720 (69.3 percent), gender type for 905 (87.1 percent), and both for 714 (68.7 percent).

The number of a cappella groups grew most dramatically in the late 1980s and throughout the 1990s (see fig. 4.1). By 1980, there were approximately 110 ac-

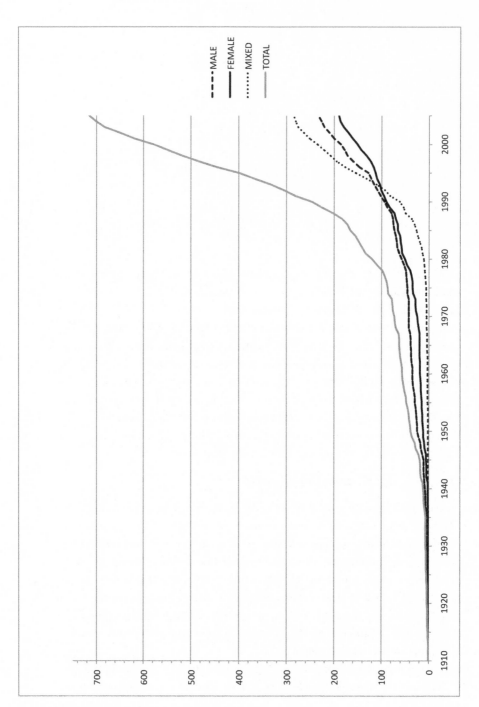

Fig. 4.1. Yearly totals of collegiate a cappella groups, by type, 1909–2005.

tive groups. These included the Whiffenpoofs (1909), Spizzwinks(?) (1914; the question mark is part of the name), and Alley Cats (1943) at Yale University, as well as the Smiffenpoofs (Smith College, 1936), the Kingsmen (Columbia University, 1949), the Friars (University of Michigan, 1955), the Beelzebubs (Tufts University, 1962), and the Clef Hangers (University of North Carolina at Chapel Hill, 1977). Of those 110, 53 were men's, 47 were women's, and 10 were mixed groups.

Most early a cappella took place at elite institutions in the northeastern United States. The Ivy League hosted 26 groups, with Yale's 11 more than double any other of the elite eight. But other institutions in that part of the country, such as the Massachusetts Institute of Technology, and Smith, Vassar, Williams, and Wellesley Colleges also had groups. These schools were among the last to embrace coeducation, which may explain the paucity of mixed groups. As the Men's Octet (University of California, Berkeley, 1948), the Gentlemen (University of Virginia, 1953), and the Mendicants (Stanford University, 1963) demonstrate, however, a cappella groups did exist outside the Northeast, just not with the same geographic concentration.

The 1980s saw the total number of groups double, while mixed groups made significant gains. The decade ended with 225 groups: 88 men's, 83 women's, and 54 mixed. The geographic scope also widened, with groups established at institutions such as the University of Vermont (the male Top Cats, 1980), Washington University in St. Louis (the male Pikers, 1985), York University in Toronto (the mixed Wibijazz'n, 1988), and the University of Georgia (the female Noteworthy, 1989), and additional groups founded at West Coast universities such as the University of California, Berkeley (the mixed Artists In Resonance, 1988) and Stanford (the mixed Talisman, 1990, specializing in world music).

Within the next ten years, 318 new groups had been established, including 90 men's, 60 women's, and 168 coed ensembles. More groups were founded in the period 1990–99 than in the prior eighty-one years. By 1994, mixed groups outnumbered both men's and women's ensembles. Figure 4.2 shows the number of new groups established each year and the rate of growth. The most new groups were established in 1996, when 46 were formed in a single year.

When accounting for the 714 groups for which I had both the founding date and gender data from 1909 up to and including 2008, the final breakdown was 236 men's, 191 women's, and 287 mixed. Of the 905 groups for which I found gender information (including the hundreds of groups for which I could find no founding date), 298 were men's, 246 were women's, and 361 were mixed groups.[3]

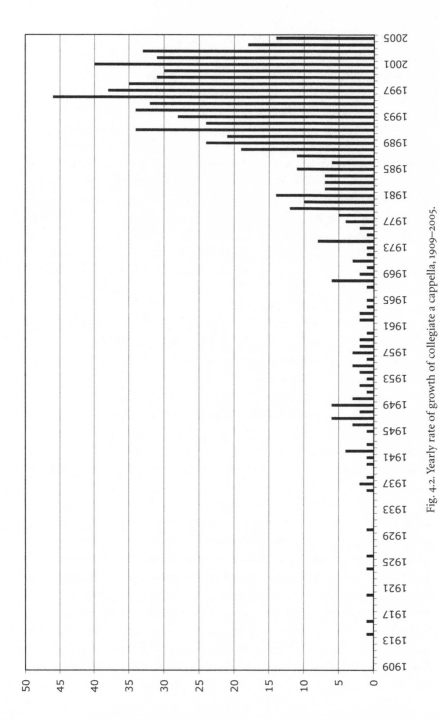

Fig. 4.2. Yearly rate of growth of collegiate a cappella, 1909–2005.

Collegiate a cappella is a trend that feeds on itself. Many groups are founded by individuals familiar with groups at other schools who seek one at their own institutions. This was the case with Amazin' Blue at the University of Michigan. Founder Mike Wang had been a member of Mixed Company, a coed group, as an undergraduate at Yale, and on his arrival at Michigan for graduate study in 1986 found no mixed groups to join. After advertising with posters on campus, Wang held auditions in January 1987 and soon thereafter began rehearsals for the new group, originally titled The Amazin' Blue. ("The" was quickly dropped, while the rest of the name is a pun on Michigan's school colors, maize and blue.)[4]

After singing in both his high school and church choirs, Adam Bower sought a musical outlet during his freshman year at Kalamazoo College in 1992. While attending a performance by Gold Company, a jazz-oriented vocal ensemble at nearby Western Michigan University, he was inspired. He and a friend took action.

> We decided that we would start our own singing group on campus . . . We wanted a group that had good talent and loved to sing. We also wanted to focus our efforts on up-beat and somewhat popular music in a small ensemble setting. We advertised the coming of the group throughout campus and waited. As spring quarter rolled around, we found interest to be high in such a group, and thus was born the first installation of the Aqua Pelicans, a mixed-voice a cappella ensemble.[5]

Bower's group lasted several years before disbanding. When I joined the Kalamazoo College faculty in 2007, a few professors recalled the group, but none of the students did.

In other cases, a cappella groups are started by students who were rejected by the existing groups at their school. When I began singing with Amazin' Blue in 2001, I was told that another mixed group on campus was founded precisely this way; the coed Dicks and Janes were established in 1996 after a musical theater student failed to win a spot at Amazin' Blue's auditions. His new group has since become well respected on campus, regularly competing in the International Championship of Collegiate A Cappella, as well as earning selections for the *Best of College A Cappella* compilation album in 2002, 2003, and 2004. By the end of my time in Amazin' Blue in the spring of 2007, the origins of the Dicks and Janes were essentially forgotten, and even recent Dicks and Janes alumni could not confirm the story (although the founder eventually did).

These examples illustrate a cappella's limited institutional memory: as members graduate, their experiences and memories are sometimes passed on to younger members, but, like any oral history, they may be distorted, misremembered, or simply forgotten. Sometimes reminders are left behind. The Harvard Callbacks were founded by a group of singers who met during the second round of auditions (known as "callbacks") to other Harvard groups.[6] We can therefore conclude that a cappella groups often form through individuals' encounters with other groups. There is, however, more to a cappella's late-twentieth-century explosion than simply tales of encounter.

Music Education, Within School and Without

The twentieth century saw great changes in music education in the United States. *A cappella* choirs gained prominence in high schools during the first half of century, for several reasons. Beginning in Kansas in 1914, high school choral ensembles started participating in organized competitions. This "contest movement" stimulated the organization of glee clubs and granted them a measure of respectability just as choir directors were competing for recognition with growing instrumental ensembles at their schools. The 1928 meeting of the Music Supervisors National Conference was dubbed a "singing conference" and featured numerous high school *a cappella* choir performances and a quartet contest. For the next seven years, the MSNC hosted the National High School Chorus. Music publishers also realized the sales potential of high school choirs and began advertising in music education journals, which spurred interest and activity.[7]

This *a cappella* movement was not without critics. Some complained the repertory was old and antiquated; twentieth-century pieces were generally not programmed. Others challenged the mostly religious character of the *a cappella* repertory, which sat somewhat uncomfortably in the secular public school curriculum, since many of the selections consisted of church music, even if set by prominent European composers of earlier eras. Finally, some simply found the performances boring; one choral society director complained that he left *a cappella* concerts "with a certain bored admiration" of the performers' skills. As the movement waned, instrumental accompaniment regained some prominence, and eventually accompanied and unaccompanied choral singing settled in balance. But *a cappella* singing had been firmly established in the curriculum from which many college-bound students emerged.[8]

Choral singing became a serious pursuit at the college level as well. In 1912, at St. Olaf College in Northfield, Minnesota, F. Melius Christiansen established a pioneering and highly successful college-level *a cappella* choir. Not unlike the Fisk Jubilee Singers, his ensemble quickly began touring to raise funds for the school. Musically, Christiansen's choir was noted for its straight-tone singing, which inspired legions of high school choir directors to adopt a similar practice of avoiding vibrato.[9] In addition to the St. Olaf Choir, Leonard Van Camp credits the Northwestern University A Cappella Choir and the Westminster Choir with leading the *a cappella* choir movement at colleges and universities. College glee clubs, which had been touring for decades, increasingly came under faculty direction, which indicated a heightened level of seriousness and professionalism. They also engaged in competitive singing: a 1914 contest featured glee clubs from Harvard, Columbia, Dartmouth, and the University of Pennsylvania.[10]

Off campus, conductor Walter Damrosch's Musical Art Society of New York is credited with invigorating *a cappella* singing in the United States around the turn of the twentieth century. The society's performances, from 1894 to 1920, consisted mostly of European and Russian classical music and folk songs. The 1920s also saw a string of successful Russian choirs tour the United States, which kept *a cappella* singing in the public's ears. In 1922, the *New York Times* observed the interest in Russian folk songs and remarked that the Ukrainian National Chorus was frequently "hailed as a 'human symphony orchestra'" during its performances. Following a European tour, the chorus continued to the United States, where, in addition to the usual New York venues, it offered performances, by request, at the Hampton Institute "before the 900 students, who in turn sang American folk songs and negro 'spirituals' to these artistic strangers from Russia."[11]

In the second half of the century, music education continued in public schools but faced certain challenges. A post-Sputnik emphasis on science threatened to draw attention away from the arts, while a gap between the school repertory and the music that students enjoyed at home grew increasingly perceptible. The period 1950–70 saw "general music" classes increase in frequency and importance, and many music educators embraced a more diverse repertory, including jazz, blues, folk, and rock.[12] After the Tanglewood Symposium of 1967, the president of the Music Educators National Conference (successor to the MSNC) announced the MENC's endorsement of popular music in music education. Just two years later, at the Youth Music Institute at the University of Wisconsin, students taught popular music to high school music teachers in order to improve educators' fluency in those idioms.

"College Life," Coordinate Colleges, and Coeducation

Beginning just before the *a cappella* movement and continuing through it, American college campuses saw the development of "college life," as particular cultures became rooted at colleges and universities, complete with their own social rules, styles of dress, and lingo. It began slowly, however. In the early 1800s and the antebellum period, college students were busy nearly every hour of the day. Early morning chapel service was followed by a class before breakfast. Classes continued until lunch, the afternoon was filled with additional classes or recitations, and additional tutoring or supervised study followed the evening meal until bedtime. This regimen, in place at Dartmouth College, for example, enabled the college to effectively control all aspects of a student's life, leaving little time for unsanctioned activity or idle wanderings. When students had spare time, it was commonly devoted to religious organizations, such as the Moral Society at Yale or the Theological Society at Dartmouth, or literary societies and debating clubs.[13] As the century wore on, additional activities, including musical ones, were added to this list. Thus, "college life" emerged as an increasingly elaborate student world parallel to the curricular world of the college. "For many undergraduates," writes John Thelin, "compliance with the formal curriculum was merely the price of admission into 'college life.'"[14]

Around the turn of the twentieth century, the concept of "college life" grew popular off campus. The American public's fascination with the "goings on" on campus—with its own fashion trends, vocabulary, and crazy antics—could be seen in national magazines such as the *Independent* and *Atlantic Monthly* (and would continue later in the century with such films as *Animal House* [1978] and its imitators). Around this time, many college colors were selected, mascots chosen, and college songs and hymns composed.[15] With the image of the "college man" firmly planted in the American national imagination, the extracurricular pursuits of college life became something for college-bound high school students to aim for and dream about and, once achieved and realized, enjoy to the fullest. For musically inclined and experienced high school students, a collegiate singing group was one way to fully enjoy the college life they had earned.

Of course, in the early twentieth century, most of those enjoying college life were white men. Early single-sex a cappella groups, such as the Whiffenpoofs, were founded at schools that admitted only one gender. And although men's groups comprise most examples of early collegiate a cappella, music was not absent from women's colleges. In fact, traditionally, it was a key component of women's education. Such instruction, Helen Lefkowitz Horowitz explains, was "foremost among the necessary accomplishments to 'finish' a woman for polite society." Well-regarded women's colleges of the nineteenth century typically devoted significant portions of their faculty to music and the arts.[16] Extracurricular singing also became a staple of college life for women around the turn of the century, as an account of the "frenzied existence of a 'popular junior or senior'" at Barnard College illustrates: "After her morning classes, the girl tries to do everything at once. She goes upstairs to song-practice and wonders, as she joins the vehement '*Rah,* rah for *dear* old *Barnard!,*' why the dean wants to see her immediately."[17] Singing was also an integral part of the rituals of college life, such as Tree Day at Wellesley.[18]

The integration of women into American higher education, an effort necessary for the establishment of women's and mixed a cappella groups, was a long and difficult process. Women's colleges were a first step. These schools hosted their own a cappella groups, such as the Smiffenpoofs at Smith College (a play on the name Whiffenpoofs). Another step was "coordinating colleges," institutions connected to a men's college and designated specifically for women. These schools also boasted their own groups. For example, the Chattertocks were established in 1951 at Pembroke College, Brown University's coordinating college. The group began when the girlfriends of the members of the all-male Brown Jabberwocks (1949) grew irritated that their boyfriends were spending much of their time rehearsing for an upcoming talent show. The women formed their own group, crafting its name as a play on that of the men's group. After taking first prize in the talent show, the women continued to sing together.[19] Pembroke officially merged with Brown in 1971, and both the Jabberwocks and Chattertocks continue as separate groups.

Land-grant universities in the Midwest and West led the integration of women into the same institutions as men in the 1850s, 1860s, and 1870s, beginning with the University of Iowa in 1855. The University of California accepted women in 1870, while Stanford University was coeducational from its founding in 1891. Between 1880 and 1900 the portion of American institutions of higher education that included some form of limited coeducation went from about a third to roughly three-quarters.[20] Still, female students were regularly ridiculed by classmates, forced to sit at the back of lecture halls, and subjected to other forms of discrimination. "Tracking into particular courses and majors," explains Thelin, "discouragement from some fields, and, above all, exclusion from extracurricular organizations and activities were the disappointing realities of coeducation" at the time.[21] Moreover, the actual number of female college students, as a percentage of American women aged eighteen to twenty-one, remained rather low: 1 percent in 1870 and 2.5 percent in 1890.[22]

The period following World War II saw a significant rise in the number of students on campus, for reasons such as the G.I. Bill. Thus, a small increase in the number of a cappella groups during this time may be explained by the sudden and massive increase in the sheer number of students in college. As the century continued, applications to colleges grew, as did acceptances. In 1960, 40 percent of high school seniors received a college acceptance letter, and by 1991 the number was up to 61 percent. Women, in particular, began attending college in much greater numbers. In 1978, there were an estimated 5.6 million women attending college in the United States; by 1991, the number was 7.8 million. Fifty-three percent of all baccalaureate degrees awarded in 1989 were given to women.[23] Yet the Ivy League, where some of the oldest a cappella traditions are rooted, largely lagged. Princeton and Yale began to admit women in 1969, Brown in 1971, Dartmouth and Harvard in 1972, and Columbia, the last of the Ivies, in 1983.[24] Other universities open to only men, such as Duke University, also had larger student populations than many women's colleges, which may help explain why men's a cappella groups outnumbered women's groups for so long. In 1957, 74 percent of the nation's 1,326 collegiate institutions were coeducational; in 1976, 91 percent of 1,849 colleges and universities were coed; and by 1981, 92 percent of 1,928 institutions were coed.[25] In early 2010, the College Board listed 48 women's (1.2 percent of the total), 66 men's (1.7 percent), and 3,772 coed colleges (97.1 percent) in its searchable database.[26]

Stylistic Innovations: The Case of the Tufts University Beelzebubs

While the rise of "college life" and the gradual integration of American higher education were important foundational developments for the collegiate a cappella explosion of the 1980s and 1990s, musical developments were important as well. The Manhattan Transfer's *Mecca for Moderns* (1981), Billy Joel's "The Longest Time" (1983), Bobby McFerrin's "Don't Worry, Be Happy" (1988), and Boyz II Men's "It's So Hard to Say Goodbye to Yesterday" (1991) demonstrated, in various ways, the potential for vocal pop music, and young amateur musicians stood a good chance of hearing these songs before matriculating to college or university.[27] Their impact did not go unnoticed. In a 2002 newspaper article, the director of choral music at Cornell University is quoted crediting "the close harmony, equal-voice style popularized in recent years" to "groups like 'N Sync, the Backstreet Boys and Boyz 2 Men [sic]," as well as McFerrin's success at "sophisticated instrumental sounds."[28] At the same time, the emerging genre of rap boasted a distinctive technique—beatboxing—which helped musicians maintain a strong rhythmic backing to their songs in a way that mimicked drum sounds.

Thus, by the time of the a cappella explosion, college singers could draw on the part retro doo-wop, part barbershop character of "The Longest Time," the instrumental imitation of "Don't Worry, Be Happy," the "equal-voice" blend of "It's So Hard to Say Goodbye to Yesterday," and the percussive practices of hip-hop's beatboxing. This combination enabled them to embrace popular music genres like rock and pop, which would otherwise be off-limits to close harmony groups because of their instrumental textures and rhythmic drive. For a cappella singers, these popular songs modeled a vocal style that did not require instrumental skills, instruments or other equipment, or significant financial resources. And they could meet just about anywhere to do it.

An excellent example of these developments may be found in the Beelzebubs, which has been called "the most famous collegiate a cappella group after the Yale Whiffenpoofs" (the Beelzebubs' founder, Tim Vaill, is in fact the son of a Whiffenpoof).[29] As a reference to the devil, an image the group has embraced on the covers of its albums and in its logo, the group's name recalls the high jinx and pranks associated with both the evil religious figure and the fun-loving "college man" of earlier eras. The group's repertory consisted mainly of barbershop, doo-wop, gospel, and jazz tunes from its 1962 founding until the 1970s, when it began performing pop and rock songs. But Foster Street, the 1991 album featuring the group's repertory from the 1990–91 academic year, marked the most significant shift.

Before beginning Foster Street, Deke Sharon, a member of the group, had received a copy of a cassette tape (compiled by Rex Solomon, a student and a cappella fan at nearby Brandeis University) filled with collegiate and professional a cappella recordings of the Yaz song, "Only You." To his ear, they all sounded the same. Moreover, "the monotony was reflected in many ways by the lack of diversity in the sets I saw when performing with other college groups," he told me. "We would sit in the back row of a show at UPenn and within the first three notes we'd know what the song was."[30] He asked himself and his group, why not do something different?

Looking beyond earlier arranging styles, the songs recorded on Foster Street embraced the driving, rhythmic nature of popular music in an explicit attempt to emulate its sound *a cappella* to a much greater degree. At the same time, the singers tried to capture the excitement of the Beelzebubs' live performances. They were frequently "treated like rock stars on other campuses," Sharon said, because their arrangements and performances were more exciting than those of other groups. One crucial element in this project was the expanded scope of the arrangements, from typical four-part settings reminiscent of barbershop and doo-wop to individual parts for individual voices, each of which had an instrumental function. Referring to legendary record producer Phil Spector, Sharon, who arranged just over half the songs on the album, said he sought an "intricate wall of sound rather than block chords."

A second aspect of the Beelzebubs' approach was the use of vocal percussion throughout the songs. Bill Stone, who sang with the group from 1985 to 1988, described the singers' approach to vocal percussion before *Foster Street*.

> The vocal percussion thing took off right after I left—that is, as a continuing line in the song. There were certainly vocal percussion interludes [while I was in the group], but nothing like the sort of driving beat that vocal percussion provides today. The percussiveness was provided by the bass back in the late '80s.

Thus, before 1988, vocal percussion was used as an effect, "as a splash of color rather than an integral part of the arrangement," as Sharon put it, offering two examples: a hi-hat " 'tss-t-t tss-t-t' at the beginning of a jazz tune, or a 'dig-i-dy-boom' as a drum fill-in between sung passages." It was not considered important enough to warrant devoting a singer's voice to it exclusively for a whole song. But on *Foster Street*, it appears throughout the songs. On some tracks, Sharon has as many as four members providing percussion sounds simultaneously.

A third element was the inclusion of vocal sounds thought to better emulate instruments such as guitars. Members of the Beelzebubs sing overtly nasal diphthongs to imitate the prominent guitar lines on James Taylor's "Your Smiling Face," for example. But beyond modifying their vocal timbre, the singers infuse their album with an instrumental-like sense of rhythm. Although block chords do not disappear entirely, gone is the fondness for long, sustained chords or vocal homophony. Basses sing rhythms suggesting a driving backbeat while tenors provide quick off-beat patterns akin to those of a rhythm guitar. Parallel fifths, reflecting the voicing of a guitar "power chord," are widely used while interior voices provide entire phrases of rhythmically intense, repeated sixteenth notes. These techniques departed considerably from earlier vocal styles as exemplified by the "Whiffenpoof Song," "Tiger Rag," "In the Still of the Nite," or any of the commercial *a cappella* hits of the 1980s and 1990s. Instead, they signaled the beginning of a cappella as a vocal style historically rooted in, but distinctive from, those that came before.

The Institutionalization of A Cappella: CASA, the CAN, and the CARAs

If increasing college enrollment and greater integration in higher education provided the students that would form collegiate a cappella groups, and a string of popular *a cappella* hits served as models that newly formed groups could adopt, what sorts of results followed from the a cappella explosion of the 1980s and 1990s? Two important ones include the formalization and professionalization of the movement and the creation of a larger sense of community through institutional structures (such as competitions), some of which were Internet based.

Deke Sharon's efforts to organize the a cappella movement in the early 1990s helped to formalize it, but this depended on encounters between groups. He began with a list of collegiate groups that the Beelzebubs maintained, which it would use to send letters of introduction, invitation, and solicitation for performance opportunities. Indeed, the Beelzebubs' willingness to travel near and far to perform at other colleges helped to ensure that Sharon's musical innovations were not confined to the Tufts University campus.

But he took things a step further, starting a publication, the *College A Cappella Newsletter,* in his dorm room in December 1990. (Because professional groups, which numbered far fewer than collegiate groups, also used it as their forum and were featured in its articles, he soon renamed it the *Contemporary A Cappella News.*) He combined the Beelzebubs' contact list with one compiled by Solomon to expand his subscription base. "The *CAN,*" as the newsletter became known, was most important as a means for a cappella groups to communicate with each other, enabling the spread of information and ideas among formerly isolated ensembles. In 1995, Bower wrote about how his subscription to the *CAN* provided "all sorts of information regarding singing and practicing techniques, arrangements, other groups and their activities, etc."[31] Its pages provided articles about a cappella recordings, interviews with professional a cappella musicians, reports from various concerts around the country, and a classified section that enabled groups to coordinate performances—and parties—with each other. For example, in the December 1991 issue, members of the "TREBS" from Oberlin College expressed their "serious wanderlust" and interest in visiting schools on the East Coast during their upcoming spring break tour. The Conn Chords of Connecticut College billed itself as "a group that loves to travel . . . planning an East Coast tour," and warned potential hosts to "prepare for the party of a life-time." The members of 36 Madison Avenue, from Drew University, as well as the Beelzebubs, the Georgetown University Gracenotes, the Skidmore College Son-neteers, and the Salem College Archways, all sought hosts for spring tours or in-vited touring groups to join them in concert.[32]

A cappella groups were joining forces for combined concerts well before the *CAN*, however. Following the Whiffenpoofs, several other groups were founded at Yale in the first half of the twentieth century, resulting in a critical mass. This created an environment in which groups could sing with each other at events such as the Whiffenpoof Jamboree. Groups from other colleges were also in-vited. As groups interacted, leadership and arranging skills were demonstrated, honed, and shared. Moreover, arrangements themselves were exchanged: "[S]ome of the Whiffs from the late 1950s recall free borrowing of arrange-ments by and from other groups."[33] Decades later the *CAN* integrated these lo-cal events, creating a wider network than was previously in place.

After his graduation from Tufts and the New England Conservatory in 1991, Sharon founded the Contemporary A Cappella Society of America (CASA). The *CAN* became the CASA's primary organ, as is evident by the early inclusion of "the official newsletter of CASA—the contemporary a cappella society of amer-ica" [*sic*] in its title bar (which by late 1991 had replaced the earlier slogan, "I have no idea what you're talking about—what the hell is a 'cappella' anyway?"). In 1992, the nascent organization offered its first Contemporary A Cappella Recording Awards (CARAs), using Collegiate, Semi-Pro, Unsigned Pro, and Signed Pro as award categories, within which Best Group of the Year, Best Album, Best Song, Best Arrangement, and Best Soloist awards were given for men's, women's, and mixed groups, in addition to an award for Funniest Collegiate Group. The CARAs were modeled on other popular academy awards, such as the Grammys, but acknowledged their obscurity with sarcastic humor by invoking frequent Os-cars host, comedian Billy Crystal, and expressing a desire for trophy statues with an a cappella twist. The *CAN* article announcing the first CARAs begins:

Ladies and gentlemen, we're pleased to present to you the recipients of the first CARAs. One day, we hope to be a nationally televised event, complete with Billy

Crystal, excruciatingly poor choreographed nightmares, and little statues of gold people with a pitch pipe for a head. For now, we'll have to settle for our dreams, and this lovely sixteen page newsletter, complete with satiristic [sic] comedy.[34]

Today, CARAs are awarded in various categories, such as Best Album and Best Song within two broad areas, Scholastic and Non-Scholastic, which separate high school and collegiate groups from professional ones. The Scholastic area also includes Best Solo and Best Arrangement categories for men's, women's, and mixed groups.

Early issues of the *CAN* reveal two important influences on a cappella at the time: professional a cappella groups and a popular documentary on pop and R&B vocal groups. Of the professional groups, the first is the Bobs, a San Francisco–based vocal quartet formed in 1981 and recipients of the first Professional category CARA. At the time, the four members of the Bobs had been together for ten years and recorded five albums on the Rhino, Kaleidoscope, and Tradition and Moderne (Germany) labels. Their repertory contained both original songs and covers; their version of Lennon and McCartney's "Helter Skelter" was nominated for a Grammy in 1983.

"Kiss Him Goodbye," a 1987 Top 10 hit by the Nylons, earned the Toronto-based quartet a significant following among a cappella singers. Sharon describes the group as having had a "proto-contemporary sound" at the time, incorporating a drum machine and an arranging style "with one foot in doo-wop and one foot stepping into what became contemporary a cappella." Mike Schwartz, who sang with the Highjinx and founded the all-male Bear Necessities as an undergraduate at Brown and later directed VoiceMale during graduate school at Brandeis, recalls that when he began singing in the Highjinx in 1988 most groups on campus were covering the Bobs, the Nylons, and the R&B group the Persuasions. Barbershop was still a strong influence, too. But over the course of his a cappella career, 1988–92, more and more groups embraced rock and pop songs.

The second influence seen in the *CAN* is Spike Lee's Public Broadcasting Service (PBS) documentary, *Spike & Co.: Do It A Cappella*, which aired on October 5, 1990. The broadcast featured music from and profiles of numerous professional vocal groups, including the Persuasions, Ladysmith Black Mambazo (the South African isicathamiya choir that recorded with Paul Simon on his *Graceland* album in 1986), the Grammy-winning gospel vocal group Take 6, and Rockapella, a collegiate-style professional group that would famously sing the theme song to the children's television game show *Where In the World Is Carmen Sandiego?*[35] The documentary was so influential, in fact, that by early 1992 the soundtrack was inducted into the CARAs "hall of fame."

> Years from now, historians will look back on *Do It A Cappella* as the first significant step in a cappella's acceptance into mainstream pop culture. In presenting the PBS special that produced the soundtrack, Spike Lee and Debbie Allen lent their credibility to the genre as a whole. The juxtaposition of traditional groups (Ladysmith Black Mambazo), seasoned veterans (the Persuasions, Take 6) and relative newcomers (Mint Juleps, Rockapella, True Image) demonstrated the richness of a cappella's past and the vitality of its future, to a completely new audience. The soundtrack presents this diversity beautifully. Ladysmith points to the genre's African origins with "Phansi Em Godini" and "The Lion Sleeps Tonight." The journey through African-American gospel music is reflected in Take 6's "Get Away Jordan." The Persuasions trace the path through doo-wop and soul with "Looking For An Echo." Finally, we see the funkified complexity of the present in True Image's "I Need You," the Mint Juleps' "Don't Let Your Heart," and Rockapella's "Zombie Jamboree." If we had to pick one album to represent contemporary a cappella to someone who's never heard a note, this would be the one.[36]

The CASA also helped promote a cappella's growth through arrangements. In the late 1980s and early 1990s, Sharon explains, a cappella arrangements were difficult to find. Most commercially published arrangements were in either the barbershop or doo-wop styles, so the CASA began archiving arrangements for its members' use, combining the private collections of Solomon and the Beelzebubs. Sharon recalls many groups, such as the Duke University Pitchforks, using the CASA arrangement library as a source for their early repertory. The later publication of the *Contemporary A Cappella Songbook* further provided repertory to new groups, as well as those unable to arrange new music for themselves.[37]

Spreading the Word: The Internet, the RARB, and the Competitions

The *CAN* and the CASA were two points around which a cappella singers could gather as a community, even if it was often an imaginary one.[38] Other structures supporting this community followed in the form of competitions and sites on the increasingly popular Internet. Technologies such as e-mail, Usenet discussion boards, and the World Wide Web became more and more accessible as college and university campuses provided fast connections to this worldwide computer network. In the early 1990s, a cappella enthusiasts shared messages containing questions, tips, and discussions of recordings and performances on the Usenet bulletin board rec.music.a-cappella. In an interview, San Francisco–based recording engineer Bill Hare strongly emphasized the importance of the Internet in a cappella's growth.

> While people like Deke [Sharon], Don [Gooding], and myself were doing pioneering things independently of each other, I cannot stress enough the role that the invention and use of the Internet had during this time, several years after our independent groundwork. If it weren't for this new form of instant information gathering, most groups would have remained islands unto themselves—I know the Stanford groups for the most part didn't know there were any other groups out there before this time. In a way, Deke invented the original intergroup net by trying to put together a database of the other groups out there, using telephone and written correspondence—I was really impressed when I got a letter from this kid Deke Sharon in Boston who had heard my work with the Mendicants from all the way over in California.

In 1994, the Recorded A Cappella Review Board was established as an online archive of *a cappella* recording reviews. With its founding, the a cappella community gained a definitive critical apparatus. The reviews were (and continue to be) written by "a cappella performers, creators, and fans from across the continent."[39] It is not unusual to find quotes from the RARB's reviews featured prominently on an a cappella group's website, suggesting that the reviewer's praise, like any review incorporated into public relations materials, legitimates the group's musical efforts. The other important aspect of the RARB is its discussion forum. Like the older Usenet board, the RARB forum creates an active virtual space for ongoing conversations on all things a cappella, to which anyone can contribute. New group members routinely sign onto the discussion forum seeking advice, which the older, more experienced contributors gladly offer. Where the efforts of Sharon and the Beelzebubs expanded the group's network beyond its own campus and locale, the RARB and CASA translates the same effort globally.

In 1995, the annual *Best of College A Cappella* (*BOCA*) series of albums began as a project headed by Sharon and Adam Farb, a 1994 Brown University
graduate who had sung with the Brown Derbies. It was not the first time
recordings by various collegiate groups were collected in one place, but it was
significant because of its scope and intent. The first volume, *BOCA 1* (1995), featured mostly early 1990s recordings by groups in the Northeast such as the
Whiffenpoofs, Brown Derbies, and Beelzebubs, as well as entries by groups
from other parts of the country, such as the University of Virginia Gentlemen,
the University of Michigan Amazin' Blue, and the Stanford University Everyday
People and Fleet Street Singers.

In later years *BOCA* became a commercial venture and a promotional project within and on behalf of the a cappella community. Since 1999, it has been
produced by Varsity Vocals, one of numerous a-cappella-related companies
formerly owned by Don Gooding, an alumnus of the Yale Sons of Orpheus and
Bacchus (SOBs) and founder of an a cappella sales catalog. Sharon, who was
joined on the selection committee by Gooding for several years, has regularly
reminded a cappella enthusiasts that they are not the intended audience for the
compilation. He told readers of the RARB forum in 2004, "*BOCA* is more to
generate new fans than it is for you guys (sorry!). Y'all already know what your
favorite 20 tracks are!" A few months later he added, "Truth is, we don't pick
BOCA tracks for the people on this forum."[40] Still, *BOCA* carries considerable
respect within the field despite the appearance of other compilations in part,
perhaps, because of its longevity and the prestige of the individuals behind it.
(*BOCA*'s effect on the a cappella community and its musical practice are discussed in chapter 9.)

In 1996, Sharon and Farb established the National Championship of Collegiate A Cappella, a live competition. Drawing from regions around the country,
the finals were held at Carnegie Hall. Within a few years, it grew to include
groups outside the United States, such as Wibijazz'n from York University
(Toronto), and changed its name to the International Championship of Collegiate A Cappella (ICCA). Varsity Vocals purchased the tournament from Farb
in 1999. The 2006 competition season expanded further to include groups in
the United Kingdom from St. Andrews, Cambridge, and Oxford Universities
(Oxford's men's group, Out of the Blue, took second place at the finals.) And
the 2010 season included competitors from Pretoria, South Africa, plus a "wild
card" semifinal in which groups were judged based on video recordings of their

performances earlier in the competition. For the past few years, the finals have been held at Lincoln Center in New York City.[41] (The ICCA is discussed in greater detail in chapter 7.)

Coda: A Cappella's Meaningfulness

Institutional structures such as the *CAN*, CASA, RARB, *BOCA*, and ICCA connect a cappella musicians to one another, enabling them to share in the production of an "imagined world" of collegiate a cappella and feel like active participants in a community.[42] Yet pointing to the a cappella explosion, the historical and musical developments that provided its foundation, and the results that followed does not fully explain how this sense of community or subculture arose,[43] how the regular, annual events of the a cappella calendar became important to actual people. In other words, why did these things become significant or meaningful?

In her study of British barbershop, Liz Garnett discusses the "ritual function" of songs. On one hand, the songs barbershop choruses sing contain lyrics, which can be interpreted as messages or embodiments of particular values or ideologies.[44] They can be "read" as a form of textual analysis, and Gage Averill examines the ideologies found in the lyrics of the American barbershop repertory and relates them to the values embodied by the quartets that sing them, and the same is done elsewhere in this book.[45] But Garnett makes a second argument, even more relevant here: the regular repetition of the songs provides a sense of stability and continuity, which can be felt even by those who may resist their lyrical messages.[46] (This idea might be similar to some types of musical religious practice in which worshippers may not understand the words but find a sense of spiritual purpose in the routine of prayers.) The passion with which singers pursue their barbershop activities, in their own chorus's performance and in competition with other choruses, evinces the meaningfulness of the community created by this ritual function.

The same logic can be applied to a cappella. As it became possible for groups to more easily coordinate with each other, sharing ideas about music, group organization, recording techniques, and myriad other topics, singers could regularly sense that they were not alone in their musical activities but instead part of a larger community. They could rely on other groups and the CASA for arrangements and on the *CAN* for news from around the a cappella world. The RARB realized the community virtually. Meanwhile, the annual cycle of *BOCA* and the ICCA—Garnett specifically cites the importance of competitions—created a calendar of regularly occurring a cappella events beyond those of individual groups.[47] They were not just musical gatherings but also goals toward which groups would work, sometimes for months at a time. The institutionalization of a cappella thereby provided the routine that legitimated the practice, during which singers could literally "do it a cappella."

PART II

Contemporary Collegiate A Cappella: Performance, Technology, and Community

CHAPTER 5

Musical Components and
Their Social Motivations

The past few chapters argue that today's collegiate a cappella is deeply rooted in several traditions going back at least to the beginning of the nineteenth century if not to the earlier colonial period. The remaining chapters show, then, how contemporary collegiate a cappella is contingent on its particular historical moment. It could only look, sound, and feel the way it does because it followed the advent of a relatively recent and supremely potent form of American cultural expression: rock music.

Of course, as a *musical* practice, a cappella depends on the creation of sounds, which are made and organized using particular methods. Ultimately, the sounds, the effort put into their creation, and the meanings attributed to them are linked. This chapter explores the sounds, their methods of production and organization, and their social significance, focusing on how ideas of emulation and originality play into the musical practice.

The Arrangement

Making music in a collegiate a cappella group begins with an arrangement, which usually takes the form of a document written in music notation, indicating which of the group's voice parts will sing which pitches and rhythms while accompanying a song's soloist. While some groups sing commercially published arrangements, most create their own. Arrangers typically begin by listening closely and repeatedly to a song's original recording to determine the necessary instrumental parts, chord structures, and other distinctive aspects to incorporate into their arrangement. Occasionally, they download MIDI arrangements of songs from the Internet to use as models.[1] Only rarely did I hear of arrangers using commercially published piano and vocal arrangements for reference.

Although some singers bring considerable musical (and perhaps even compositional) experience to their group, a cappella arrangements can be different from other choral arrangements, so some additional instruction is necessary. Most arrangers learn by observation; they see, sing, and experience the arrangements already in their group's repertory and discern their basic components and effective aspects. That is how I learned to arrange. Some groups take a more active role in training arrangers, however. In Company B, a mixed group at Brandeis University, all first-time arrangers partner with an experienced one to learn the process. (Arranging is discussed in more detail in chapter 8.)

Most barbershop and many traditional Western choral arrangements feature four voice parts. Many a cappella groups expand both the number and function of voice parts in their arrangements, however. This difference may be traced, at least in part, to the fact that a cappella music replicates the music of a rock band, in which several instruments with different timbres usually accompany a lead singer. Brandeis University VoiceMale's arrangement of Michael Jackson's "Human Nature" is a good example. At the time I learned it, the group had eight members, so the arrangement calls for six background singers, one vocal percussionist, and the lead soloist. Members of VoiceMale take pride in the fact that each sings his own part. "It doesn't take sixteen people to sing a four-note chord," Drew, the group's music director, told me, echoing a motto he learned from a predecessor. That is, once singers are assigned to each necessary chord tone, the others are better used to serve other functions, such as imitating instrumental riffs from the commercial recording.

In VoiceMale's "Human Nature," which itself is based on a 2004 Boyz II Men recording of the song, four voices provide the basic background chords and rhythms (in example 5.1, the "acoustic guitar" staves, abbreviated "Ac Gtr"), while another sings the muted guitar's melodic interjections ("Muted Gtr"); the sixth background part is sung by the bassist. By using more than four parts, VoiceMale effectively mimics Boyz II Men's (and to a lesser degree Jackson's) recording, including sparse chords providing the basic harmonic background and an additional solo guitar whose lines punctuate the lead. Other a cappella groups use this technique as well, even if more than one voice sings each part.

Example 5.1. Excerpt from Brandeis University VoiceMale's arrangement of "Human Nature," verse. (Transcribed from field recordings by the author.)

Thus, rather than reducing or adapting a piece to the standard choral medium, as many traditional choral arrangements do, the goal here is to create a vocal original by expanding the medium itself.

As most songs have only one soloist, singers spend much of their time singing (often repetitive) background parts. So while a cappella arrangements maintain a distinction between the lead melody (on which listeners focus) and its accompaniment (which serves as background or support), background parts often incorporate various devices to ensure that they are not simply "background" and to provide variety for the singers. VoiceMale called one such device a "bell," a term derived from barbershop describing voices entering in succession to form a chord. In "Human Nature," while the background parts mostly consist of offset and overlapping, rhythmically identical patterns (see example 5.1, "Ac Gtr" staves), bells occur at the end of each phrase during the verse, when the rhythmic pattern is replaced by arpeggios performed by four of the voices (see example 5.2). These mimic the arpeggiated guitar figures in the Boyz II Men recording while providing a textural change, from an overlapping

Example 5.2. A "bell" from Brandeis University VoiceMale's arrangement of "Human Nature." (Transcribed from field recordings by the author.)

rhythmic motive to broken chords, signaling a formal transition and hinting at the upcoming repeat of the verse or the downbeat of the chorus. Moreover, they create moments of interest, as well as a challenge—interest because there is something new to sing and challenge because the passages require precise rhythmic coordination and close listening. Overcoming such challenges and mastering these tricky passages takes time—the better part of a two- or three-hour rehearsal—and results not only in more interesting music for the singers but also a valuable sense of accomplishment.

Syllables

One of the most distinctive aspects of collegiate a cappella arrangements is their vocables, the presumably meaningless words comprising most background parts' lyrics. A cappella singers call them "syllables." Although these sounds do not necessarily carry lexical meaning, they can be mimetically meaningful. Thus, particular syllables are often chosen for a reason.

Before the 1990s, a cappella groups drew on the familiar syllable palette of glee clubs, barbershop quartets, and doo-wop groups: "doo," "bum," "bop," "wah," and open vowels such as "ooo," "oh," or "ah." If the song's lyrics suggested such opportunities, one might occasionally hear a walking bass, an imitative "beep-beep" of car horns, or a momentary impersonation of brass. Much of the time, though, the ensemble would sing as a unit, with everyone on the same rhythm, harmonizing the song's melody. For example, most of the twenty-two tracks on the Yale University Whiffenpoofs' album *The Whiffenpoofs of 1958* (1958) feature this sort of homophonic ensemble singing, even on arrangements that include a soloist. When soloists do stand out from the ensemble, the background singers most often sing the syllables "doo," "bum," or open vowels.

Throughout the 1980s, a cappella recordings increasingly adopted the texture of a band, separating the background parts from the soloist and including fewer and shorter instances of background voices harmonizing the melody. Instead, they more often functioned as accompaniment. The homorhythmic texture of earlier records also gave way to more complex rhythms, including techniques such as "bell chords," "pyramids," and "cascades" (in barbershop parlance).[2] *Safari*, the University of North Carolina Clef Hangers' 1992 album, illustrates this stylistic shift. With the exception of one track (a rendition of "Chattanooga Choo-Choo"), every song features at least one soloist, while backgrounds continually use the syllables "doo" and "ba."

An important change occurred in the mid-1990s as groups began using syllables with a *j* sound, such as "jun," "jin," "sjun," in order to more effectively emulate the sound of a guitar strum. It is unclear who used them first, but "jun" or one of its variants first appears on the *Best of College A Cappella* compilation album's second installment (1996) on tracks recorded in 1994 (the University of Michigan Amazin' Blue's recording of Mr. Mister's "Kyrie") and 1995 (the University of Virginia Gentlemen's recording of Billy Pilgrim's "Insomniac"). VoiceMale's "Human Nature," arranged in 2004, makes extensive use of this *j* sound with its syllables "jig-ga jig-ga" and "jen." Of course, the spread of "jun" was not immediate—as some groups began using the new syllables, others continued with the older ones—and today's groups have not abandoned the more traditional syllable options.

Any time a note is played on an instrument, its sound has at least three acoustic properties aside from pitch. "Attack" describes how the sound first begins, whether slowly, suddenly, or in some other way. "Timbre" is its tone color, produced by the particular combination of frequencies that make up its sound. And "decay" refers to how the sound ends, whether it fades out (quickly or slowly), stops suddenly, and so on. Since most contemporary a cappella arrangements contain parts intended to sound like instruments, it makes sense that many arrangers and singers take these properties into account, even if they lack the scientific terminology to describe them. For example, when members of the Harvard University Fallen Angels were rehearsing their arrangement of "Turn the Beat Around," they spent considerable time making sure each of the three women singing the bass line matched vowels exactly—timbre—while the rest of the singers were instructed to make sure their syllables, a series of "it'll-ow" sounds, were similarly precise—attack and decay.[3]

The term *direct emulation* may be applied when syllables are used to map an instrument's acoustic properties onto a vocally produced sound. Quick attacks, particularly those of pianos, are often accomplished with a *d* sound, such as "dun," "dum," or "den." Slower attacks, like those of some guitars or synthesizer sounds, might call for a less percussive consonant, such as *l* or a "soft *j*" (frica-tive), or they might simply begin with a vowel. The timbre of the syllable is de-termined by the vowel choice and its placement in the singers' mouths (is it nasal, rounded, sung from the back of the throat?). With its "hard *j*" (affrica-tive) syllables, VoiceMale's "Human Nature" maintains the sparse, percussive quality of the Boyz II Men version, which relies heavily on plucked and strummed acoustic guitars with short decays. An arrangement of the same song by the Cornell University Hangovers creates a smoother texture by using sus-tained chords in the background parts, which directly emulate the synthesizer sounds of Michael Jackson's recording.

Syllables are sometimes selected to capture the "mood" of a commercial recording rather than to emulate particular instruments, however. This tech-nique, which maintains an instrumental function without strictly mimicking instrumental sounds, may be termed *indirect emulation*. In my own arrange-ments, I have used syllabic combinations such as "jah-nah-nah" or "jeh-nah-doh" to suggest a dense guitar texture without specifically copying the guitar part from the original commercial release. Although such strings of syllables may not mimic instruments quite as strongly, they provide the general "feeling" or texture necessary to maintain the spirit of the original recording or the mood the arranger wishes to evoke.

Syllables also have the social effect of distinction, enabling singers to think of themselves and their group as different from others. In this way, syllable choice can be an element of personal and group identities. Certain syllables, such as those beginning with a *j* sound, can move a group's style beyond the older-sounding "doo"-like syllabic palette they may associate with glee clubs or barbershop quartets, or the official campus choir, chorus, or chorale. Reflecting on the syllabic combination "kin-diddle-ray-doh, kin-doh-doh-diddle-rai," former VoiceMale member Eli distinguished his group from the others on his campus. The source of his group's unusual syllables may have been the ethnic and linguistic diversity of its arrangers (one was from Israel, another from India), but the effect was to separate it from all others: "Nobody thinks of that kind of stuff," he said, "if you're thinking in English."

Vocal Style

The collegiate a cappella singers I worked with generally avoided vibrato, preferring to sing with a "straight tone" (sometimes called a "flat tone") while on background parts, a musical choice that also effects distinction. John Potter suggests that rock singers use vibrato as a "cultivated effect because of its association with classical singing," while "singers of more middle-of-the-road pop music will use a greater or lesser amount of vibrato according to which end of the sociomusical spectrum they wish to identify with."[4] Many singers I encountered use a lack of vibrato to distinguish themselves and their groups from choirs and glee clubs they perceive as being more "classical." They may also eschew vibrato because of its association, in popular music, with prerock singers (such as Bing Crosby and Frank Sinatra) whose cultivated crooning style sounds old-fashioned to many young audiences.

In Amazin' Blue, the use of vocal style for social distinction frequently began in rehearsal. One of the group's favorite vocal warm-ups consisted of a I–IV–V–vi–V–I harmonic pattern in four-part harmony. As it repeated, ad infinitum, the music director would call out instructions for how to stylize the next go-around. A common sequence of instructions would consist of three styles: "choral," in which the singers would exaggerate the roundedness of their vowels and raise their soft palate (thus "opening" their vocal cavities to their largest "size"); "opera," in which they would sing with the widest vibrato they could muster; and finally "Amazin' Blue," in which they would return to their customary vocal style of straight tone, moderately "open" singing. Thus, the singers embodied the differences between three different vocal styles, ending each time with the style whose name matched their own—effectively instilling a sense of musical and social identity.

For a cappella singers, the most important vocal concept is blend. Blended voices are indistinguishable from one another. Blend has been used as musical justification for the avoidance of vibrato, as Gage Averill notes in the case of barbershop: "One requirement for ringing chords [one of barbershop's stylistic goals] was the avoidance of vibrato (which would of course vary the pitch and derail any effort to lock the chord). An article on barbershop style once called vibrato 'poison.'"[5] The singers I consulted avoided vibrato for similar reasons. They often told me of the value of a singer's ability to blend, and the use of vibrato was heavily criticized in deliberations about new members.[6] Historical precedents for a cappella's emphasis on blend can also be found in the glee club tradition (vis-à-vis the straight-tone technique of the early St. Olaf choir), the African American quartet tradition, and doo-wop.[7]

VoiceMale sought a particular vocal style hinging on a strong, loud, and intense timbre. In songs such as "Human Nature," it avoided not only vibrato but also falsetto, the upper part of the vocal range. In my field recordings of the song, the singers "belt" (in chest voice) during the song's brief introduction and chorus but not during the verse, when the listener's attention focuses on the soloist. This use of belting (and volume) emphasizes passages during which the group, not the soloist, is the center of attention.

Eli explained this stylistic preference: "As part of the power of the sound that we try to put out, we very rarely put anything in falsetto. If you can hit it, unless it's supposed to be quiet, we want it powerful, we want it out there." Another member, Jon, explained that they want to sound as loud, or louder, with their seven members as other groups do with seventeen. Given VoiceMale's ideal of one singer per part, it becomes clear that in order to achieve the desired loud and intense sound while maintaining a balance between the parts each individual must sing confidently and loudly enough by himself. No one else is covering his note; there is no safety in numbers. An untrained falsetto is typically quieter than a male voice in the belt range, so avoiding falsetto makes sense as a musical choice.

But it was also a social choice. It fit the ethos of VoiceMale's identity as projected by its manner of vocal delivery. In Eli's quote, *power* is the key word, applying both to the singer's physical effort and to the identity he projects. As Simon Frith writes, "Even when treating the voice as an instrument . . . it stands for the person more directly than any other musical device."[8] Through its loudly belted performances, VoiceMale tried to project masculinity, strength, even domination. In addition, through the volume its members could produce by belting, VoiceMale distinguished itself from other men's groups (such as the Beelzebubs at nearby Tufts University), which usually consisted of more singers. In effect, the men of VoiceMale sought to prove that they were more musically potent; they could do more with less.

Not all groups shared VoiceMale's vocal style or intent. The Boston University Treblemakers preferred a more muted, more choral sound. It was unusual for the group's tenors to belt. Instead, they habitually switched out of their chest voices and into falsetto whenever they had to sing high. In October 2004, I taught them my arrangement of Maroon 5's 2002 pop ballad "She Will Be Loved." During the song's climactic final chorus, the tenor part splits into two lines. The upper line features sustained notes on a high G (G4) and a momentary A-flat and is intended to indirectly emulate a wailing, distorted electric guitar. It could have been sung by an alto, but I wanted to hear the strain in a tenor's voice, a sort of soaring gesture that would expand the emotional scope of the song as it entered its final chorus. Yet the tenors in the Treblemakers preferred, and ultimately chose, to sing the passage in falsetto. They placed the sound forward in their mouths, producing a focused, pointed timbre that came close to, but did not quite achieve, the effect I wanted. It was their preference, not a necessity, to use the falsetto's lighter vocal quality, since in other songs these same singers could hit the same pitches with the timbre I sought—as soloists. In order to blend properly, they avoided singing too loudly or in a manner that would vary significantly in timbre from the rest of the group. Moreover, the goal was not volume or domination but instead a smoother, gentler, blended sound—a goal very much in line with the social image the group sought to project.

Vocal Percussion and Gender

Vocal percussion refers to the practice of vocally emulating the sounds of a drum set, an important rhythmic instrument in a typical rock band. Singers usually create a kick drum with the syllables "doo" or "doom" placed low in the vocal range, or an unvocalized plosive "p" or "b," and a snare drum with a "kh" or a "pf." These sounds, along with "ts" for hi-hats and ride cymbals and "ksh" or "psh" for crash cymbals, can be combined with rhythmic breathing into patterns that approximate those played on a rock kit. Even if the sounds of vocal percussion, when isolated, do not convincingly imitate those of actual drums, professional vocal percussionist Wes Carroll explains, they can still assume the function of the drums when they are performed in the right rhythmic patterns.[9] During performances, bodily gestures make clear visually the instruments being imitated vocally, from "air-drums" to "air-guitars." It is especially common to see vocal percussionists make drumming gestures. Some performers believe that such bodily gestures actually improve the sound and make for more convincing performances and recordings.[10]

The practice of vocal percussion is widely perceived as a male domain. Talented female vocal percussionists seem to require qualification, such as "she's rockin' it *for a girl, for a chick,*" as Alyson, a Fallen Angels alumna, put it. Despite knowing talented female vocal percussionists, including one who had recently been a member of their group, most members of the Fallen Angels avoided vocal percussion parts. Many made it a point not to develop such skills. The perception of vocal percussion as inappropriate for women is so widespread that Carroll had to address it directly in a column published by the Contemporary A Cappella Society of America (CASA), writing, "[T]here is no physiological way in which I rely on my gender to perform vocal percussion. (Period. Full stop!)" He saw the paucity of female vocal percussionists and the persistence of the question "Can women do mouthdrumming?" as a result of the ways in which the "art" of vocal percussion has been practiced; he called it "combative in flavor if not actually in practice (witness 'beatbox battles' and such)."[11] Vocal percussion certainly draws on culturally embedded ideas associated with its male-dominated hip-hop history even if contemporary agents like Carroll seek to weaken those gendered associations.

Claims that women's vocal percussion is somehow weaker often point to physical factors first. Carroll's statement notwithstanding, female singers' reluctance to take on vocal percussion parts, or their ineffectual performance of them, is frequently attributed to a lack of depth in the female vocal range, resulting in a weak bass or kick drum. Fallen Angels member Debra told me, "We try to push people to do it, but I mean obviously I don't have a bass [voice], you know? I can do everything on top just fine: I have a hi-hat . . . I [just] can't do a bass [drum]." When women perform vocal percussion, fellow singer Charlotte described the overall group sound as "more hollow," and Chimnomnso, another member of the group, agreed.

Importantly, Carroll's mouthdrumming technique does not actually rely on physiological features like the larynx or chest resonance. Instead, he uses vocal articulators (lips, tongue, etc.) to produce quiet sounds that are immediately picked up by a microphone and amplified. In the world of collegiate a cappella, however, this technique is not widely used, probably because groups often perform without microphone amplification. Instead, most collegiate vocal percussionists rely on the larynx and chest resonance as a sound source.

But the problem of women's vocal percussion is also visual. When I asked Alyson why she thought the women in the Fallen Angels were so reluctant to do vocal percussion, she replied, "Some people think they look funny or sound funny. I always did this thing that everybody laughed at when I tried to do the ["pff" snare] thing. I guess I scrunch my face; I don't know what I do but apparently it's hilarious." Moreover, developing vocal percussion skills requires practice. On the Recorded A Cappella Review Board (RARB) forum, Kurt, a vocal coach and a cappella clinician, observed that male vocal percussionists tend to practice more than their female counterparts do.[12] Alyson would have agreed. "It's one of those things that you have to go home and you have to do it all the time," she said. "And I'm not willing to walk through the subway" making vocal percussion sounds. The concern with "looking funny" is grounded in the experience of, and potential for, social embarrassment, and Alyson was not the only one concerned. When one of the freshman members of VoiceMale attempted vocal percussion for the first time, the other men found his facial expressions particularly amusing; he became the subject of many jokes in the weeks that followed.[13]

From the perspective of one woman in the Treblemakers, vocal percussion is a matter of power, as the percussionist is the most powerful member of the group during a performance.[14] He—she nearly always referred to the percussionist using the male pronoun—controls the tempo and the "feel" of each song in a way neither the soloist nor the music director can. When members singing background parts are instructed to listen to each other in order to ensure a performance's success, they are typically told to listen to the basses for tuning and to the percussionist for tempo, not to the soloist. To be effective, this Treblemaker explained, vocal percussion needs to be loud enough to be heard over all the singers. If one believes that men have superior chest resonance and therefore greater volume, then it is easy to conclude that a group can best present itself if a male member provides percussion. Weak percussion leads to weak performances, which reflects badly on the whole group, so the logic goes.

The power attributed to vocal percussion lines up with the masculine character other scholars find in rock music, which Sara Cohen argues is "actively produced as male."[15] This character may result from the exclusion of women from the music industry or scholarly accounts of rock music.[16] Or it may derive from a gendered quality attached to specific genres or instruments.[17] Frith and Angela McRobbie consider rock "a framework within which male sexuality can find a range of acceptable, heterosexual expressions."[18] Indeed, "if you want to sing with girls, join a co-ed group," members of VoiceMale said half-jokingly, but "if you want to sing *to* girls, join VoiceMale." This distinction stems from the idea that social capital is generated by the act of performing music in ways that promote the desirability of the male performer.[19]

In rock, Mary Ann Clawson writes, "power is derived from sound . . . Playing rock music is by definition an act of aural-spatial domination."[20] The requirement that vocal percussion be deep and loud can be understood as such domination. Clawson draws on David Whitson's work on sports teams, which stresses the importance of the body in the development of male identity. "To learn to be a male is to learn to project a physical presence that speaks of latent power," which can be accomplished through "learning to use the body in 'forceful and space-occupying ways'" involving "practiced combinations of force and skill" of which vocal percussion is a good example.[21]

"Be the Song": Emulation and Originality in A Cappella

One of the goals of collegiate a cappella is to sing songs the audience knows and hopefully loves. A successful arrangement must preserve important harmonic, rhythmic, and melodic aspects of a song's commercial recording, so a certain degree of emulation is necessary to achieve this goal. Julia and Lianna, from Company B, agreed that arrangements closely mimicking commercial recordings help determine a song's success in performance.

> J: The reason that we try to stay so true to the song is so that when we sing it, it sounds like the song. We want our arrangement to *be the song,* just a cappella. You know, we don't want to change it [from] the way the artist intended it to be. So—
>
> L: And then the audience really catches onto it—
>
> J: Yeah.
>
> L: —and they really like the way it's *just* how they heard it on the radio.

Their language reveals that they are talking about the *sound* of an artist's commercial recording. To them, it is obvious that the "song" is the recording, which needs to be reproduced accurately to satisfy audiences. (While the singers and arrangers I worked with never talked about their arrangements in terms of "authenticity," this concept has been particularly important to scholars assessing the ideologies behind popular music and may therefore represent a point at which a cappella and scholarly discourses connect.)[22]

How do arrangers get their songs to emulate commercial recordings? Many start with transcription, simply notating for voices what is played by instruments. Anna Callahan, author of an arranging manual specifically for collegiate a cappella, proposes a continuum on which she locates three types of arranging: "transcribing," what she calls "transanging," and "true arranging." Her language seems to place the greatest value on the latter.

[Transcribing:] the act of listening to something and writing down exactly what you hear.

[Transanging:] to convert a song originally played with instrumentation into an a cappella song without substantially changing the melody, harmonic structure, or style. Transanging often involves restructuring, simplification, range adjustments, syllable assigning, and other modifications of the original, but is always replicating the original version.

[True arranging:] This is the type of arranging that I call "true" arranging, not because transcribing and transanging aren't useful, difficult, or creative, but because this type of arranging allows you the freedom to really express yourself. [Includes dramatic changes of style, mood, meter, form, and dynamic growth.][23]

Callahan's terminology suggests that emulation alone fails to produce "true" a cappella or allow arrangers and singers "to really express" themselves, and others agree. For example, in a 2004 discussion on the RARB forum, one arranger criticized "strictly imitative charts." He wrote, "I agree with those . . . who are tired of literal transcriptions of pop tunes. That's not art, it's math. I don't want to go to math concerts."[24]

Still, at its core, a cappella carries an emulative imperative.[25] The techniques I have described serve, in many cases, to meet it. However, oftentimes arrangements are expected to show some signs of departure from the original commercial recording, even if they are small or difficult to notice. This may be one of things that make a cappella a fun, vibrant musical practice—and a different experience than just listening to commercial recordings. Thus, an adequate a cappella arrangement (and performance) sounds like the song's commercial recording, but an excellent one presents the song in a new way that pays homage to the original while adding something unexpected.

Aside from VoiceMale's "bells," there are other techniques that keep singers and listeners interested, challenged, and happily engaged with the music, including musical quotation, formal expansion, textural variation, the sharing of melodic material across voice parts, and a soloist's reinterpretation of a song's lead, to name only the most common. The first two explicitly change the song through the introduction of new musical material. The other three can be used in the pursuit of a cappella's overall emulative goal or as ways to bring a new interpretation to a song. All can have social implications.

Musical quotations reference other songs within an arrangement. Sometimes other material by the same recording artist is borrowed; an arranger might use lyrics from one song as background syllables to another song. At other times he or she may quote an entirely different musical source, with arrangement and source having only a common harmonic framework. In its recording of "Let Me Entertain You," originally recorded by British rocker Robbie Williams in 1997, VoiceMale quotes Steppenwolf's "Magic Carpet Ride" (1968). A second soloist sings the Steppenwolf lyrics ("close your eyes girl, look inside girl / let the sound take you away") while impersonating the raspy quality of that song's lead. At the quotation's introduction, all background rhythmic activity ceases, allowing the listener to focus entirely on the Steppenwolf interpolation with only a backing of block chords. Then the Williams song's refrain ("let me entertain you") returns in the primary soloist's voice while the Steppenwolf lyrics continue more quietly as a harmony line. The result is not a Williams-Steppenwolf medley but a brief reference to the second song that folds into the fabric of the first.

The prevalence of musical allusions in a cappella suggests not only the playfulness of the genre but also an appreciation of intertextuality's complexity. Whether or not the audience recognizes the quotation and appreciates its significance depends partly on how apparent it is. If executed by a soloist, it makes a direct and apparent association with the secondary song. If it appears only within the background parts, then it remains "insider knowledge"—another social distinction—and a feat of musical fusion of which the singers, themselves, are proud but that remains mostly hidden to listeners.

A related technique involves changing a song's form by adding new, rather than borrowed, musical material. An arranger from Amazin' Blue added a new, scatlike section to the Sting song "If I Ever Lose My Faith In You" that featured the group without a soloist. Each background part entered separately, as if announcing its presence and independence from the other parts. The background singers were thereby featured for a moment before the soloist, and the song's

original form, returned. By basing this new section on the cyclic harmonic progression of the song's coda (iii–i) and by avoiding the introduction of new
lyrics, this technique allowed the formal expansion to emerge organically
rather than seem imposed.

Since the 1990s, a cappella has drawn a fundamental distinction between
the role of lead soloist and background singer through the articulation of
words: the former may do so, while the latter usually does not. One technique
used to create a textural variation is the sparing but striking use of the whole
group as a homophonic choir. After spending most of a song singing instrumentally functioning background syllables, the entire group may explode, for-
tissimo, in dense harmony, singing the lyrics along with the soloist, creating a
dramatic statement and weakening the lead/accompaniment dichotomy.[26] This
"momentary choir" technique is prevalent in the a cappella repertory, but related techniques of varying an arrangement's texture also include passages during which the basses drop out (leading to a distinct textural change and the opportunity to make a musical event out of the bass section's return) and other
moments of marked contrast between polyphonic and homophonic passages.

A particularly important technique involves having two or more parts coordinate, often antiphonally or in a hocket, to create a single melodic line. The
"instrumental" section of the Treblemakers' arrangement of Rufus Wainwright's "Instant Pleasure" reveals such an exchange (example 5.3). The altos
begin by directly emulating the distorted guitar solo in the original recording
using the syllables "bair ner ner" and are answered a measure later with an
arpeggio articulated by the tenors, altos, and sopranos. After this figure repeats,
the harmony changes (from I–V–IV to the double-plagal I–^{b}VII–IV–^{b}III–
^{b}VII^6–I) and the tenors seize the melody before the sopranos finish the phrase.
In my fieldwork, I found that singers especially enjoyed moments like this. Creating a single melodic line fosters visual and aural communication and thereby
enhances the performance's social dimension.

Finally, the personal prerogative of the soloist offers a prime vehicle for
originality. He or she need not simply imitate the recording artist's performance, although some fidelity to the commercial recording is fundamental to a
cappella's emulative goal. Small melodic or timbral, or even visual, variations
allow soloists to give their performance "its own personality," as Julia and
Lianna put it. This idea aligns with George Plasketes's writing on the process of
covering, which he describes as an "adaptation, in which much of the value lies
in the artists' interpretation." In this recontextualization, "Measuring the inter-

Example 5.3. Excerpt from the Boston University Treblemakers' arrangement of "Instant Pleasure" showing soprano, alto, and tenor parts coordinating to create one melodic line.

preter's skill, in part, lies in how well the artist uncovers and conveys the spirit of the original, enhances the nuances of its melody, rhythm, phrasing, or structure, maybe adding a new arrangement, sense of occasion or thread of irony."[27]

Social Motivations for Stylistic Goals

The methods collegiate a cappella groups use to make their music, and the social effects created by the resulting style, begin to illustrate some of the social meanings attributed to sounds within the musical practice, such as distinction. But what else motivates a cappella's stylistic goals? One answer may be economic: in the crowded arena of student activities, a cappella groups must compete with each other and other student clubs for financial and human resources while maintaining those they already have. By filling their repertory with covers, a cappella groups give their audiences—which may otherwise be limited only to roommates, friends, and family—something familiar, adding motivation to attend performances. Covers also provide constraints on and conventions for expression: the audience already knows how the song goes, so the thrill comes from how the group will do it in a new, vocal-only medium. Moreover, a song performed by an a cappella group is often not immediately recognizable based on the first few measures of its introduction. Typically audience members wait for a recognizable melodic, harmonic, or rhythmic snippet—the song's hook, perhaps—before recognizing the song. In my research, concert programs only rarely listed the titles of the songs to be performed, so recognition was based entirely on aural perception. In performance, then, a cappella groups enable a pleasurable sense of discovery as audiences identify familiar songs.

Few a cappella groups collect dues from their members, and most rarely find their school administrations to be sufficient sources of funding. Ticket and album sales therefore comprise most of a group's revenue, but economic success also depends on constant recruitment efforts, whether active (seeking out new members) or passive (staying visible to prospective members). On campuses where a cappella thrives, the perception of a diluted talent pool and heightened intergroup competition can be intense. A group must ensure its continued survival and success by attracting and training showstopping soloists, skilled arrangers, and future leaders through its performances. Every time it performs a popular or familiar song, or quotes another song in an arrangement, it not only shows off the skills of its musicians but also creates an opportunity for connection with potential members.

As a voluntary activity, a cappella group members have to feel valued in order to participate. As one singer from the University of Pennsylvania Counterparts told me, "[Y]ou can sing doo's and da's only so long before it stops feeling fulfilling." When a group "gives" a member the spotlight (e.g., a solo), it is implied that the other singers believe that that member's is the best voice for that song and have confidence in his or her ability to execute it successfully on their behalf. Most groups determine each song's lead soloist by holding internal auditions, judged by those members not auditioning. In some groups, an important factor in this audition process is whether any of the candidates already have solos in the group's repertory (or, importantly, if any do not), revealing that the distribution of solos is important socially. Frith's metonymic treatment of the voice/instrument as the person is instructive here. With a share of the spotlight comes the social implication that the individual's voice is important, not only as a singing voice but as a person.

In some songs, the melody is split among several soloists, each taking succeeding sections. Such distributions are often an effective way of honoring several members at once, although those members may be acutely aware that they sing only part of a song. Soloists represent their group to the audience, including prospective members. By presenting several individuals as soloists, a group can access a larger social network in its audience. As Drew explained: "If everybody has a solo, the audience gets to feel like they've met everybody, and that's a better performance. That makes them feel closer to you than if two people are singing all the solos and the rest of the guys are just faceless, nameless guys in the back singing 'doo-wop, doo-wop.'"

The economics of time also play an important role. Each singer has many obligations—academic and social commitments, family needs, religious practice, and so forth—which may conflict with those related to a cappella. When I asked singers what they gained from their experience in an a cappella group, the most common answer, after the creation of community, was better time-management skills. Since membership in an a cappella group is not legally binding, members may theoretically quit at any time. One might think of a cappella participation as a cost-and-rewards phenomenon, implying a sort of psychological ledger by means of which individuals determine whether they are sufficiently satisfied with their experience to remain in a group. Personal enrichment, the enjoyment of singing, and self-actualization have been demonstrated as the rewards of barbershop singing.[28] The a cappella case also suggests the support of a similarly liminal community, leadership experience, and the feeling of being valued by one's peers. In barbershop, common costs are disappointments in competitions, dislike of group leadership, and frustration with varying levels of commitment among other singers—conclusions that largely apply to a cappella.[29] But for each individual, the weights of the various costs and rewards differ. While I sang with Amazin' Blue, the sharing of the spotlight (and the implied value of individual voices) strongly affected individual members' decisions to remain.

Sharing the spotlight also allows singers to tap into the powerful cultural archetype of the "rock star," a figure with considerable social capital, especially in youth culture. For many, it is simply good fun to create a virtuosic or spectacular vocal-only rendition of a familiar musical icon. But beneath the pleasure of performance may lie the process Frith and R. J. Warren Zanes call "identification," which occurs when a fan (or fanatic) either desires the popular artist or desires to be the popular artist and then enacts that desire through mimicry.[30] As one a cappella singer told me in a 2005 interview:

> Every girl secretly wants to be like Britney Spears. You see someone dance—and I'm not saying risqué—but you see someone be so confident and dance like that and sing and really belt it out, and have so much energy, and you're just like, "I want to be like that." And, "if I join that group, I will be."

The vocal techniques and bodily gestures that singers perform facilitate identification. They enable the singer to assume a rock star's persona or act like the rock star playing his or her instrument. Moreover, through direct emulation, syllables enable the singer to be the rock star's instrument.

Collegiate A Cappella and the Discourse of Musical Recontextualization

The term *emulation,* defined by the *Oxford English Dictionary* as "the endeavour to equal or surpass others in any achievement or quality," nicely captures how collegiate a cappella uses certain techniques, which might be described as "imitation" or "mimicry" (especially if the instrumental function of the vocal parts is clear), in order for the vocal-only presentation of a song to "equal" the commercial recording.[31] Other techniques, such as offering new musical ideas, aim to "surpass" the commercial recording. Although emulation and originality have an inherent tension and sometimes contradict each other, both pervade a cappella.

At the same time, the practice of "covering," recontextualizing musical material from one setting to another, is essential. When scholars have addressed covering, they usually distinguish between at least two types, although terminological agreement has been elusive. (Only some refer to recorded sources, a key element of a cappella.) David Horn separates covering (a "close approximation to an original") from "interpreting" (which "may possibly involve that, but does not have to"), while Serge Lacasse associates "interpretation or reading" directly with covering ("a rendering of a previously recorded song that displays the usual stylistic configuration of the covering artist").[32] Deena Weinstein contrasts the terms *cover* and *version*, differentiating the two by their reference to preexisting material: a cover references a particular recording of a song, while a version references the underlying song itself.[33] Weinstein's cover/version dichotomy may provide the most specific terms, but how does it square with processes discussed here?

A cappella shows that categories such as "cover" and "version" sometimes blur. A cappella groups emulate particular performances of songs (created or captured on particular recordings) while simultaneously denying the very instruments used in those performances. And when an a cappella group strives to re-create aspects of a recording—such as in VoiceMale's arrangement of "Human Nature," whose guitar lines appear more prominently in Boyz II Men's recording of the Michael Jackson song than Jackson's—it would seem the group is aspiring to cover. At the same time, some techniques of originality, such as interplay between background parts or reinterpretations of the lead melody, suggest an effort to version. Yet because they alter basic building blocks of the piece, other techniques of originality, such as musical quotation and formal expansion, undermine the case for a cappella as a versioning practice. Similar difficulties arise when the scope is limited to syllables, as direct emulation suggests covering while indirect emulation may imply versioning.

The previously proposed schemes defining the act of musical recontextualization also largely fail to account for the social aspects of musical practice.[34] Does it matter to musicians whether they are covering or versioning? My research shows that other issues are in fact more pressing. Therefore, the remaining chapters turn increasingly to those topics, beginning with trust and support, power and social capital, and identity in a cappella rehearsals.

CHAPTER 6

In Rehearsal: A Cappella's Social Performance

Most of the time collegiate a cappella singers spend with their groups is devoted to rehearsal, usually between six and ten hours per week in two or three sessions on alternating nights. The University of Michigan Amazin' Blue rehearsed three times per week for a total of seven hours, the Harvard University Fallen Angels for two hours three days a week, the Boston University Treblemakers for three hours twice each week, and Brandeis University VoiceMale for three hours once and two hours twice per week. It makes sense, therefore, to include the rehearsal in an investigation of a cappella. Thus, this chapter has three goals: to offer a sense of what it is like to participate in such a rehearsal; to discern what rehearsals tell us about a cappella groups, their behaviors, and their beliefs; and to challenge the idea that rehearsals serve a purely preparatory function. Such an examination reveals how the social activity that fills rehearsal is not a distraction from the music but a crucial foundation for each member's sense of belonging to a community and can help guide singers through the rite of passage known as college. In the rehearsal, a group's social, political, and musical practices are negotiated and propagated. These practices, in turn, contribute to groups' conceptions of their style and identity.

Earlier studies of rehearsals have not always embraced this perspective. Much published work on vocal ensemble rehearsals in the West consists of manuals intended to help choral directors and conductors prepare music for public performance.[1] Some scholars, such as Richard Schechner, have viewed rehearsals as a time to prepare performances, a "way of selecting from the possible actions those to be performed."[2] Yet in my view, a cappella singers not only select actions to be performed but also come to an agreement on *how* they are to be performed and what their performance means socially and musically. Indeed, this perspective is supported by other studies, such as Carol E. Robertson's work with the Washington, DC, Area Feminist Chorus.[3] And while the idea that musical ensembles serve social functions is certainly not new with a cappella, the liminal setting of higher education presents a context different from those, like Robinson's, already explored in the literature.[4]

The following "thick description" of a Fallen Angels rehearsal and the analyses that follow stress that group's marginality in Harvard's a cappella scene. This "outsider" status highlights certain political aspects of the campus a cappella community and the strategies groups develop to deal with them. And while some of the Fallen Angels' practices are particular to that group, most differed little from those I observed in groups on other campuses, including those at the center of their campus scenes.

Rehearsing with the Fallen Angels

Just before seven o'clock in the evening, I arrived at Leverett House, a Harvard University dormitory situated near the Charles River in Cambridge, Massachusetts. Following a student through the building's front door, I made my way across a small foyer, to the left, and down a few steps to the Junior Common Room, a lounge used for meetings, receptions, and other events, featuring a grand piano, comfortable couches and chairs, and a fireplace. There I found four of the Fallen Angels gathered around the piano.[5] Jennifer, the group's president, was a junior from Tennessee. She stood next to Susan, a senior and the group's oldest and most experienced member. While no longer holding an official leadership position, Susan's knowledge of the "ins and outs" of Harvard a cappella and the group's past successes and failures made hers a valuable, if soft-spoken, voice. Standing at the piano was Debra, a junior who recently finished serving as the group's music director, and freshman Anne, who currently shared that post with junior Candace.

Soon the rest of the women arrived, right on time for the start of rehearsal. As a group, their diversity roughly tracked with that of the student population of Harvard College. At least two of the twelve members were of Asian descent, one was Persian, and one was African American.[6] All were American citizens, and all had gone to high school in the United States, except for one who had attended an American international school in Beijing. Beyond music, their interests were similarly diverse. Debra spent all her waking hours, it seemed, in a biology laboratory. Maggie, a freshman from a nearby Boston suburb, played on the women's soccer team. Freshman Rebecca spent her time organizing the Harvard Model United Nations conference. And sophomore Danielle was active in a student political club. Singing with the Fallen Angels was thus one of many extracurricular pursuits for these young women.

During the 2004–5 year, the Fallen Angels was one of two women's a cappella groups at Harvard. The other was the Radcliffe Pitches, which some of the Fallen Angels considered a cross-campus rival and a group they portrayed as having older musical tastes (e.g., doo-wop, vocal jazz).[7] The Fallen Angels therefore billed itself as Harvard's only women's *contemporary pop* a cappella group. It also differed from the other Harvard groups because, at the time I joined it, the group was fairly new (only four years old). As a result, it had not yet been fully accepted by the rest of the Harvard a cappella establishment. It was often excluded from events to which the other groups were privy, such as coordinated auditions; official programs for admitted students, freshmen, and graduating seniors; and, most important, regular access to the most coveted venue on campus, the Sanders Theatre.[8]

The members of the Fallen Angels generally acknowledged the identity ascribed to their group: upstarts on the fringe of Harvard a cappella (whether intentional or not, their group's name also fits this image). They had neither a track record of audience draw and staying power, a prerequisite for access to Sanders, nor proof of musical excellence demonstrated through competition success, critically acclaimed recordings, or historical longevity. Yet they embraced this "outsider" status, adding positive self-attributed traits that separated them further from their cross-campus musical peers. The pursuit of musical excellence, according to them, should not overtake the pursuit of musical camaraderie and pleasure. In their view, many of the older, more established groups at Harvard inverted these priorities, resulting in musical experiences that may have sounded good but were less enjoyable for the singers.[9]

Jennifer called the rehearsal to order, and we sat on the chairs and couches across the room from the piano. A few of the women had arrived directly from the dining hall carrying trays with dinner plates and small desserts to share. Fallen Angels rehearsals always began with "check-in." One by one, each member would talk briefly about recent events in her life, share a funny story, or vent a frustration. Often the others responded with advice for the academic and, more frequently, social situations described. From the start, I was included in check-in, too, although my first few weeks with the group were sometimes marked by moments of tension, as some women were reluctant to share intimate details of their lives with me—a man—in the room. While eventually becoming less noticeable, this anxiety never quite disappeared. As the months passed I found myself sharing more details of my personal life, as were the Fallen Angels women. Check-in was comfortable and supportive. No one was forced to talk, but everyone usually did. The whole process usually took between ten and fifteen minutes.

The next task was business. For about ten minutes, Jennifer discussed performance requests ("gig proposals") the group had received. Given the variety of activities each member pursued, gigs had to be scheduled carefully. Thinking ahead to their upcoming concert, they needed to decide certain details so advance preparations could be made. Most important, they needed a concert theme. A good theme could translate easily into a catchy (and/or funny or punny) title, appropriate costumes, humorous skits, and posters for publicity. Their previous concert had been titled "Angels: Most Wanted," a parody of crime-reporting television programs featuring short sketches in which members became "notorious" for humorous "crimes" like vanity or petty theft (see fig. 6.1).

They decided to invite the Din & Tonics, a men's a cappella group at Harvard, as their "guest group" or opening act, a social and strategic choice. Some of the women were friendly with a few of the men and planned to use these connections to interest them in the gig. Usually a guest group sings one fifteen-minute set—two to four songs—at the beginning of a concert, after which the host group performs. Sensing their marginal place in the campus a cappella field, the women proposed to sweeten the deal for the men by offering them *three* sets, tripling their stage time. Booking them was important. If an established and respected group like the Din & Tonics chose to associate with the Fallen Angels musically, it would boost the Fallen Angels' standing on the campus scene. If all went well, not only would the Din & Tonics' popularity draw an audience that would not otherwise attend a Fallen Angels concert, but the whole affair would pull the Fallen Angels in a little bit from the margins of Harvard a cappella.

Energized by the musical and political possibilities of their upcoming concert, they began the singing portion of the rehearsal. At this point, Anne took over. The others stood in a circle in the center of the room and faced inward toward each other. Anne played a pitch and a major chord on the piano to orient the singers to the key. Then she modeled a brief vocal exercise to begin warm-

Fig. 6.1. The Harvard University Fallen Angels' "Angels: Most Wanted" concert poster, 2004. (Courtesy of the Fallen Angels.)

ing up their voices, a common choral practice. The rest of the group immediately chimed in. "Listen to each other," Debra instructed, "and match vowel shapes." A few women nodded slightly, acknowledging Debra's comment. Eyes darted about as singers visually measured the curvature of their friends' lips and the shapes of their mouths, attempting to match them exactly. Some of the younger members looked to Susan or Jennifer, perhaps assuming that their manner of vocal production was more correct.

After two more warm-up exercises, the repertory-based portion of the rehearsal commenced. Anne stepped away from the piano to join the circle and announced a song title, "Band of Gold." The group had been singing this one for a several semesters. But like all a cappella groups, the membership changed over time, so adjustments were necessary. Jennifer, the song's arranger, reassigned Anne to sing the background part formerly sung by Maria, a member who had recently taken time off from the group. It was a treble-range countermelody that included several passages of lyrics in harmony with the song's lead ("the solo"), which Jennifer sang. It differed substantially from the lower-range, rhythmic or basslike parts assigned to most of the singers. Anne asked Jennifer for help in learning the part, and Debra soon joined them, consulting the notated score of the arrangement ("the music"), as well as teaching aurally and from memory. They used the piano for reference, but mostly the two older members just sang the part to the younger one, who repeated it back. Then all three sang the passages together to make sure Anne knew them before inviting the rest of the group to join in.

Candace conducted as they ran the entire song with Anne on her new part, Jennifer on the solo, and all the background voices singing. As they sang, nearly everyone made the same physical motions, bending a knee slightly on each beat, alternating left and right. The whole group moved together, physically entrained through the music. Debra stood by Anne, singing her new part during tricky passages. Meanwhile, Jennifer's solo did not follow precisely, creating a rhythmic clash that the women found humorous but confusing. Who should they follow, the soloist or the conductor? Who controls the flow of the music?

After a second time through the song, Anne asked Jennifer what sort of "tone" she should use when harmonizing with the solo. She offered two possibilities: "Motown," indicating a pop sensibility with appropriate scoops and styling and limited use of vibrato; or "chorally," with a stronger emphasis on rounded vowels, precise attacks on each pitch and execution of each rhythm, and some moderate vibrato. Jennifer chose Motown. Debra added that Maria used to sing it "chorally" as a matter of habit. So the substitution of Anne's voice meant not only a change of personnel but also a change of timbre and style on an important harmony part.

During this exchange, I heard a few others discussing a potential theme for the upcoming concert, "prom night." The idea offered several possibilities: they could sing a medley of popular songs about high school or one comprising songs that were popular while they themselves were in high school; the Din & Tonics could be the Fallen Angels' "prom dates," with dancing couples grossly (and humorously) mismatched in their relative heights; and the women could perform skits parodying recent films set in high schools, *Mean Girls* and *Napoleon Dynamite*.

Following one more run of "Band of Gold," the rehearsal ended. Most of the members gathered their belongings and left in small groupings. A few stayed behind for a meeting to work out administrative details for upcoming events, including the concert. I moved with them into the Leverett dining hall, where we grabbed something to drink, plus a few cookies to snack on, and began talking business.

Trust and the Performance of Social Support

In some ways the Fallen Angels rehearsal was typical, including elements common to all rehearsals I observed, such as the business discussion, warm-ups, and time for learning and practicing songs. In other ways, such as the degree to which the group members institutionalized and made explicit their social support for each other, it was exceptional. Check-in was a standard part of their rehearsal structure but unique among groups with which I worked.

Susan once told me that check-in had begun with Alyson, a Fallen Angels founder and a psychology student familiar with peer-counseling methods. After an episode of severe disagreement, she brought the idea to the group. Its importance became clear on two occasions when it was removed because the members sought to reinstate it. During an organizational meeting in mid-September, Jennifer suggested that check-in was an inefficient use of rehearsal time. She sought alternatives, such as not doing it at every rehearsal or having only a few members check in during each rehearsal. But the others resisted changing the routine; for most of the members, check-in was a brief yet important time to connect, to learn what was going on in each other's lives, and to give and receive support. Then, during the final weeks before their fall concert in early November, check-in was temporarily suspended while the group held extra rehearsals. Susan recalled:

> Before the fall concert, for about two or three weeks . . . check-in was taken away because we needed to focus on the music. People were miserable. I could see it . . . [P]eople were so used to, when they come to the Angels, seeing a loving environment and an environment that they can really build from that I feel like we almost *rely* on having check-in. They *save* stories to tell at check-in. It's really endearing. I just think it's something for our group that's been really important.

For the Fallen Angels, the social support offered by check-in was often more important than musical perfection. In fact, Alyson maintained that members remained committed to the group, in spite of its lack of musical accomplishments relative to other Harvard groups, precisely because of the environment check-in fostered.

> There has to be something other than the music that pulls you back. There has to be, otherwise you'll stop coming, right? We're not good enough for that to be a total reward—there's no kickback in that . . . [In the Fallen Angels,] the *people* really have to bring you back, otherwise you'd just stop coming. So in doing that you sacrifice some of the things . . . [Y]ou quote-unquote "waste time" with check-in, you sacrifice some sound quality. But meanwhile I'd say for most everyone in the Angels, the Angels have been such a source of support or have taken on such a strong emotional role in their lives that those few missed notes or whatever just don't even compare to what . . . you gain.[10]

Similarly, Susan emphasized that her best memories of a cappella came from Fallen Angels rehearsals, especially from check-in. As Jennifer's and Debra's actions illustrate, however, this view of check-in was not universal. Some members valued musicality highly—to the extent that they occasionally considered check-in dispensable.

Through check-in, the women share knowledge and experience, both academic and social. If one is anxious about an upcoming exam, for example, another, who may have taken the course in a previous semester, will offer advice. The women also help each other to reflect on and interpret various interpersonal situations, especially those involving dating. These conversations create a body of knowledge that all members of the group share, equipping everyone with the same information and skills in order to navigate their academic and social environment. Check-in thus creates the kind of homogeneity critical to what Victor Turner calls "communitas," the sense of belonging felt by a group of people undergoing the same process of transition or transformation, during which the structures of their earlier lives are removed.[11]

The student singers of the Fallen Angels go through at least two types of transition during their time in the group. First, they move in their daily lives between the academically structured world of the university, with its clear and formal hierarchies of age and rank, and the musical world of their group, where power asymmetries, while still present, are socially minimized through check-in, circular physical formations, and democratic self-governance. Second, in a broader sense, the undergraduates are slowly shifting from their senses of self prior to enrollment in college toward new, adult identities as they are (re)formed through the process of higher education, itself a rite of passage in American culture, particularly for the upper middle class.[12] The invocation of films set in high schools and the temporary embodiment of their characters through skits and songs reinforce the notion that, for the Fallen Angels, those roles and behaviors are a thing of the past.

Research shows that students preparing for college anticipate creating a new system of social support in order to ease the transition toward independence. The new system replaces the family, at least partially, while also serving as a testing ground for new identities.[13] Systems of social support within a cappella groups, as well as groups like fraternities and sororities, serve just this function. The differences discussed later, mostly relating to the gender makeup of the group, speak to the various ways in which those systems operate but in all cases reveal them to be in place. Fraternities and sororities may in fact be the archetypal collegiate social support system; many singers, such as Alyson, frequently described their group as a family, fraternity, or sorority.

A sense of communitas is routinely and habitually reinforced in nearly every Fallen Angels rehearsal with check-in, whereby social support is provided structurally and performed verbally through mutual expressions of understanding.[14] As Anthony Giddens explains, routine provides conventionalized modes of interaction people use to connect episodic events in their everyday lives and control the threat of dispute.[15] What results is a sense of safety and trust in interpersonal relations. For the Fallen Angels, the routine of check-in and its content help to foster this trust. Under these circumstances, members feel free to share private information, such as fears, frustrations, or flirtations, because they have a mutual understanding with the other women in their group. Deborah Tannen calls this verbal demonstration of understanding "troubles talk." For many women, this practice maintains power symmetries by "sending the metamessage 'We're the same; you're not alone.'"[16]

Trust extends in two directions. The singers in the Fallen Angels emphasized social support and trust, then extended it to their music. But it can also start musically, as singers demonstrate their musical abilities in their initial audition and later in rehearsal, and then develop socially. Dave, music director of the Treblemakers, spoke of the social trust his group members gained through the shared act of making music.

> You just sort of skip over a lot of the "getting to know you" parts of friendship when you perform music . . . You create a connection, and music is something we all can agree on, we can all put our hearts into. It's just showing who you are to the group without—it's like automatically trusting them. You give music to them, you share music. To me that's really a bond of trust because music is that powerful for people, I think.

Dave's comments hint at concepts of identity ("showing who you are") and gift exchange (with music as the gift). These two aspects are important for the formation of a sense of belonging to a group, of collective and cooperative behavior within which disputes can be managed and goals met. In this way, the group itself becomes the "medium of instruction, pleasure and empowerment," as Mary Ann Clawson writes regarding group formation in adolescent rock bands.[17] Leslie C. Gay observes similar notions of cooperative identification, ideas of group boundedness, and an egalitarian ideal in New York rock groups.[18] And Gregory Barz shows how Tanzanian choirs constitute communities best understood as "'systems' of communicative events" that "only exist in relation to the reformation, reaffirmation, and continuous expectation of that system."[19] In each case, the routine behavior of collective music making enables a feeling of connectedness among musicians.

Unlike the Fallen Angels, social bonding in the Treblemakers is primarily accomplished through music, not through verbalizing the intimate details of one's life (although talk was certainly important to the group). Moreover, both the Fallen Angels and the Treblemakers differed from VoiceMale, wherein music and friendly physicality—benign pushes, shoves, and punches—played a larger role in the group's social relations and the way social support was performed. This observation parallels Tannen's conclusion: "For girls, talk is the glue that holds relationships together. Boys' relationships are held together primarily by activities: doing things together."[20]

Yet those activities, those physical actions, have social effects. According to Mike, a former VoiceMale music director, the display of emotion, practiced in the rehearsal's musical activities, is a key element in a convincing performance. And "that leads to closeness. I definitely don't think it was something people established outside of rehearsal and then brought in," he said. "There aren't a whole lot of situations where guys can emotionally be *open*," as if to suggest that doing so risked the seemingly dangerous possibility of feminine display. Indeed, as Ingrid Monson writes of jazz ensembles, "musicians must be able to trust the musical abilities of other band members in performance, especially if they are taking musical risks."[21] The a cappella context suggests the importance of social risks. VoiceMale rehearsal thus provided a safe space for young men to express emotion and support for each other. Here the boundaries of masculinity were circumscribed socially and reinforced musically. Expressing emotion was considered to have musical benefits (a more sincere and moving performance) and social benefits (a stronger sense of "brotherhood" among the guys). But such expressions had to be made and honed carefully, in the safe and contained atmosphere of the rehearsal, before being publicly unleashed.[22]

Power, Resistance, and Social Capital

Unlike a traditional Western choir, in which all the singers follow the direction of the conductor, the Fallen Angels rehearsal shows how collegiate a cappella groups distribute power more broadly. They more closely resemble an adolescent rock band model, in that important musical aspects are self-taught and the "learning process is a peer-based experience."[23] I never heard a group's musical leader called a "conductor," and the use of conducting gestures (like Candace's), while uncommon in a cappella rehearsals, was rare in public performance (see chapter 7).

The organizational structure of the Fallen Angels was typical of the groups I encountered. Members with official administrative positions were responsible for tasks that must be accomplished in order for the group to function, while unofficial social roles could belong to individuals with seniority, popularity, or sufficient social capital. Any member might occupy multiple roles. As president, Jennifer handled external relations (performance arrangements and dealings with other groups on campus or administrative offices) and oversaw internal organization (scheduling rehearsals and enforcing standards of attendance and behavior). As music directors, only Anne and Candace matched Jennifer's power. They were responsible for all of the musical aspects of the group (approving and teaching arrangements, assigning parts, selecting songs for rehearsals and performances, and the group's overall performance quality). When opportunities for recording arose, they would supervise the process in conjunction with a recording engineer. Although most groups maintain these positions, administrative configurations vary. Other positions include a business manager (responsible for bookings), a treasurer, chairs of publicity or social events, and coordinators of concerts and tours. Many groups specify their administrative organization in written documents ("constitutions"), which may be required by their school in exchange for official recognition, student funding allocations, or access to rehearsal and performance space on campus.

Within the social reality of the group, however, such idealized structures are rarely fully realized. Regular members make their voices heard and perform their importance for the rest of the group, earning themselves social capital. In the Fallen Angels rehearsal, Debra, the former music director, exerted power with her instructional comments during the vocal warm-up exercises ("listen to each other . . . and match vowel shapes"). The nods she received confirm the efficacy of her performance and social role. Group members can also resist the power exercised by those in officially sanctioned positions. Roel, a former music director of the Dicks and Janes at the University of Michigan, explained how, in his group, an unelected member with a strong social role (earned through his demonstrated arranging skills) repeatedly took advantage of the opportunity to comment on the group's performance of his arrangements: "When we're running [a song] in rehearsal, I give comments and then ask the arranger, 'do you have any comments?' . . . Right now, because we have one arranger who arranged pretty much our whole rep[ertory], he is like a nonelected assistant music director . . . He hasn't been elected, but he feels he has to talk about everything all the time."

Another example of group members resisting the power of recognized leaders is the practice of talking in the time between the starting pitch, blown by the music director on a pitch pipe, and the actual count-off that begins a song. Among all the groups I worked with, it was understood that during this time there should be complete silence. Although it is sometimes tempting to view these noisy interruptions as benign socialization, it was clear in some cases that members saved their comments—often critical of the group's performance or its leaders—for delivery specifically at such moments in order to maximize their impact. Music directors then faced the choice of disciplining their peers or ignoring the infraction, both of which risked further distraction and the expression of discontent.[24] Ellen Koskoff observed a similar tension between official leaders and unofficial social leaders in her study of an adolescent percussion ensemble at a summer music camp.[25]

In many groups, a song's arranger assigns members to particular background parts on his or her arrangements. While singers are usually assigned similar parts on most songs according to vocal range, arrangements (such as "Band of Gold") sometimes include special countermelodies or harmonies along with the solo line, as well as vocal percussion. Through their right to assign particular voices to particular parts, arrangers have the power to shape the way the group sounds on a fundamental level: whose voice will sound when, and how. Their musical choices can influence subsequent decisions, such as staging, and ultimately affect the performed or recorded musical product. A privileged voice, assigned to a special countermelody or harmony, may also more visibly demonstrate its skill (and thus value), thereby earning additional social capital. Moreover, arrangers' ability to bring new repertory to their group can lead to conflict. Alumni of Amazin' Blue spoke of members who would sometimes arrange songs for which they were particularly strong candidates for the solo, while Debra reflected on a situation in which members of the Fallen Angels did not enjoy singing one particular member's arrangement and had difficulty explaining so without insulting her.

Solos, the ultimate privilege, are usually assigned democratically, as members decide whose voice and whose interpretation of the song will represent the group (see chapter 5). To what degree should the soloist attempt to emulate the original artist's recording? Are significant changes in rhythm, melody, phrasing, and other musical features acceptable? The answers to these questions, determined by vote tallies, reveal the group's aggregate musical values, as does a group's policy, spoken or unspoken, on whether a candidate's "possession" of other solos in the repertory should be a factor in the decision. Are members more concerned with the quality of the musical product than with sharing the spotlight among the singers? If a majority believes so, the group may simply pick "the best voice for the song." If not, they may instead offer the solo to a candidate who does not yet have one, placing less weight on the sound or musical quality of the audition and more on a sense of social and musical equality.

Deliberations over solo assignments prompted some of the most heated debates I observed. They revealed the variety of ideas regarding the balance of musicality and sociability that could exist within groups. Some groups, such as Amazin' Blue, tended to favor musicality, while others, such as the Fallen Angels, tended to favor social equality. But even in those cases and others, individual preferences did not always line up with the group's democratically determined choices.

Solos may be the ultimate statement of musical power because they place one individual's voice in a vastly more prominent role than all others. Success in a solo role validates an individual's manner of vocal performance in front of the rest of the group, rendering it a model for others to follow. In this way, that model can influence the style of singing of individual members, the whole group, or both. Thus, individual members, informed by their experience and understanding of the group's values, contribute to decisions made in the rehearsal, which have lasting consequences beyond it.

Sharing Musical Ideas

As one of the most important concepts in collegiate a cappella, an "ideology of blend" pervades the musical practice. (Of course, the notion of blend is common in [Western] vocal harmony and choral practices and not unique to a cappella. Especially in studies of barbershop singing, it entails not only musical but also social significance.)[26] In order to blend effectively, a cappella singers form their vowel sounds as similarly as possible. They synchronize their attacks and cutoffs. They know what kind of tone to use, and when: breathy, raspy, nasal, throaty (or "chorally" or "Motown"); with or without vibrato, scoops, or other ornamentation; belted or placed in falsetto; and so on. Coordination of these aspects of vocalization requires, first, awareness of one's own vocal production and that of others in one's group and, second, repetition and practice, which the routine of rehearsal provides. Each aspect is variable; singers constantly make choices about how to sing, which are influenced by the underlying ideas of what sounds good in their group and on any particular piece. The process is a negotiation-in-song: the aggregate vocal sound will, in a sense, become an average of the many subtly different, individual vocal qualities in any given group, much like the way Charles Keil describes a groove arising from an instrumental ensemble's "participatory discrepancies."[27]

During rehearsals, important knowledge about singing is passed between individuals. This transmission is all the more important because of the transient nature of group memberships. Older members train newer ones in how to sing with the group and what that sound means, framed by the group's formal organizational structure and through informal interactions during and outside the rehearsal. An individual's understanding of his or her group and what it is "all about" is dynamic, changing as he or she gains experience in rehearsals, gigs, tours, and other activities. Of course, different people may interpret and internalize these experiences differently, resulting in varying perspectives on the group they will carry with them as they rise to more prominent roles. Through the rehearsal process, certain individuals can influence the underlying concept of blend by setting an example with their own style of vocalization and through verbal directions, as the Fallen Angels example shows. The rehearsal is thus a site of negotiation, and singing emerges as a process that takes place within the context of organizational and social structures that support particular ideas of good blending, singing, and group unity, which entail minute and split-second choices.

Those choices may be guided by "habitus," Pierre Bourdieu's term for the patterns of action, learned through past experience and "transposable" to future situations, to which individuals and groups are subconsciously predisposed.[28] Judith Becker theorizes a "habitus of listening" to understand issues of musical reception.[29] Similarly, I imagine a "habitus of singing," which underlines specifically vocal production. It encompasses an individual's usual, predisposed manner of singing and the ways in which it is applied to the music of the moment. It is shaped both by past experience, whether in an a cappella group or other vocal ensemble, and by the power structures within which the singer sings.[30] Based on this experience and the immediate context, then, certain musical choices become more likely than others.[31]

Warm-ups provide an excellent example of individual and group habitus. They typically do not involve unusual syllables or rhythms that might otherwise distract singers from concentrating on their singing, so singers can observe and emulate each other, improving blend. The repetition of warm-ups from one rehearsal to the next yields similar aesthetic views toward singing, which inform notions of the group's vocal style. In the Fallen Angels rehearsal, the glances around the circle during warm-ups were an unspoken negotiation, resulting in a kind of mean or aggregate vowel placement. As Drew explained, in VoiceMale, the goal was for all the singers to function like "eight extensions of one mind."

Interpersonal competition can also motivate singers to adapt and match each other's voices. One singer in Amazin' Blue framed the experience of learning to sing with the group in friendly but competitive terms.

> There's definitely a level of competitiveness, like, "oh you can do that much vibrato, well this is how much vibrato *I* can do . . . oh you can do it that loud, well this is how loud *I* can do it." So it becomes sort of working together and sort of not, so it's almost like challenging yourself against the person who's doing it with you. So even if it's like, "well, even though it's an a cappella song and we're singing backup so we're going to do it straight-tone" . . . it becomes, "well, if they're putting a little something into it then maybe I should put a little something into it."

Crucial in this singer's description is the nonverbalized aspect of interaction. She and the two others involved in the interview all agreed that this kind of unspoken instruction plays a significant role in learning to sing with the group, together with more direct verbalized instruction from the music director and arrangers. Such nonverbalized interaction, in addition to the verbalized interaction described earlier, requires both performance and observation while enabling the sharing of ideas about (good) singing within a group, the sort of "active knowledge" Benjamin Brinner calls "competence."[32]

Vocal Style and Identity

In Bourdieu's theory, a field of cultural production is an array of positions of power based on capital and realized through practice, within which habitus is formed.[33] Between the performance of vocal competency and its observation, the rehearsal becomes a fertile ground for demonstrating and absorbing the musicianship, vocal acumen, and skill involved in singing collegiate a cappella. These performances are judged against the backdrop of the group's (and individuals') habitus of singing. Rehearsals also prepare the singers for public performances, however, through which a group displays not only its musical skill or talent but also a social persona or identity, which—as the Fallen Angels' sensitivity to campus politics and VoiceMale's purposeful avoidance of falsetto demonstrate—can be carefully crafted.

The idea of an identity based on vocal style, and the consistency of that identity/style from year to year, is more important to some groups than others.

But it is widespread throughout the a cappella community, evident from rehearsal to performance to recording. When I asked singers about their group's traditions, they often talked about particular warm-ups passed from "generation" to "generation." The importance of continuity is perhaps clearest in criticism: album reviews by the Recorded A Cappella Review Board frequently compare contemporary albums with others by the same group years earlier, even while acknowledging that none of the same singers remain.[34]

Some groups attempt to maintain a sense of stylistic continuity, and thus identity consistency, through the active involvement of alumni, who may contribute arrangements, come to rehearsals and teach songs, or even sing with current members. Off the Beat, a mixed group from the University of Pennsylvania, is a good example. With appearances on most editions of the *Best of College A Cappella* compilation albums and many Contemporary A Cappella Recording Awards, the group is widely regarded as having a distinctive sound: loud, edgy, and intense.[35] Following a major concert, a cappella groups customarily throw a party, inviting their friends. In Off the Beat's case, according to Larry (a former group president), the first hour of the party is open only to current members and alumni. During this time, the alumni sing songs from years past. Current members may recognize these songs from the group's earlier recordings, but at the party they are directly infused with their group's sounds, vocal style, and spirit.

Importantly, Off the Beat's arrangers purposefully include elements from old arrangements in their new ones. By recycling melodic, rhythmic, or syllabic motives, current members make musical connections with the group's past, a historical link encompassed in what Monson calls "intermusicality."[36] Senior members, who may have sung the song being referenced, typically explain the musical allusions to younger members during rehearsal. Then, at the party, the younger members are already familiar with distinctive features from the group's past arrangements and are more likely to recognize them when performed by alumni. Moreover, the vocal stylizations the alumni have learned, and re-present to the younger, current group, become models for future performance. In this way, the group's distinctive vocal style and identity are perpetuated.

In many traditions, the rehearsal is a standard part of the process by means of which music is prepared for public performance, the "submerged body" of a performative iceberg of which public presentations are merely the tip.[37] Just as the tip does not represent the whole iceberg, however, analyses of public performance alone do not reveal all there is to know about group music making. Collegiate a cappella illustrates how rehearsals offer individuals going through a period of life-changing social transition a sense of community and identity based on trust, routine, and a shared sense of (vocal) style. The a cappella case would also seem to confirm Koskoff's finding that "the internal process of rehearsing . . . allows the external events of rehearsal to take place," as the routine actions of learning to sing with one's group shape the sounds that are ultimately rehearsed and the routine performances of social support enable the creation of a peer community.[38] Of course, in addition to those processes, rehearsals also prepare the group for its public performances. The next chapter explores those performances, paying particular attention to humor, gender stereotypes, and gestures that link a cappella to its immediate contexts as well as to broader aspects of rock performance.

CHAPTER 7

In Performance: Gender, Humor, Gesture, and Politics

When I arrived at Cholmondeley's on a crisp autumn night at about 11:00 p.m., simply entering the building was a challenge. "Chum's," as it was called, was a student-run lounge in the historic Usen Castle at Brandeis University, offering overstuffed couches and chairs, a bar serving coffee drinks and ice cream, and a small raised platform for a stage. The event was a "coffeehouse," a fund-raiser featuring student performances to benefit another student organization on campus. The crowd roared as the men of VoiceMale were announced and, clad in dark slacks and button-down shirts, some wearing blazers or neckties, made their way to the stage. There they began their first song, the one with which they opened all their shows, "Falling Over You." "*I made up! Hunh! I made up my mind!*" they shouted, twice, punctuating their percussive chant with grunts, growls, and vocal riffs. Then they were singing. Drew kicked in on vocal percussion, and in no time bodies were moving to the beat, bouncing and bobbing, onstage and off. The thirty-minute set alternated energetic songs with humorous vignettes satirizing topics ranging from American foreign policy to the a cappella scene at Brandeis to recent video game fads. The crowd loved all of it.[1]

Live performance, like the one described above, is the primary medium of collegiate a cappella. In this chapter I propose two theories about a cappella performance: first, that it reproduces performative aspects of the world around it, namely, through the gestural language and imagery of rock music and American popular culture; and, second, that it provides a venue through which college singers comment on that world, often through comedic vignettes. Gender is a key variable in both performances, while humor and choreography serve as expressive strategies. Before going too far, however, it is useful to briefly examine how a cappella singers think about and experience such performances.

Distinguishing Performances: Gigs and Concerts

Collegiate a cappella singers often refer to some of their live performances as "gigs," much like musicians in many other popular music genres. *Gig* signifies a scheduled event for which the group receives some kind of compensation, usually monetary. It is sometimes applied more broadly to performances with other a cappella groups, such as when one group opens another's concert. A group's major performances at its home institution are more often called "concerts" or "shows."

Gigs can be distinguished from concerts in terms of repertory, publicity, and the relationship between performers and audience. At its concert, a group such as VoiceMale typically sings most or all of its repertory for the semester (usually between eight and sixteen songs). At a gig, it sings fewer songs, depending on the time, occasion, and audience (typically three or four songs in about fifteen minutes). While many groups promote their concerts using posters, signs in dining halls, chalk drawings on campus walkways, pieces in local print media such as the student newspaper, e-mail messages, website announcements, and other electronic media, and word of mouth, they are generally not expected to publicize a gig. Finally, a concert implies that the audience has come to see and hear the group. That kind of performance is socially rewarding for the singers, complementing motivations such as financial gain. Since the audience for a gig might be there for other reasons, it is more likely that the group's performance will be motivated by financial reward. However, groups also gig to keep a presence on campus for local fans and to spread their reputation by performing for new audiences. Some groups carefully calibrate their exposure via gigs; VoiceMale limited its public performances on the Brandeis campus in order to regulate demand among its fans.

Concerts are usually presented on a Friday or Saturday night in a campus venue such as a theater or recital hall, or a lecture hall, cafeteria, multipurpose room, or building lobby. Sitting in rows facing the stage, audience members—usually friends and parents of the performers plus other campus and community members—tend to listen quietly and applaud loudly between songs, while perhaps clapping or cheering during a song in response to an impressive vocal or choreographic display. Occasionally they will be more expressive, calling out the names of friends among the performers. An intermission customarily separates a concert's two halves.

A "guest group" frequently starts the show with a brief set of songs before inviting the main performers to the stage. Many groups invite their alumni to the stage for an "alumni song" toward the end of the evening; the same song is repeated at each concert. Singing the alumni song enables former members to relive their a cappella experience while demonstrating to the audience the continued vitality of the group and its legacy of performers. Group members whose graduation is immanent are sometimes honored with a "senior solo" in their final concert, a song of the senior's choosing to which he or she sings the lead. The senior solo is often preceded by a short speech detailing the senior's contributions to the group.

While concerts can yield monetary rewards, they are also typically a group's largest performance-related expense, as it may have to rent the venue, hire a sound technician, contract with campus police for security arrangements, and fund its publicity. Popular groups that draw large crowds and charge for admission can profit by several hundred dollars, but not all groups or campuses charge such fees. Sales of CDs are also generally strongest at concerts. But no one I spoke with ever heard of a collegiate a cappella singer keeping a share of a group's revenues. Instead, funds are used to cover the group's other expenses, such as future concerts, tours, and recordings. A certain level of financial continuity is thereby maintained, as each group depends on the previous year's members to support the current year's activities.

A cappella groups typically book "ceremonial gigs" throughout the academic year at events like convocation, baccalaureate, commencement, and others run by university offices and departments.[2] The employer dictates the length of the performance, formality of dress, and may even request particular songs while the group serves as an interlude in a larger program, a brief diversion or background music. Payment is exchanged for the performance itself, and CDs are rarely sold. The amount of money groups earn from such gigs varies widely. One group I worked with routinely quoted eight hundred dollars per hour (although few gigs actually lasted an hour). Others take what they can get, accepting anywhere from fifty to three hundred dollars.

"Social gigs," like VoiceMale's performance at Chum's or other student events, are a mainstay of the a cappella experience.[3] As monetary rewards for these gigs vary, if they exist at all, the chief benefits are social: demonstrating one's skill and hard work for friends and receiving recognition and compliments. These appearances also advertise the group's other live performances, such as a concert. In contrast to a ceremonial gig, groups expect greater control over the content and presentation of their performances, as well as the chance to sell their CDs.

Groups sometimes travel beyond their own campuses to perform, often to appear as a guest group or one of several groups in an invitational concert. These performances can become the focus of a whole weekend, although the distance a group is willing to travel is usually limited to a few hours of driving. When I sang with the University of Michigan Amazin' Blue, for example, we were repeatedly invited by Purple Haze, from Northwestern University, to join four or five groups from other midwestern schools in a concert each fall entitled "Best of the Midwest." Some groups go "on tour" during their schools' breaks or after the spring term's final exams and can venture farther from their home institutions than a typical out-of-town gig. In the spring of 2005, for example, VoiceMale left Boston to tour California, singing in concerts hosted by other college groups along the way. However, most groups do not regularly embark on tours due to their high costs.

Performance Practice: Conventions of an A Cappella Concert

Certain elements of collegiate a cappella performances have become common enough to be conventionalized and are reinforced both by tradition within groups and through exposure to other groups' performances. For example, while singing, groups stand in particular physical formations, the most common of which is an "arc" (sometimes called a "bow" or a "horseshoe"), a half circle or crescent shape with the open end facing the audience (fig. 7.1). Larger groups stand in two or three curved rows. Occasionally other formations are used, such as a modified arc that looks more like a *U* (with the singers on the ends facing each other more closely and directly) or standing in straight lines, shoulder to shoulder. Groups may change formations for each song. Unlike the circular formation commonly used in rehearsals, these formations enable the audience to see the singers' faces while still allowing the singers to hear each other.

While performing, singers often bounce or "bop" slightly with a bend at the knee, and perhaps also a snap, on the beat, as VoiceMale did at its coffeehouse gig. Background singers can also perform choreographic movements and gestures coordinated with the soloist, the song's dynamics, or its lyrics. For exam-

Fig. 7.1. University of Michigan Amazin' Blue in the conventional arc formation. (Photo by the author.)

ple, it is common for background singers to lower themselves physically during quiet musical passages. This helps the singers coordinate the song's dynamics and perform them dramatically and also cues the audience to these changes. Such passages are sometimes followed by contrasting ones during which the singers stand up taller and sing more loudly. Singers may enact passages from the song's lyrics even if they themselves do not actually sing words. In the Boston University Treblemakers' performance of The Knack's "My Sharona," the background singers pointed to their eyes along with the soloist's lyric, "close enough to look in my eye, Sharona." In the Boston University Dear Abbeys' performance of Styx's "Renegade," the singers searched the horizon in accord with the outlaw premise of the song.

Certain group members often have designated places in the formations. Vocal percussionists may stand apart from the group by several feet, drawing more attention to themselves and also perhaps suggesting a musical distinction between the percussion and the pitched sounds of the rest of the group. When the vocal percussionist stands with the group, he or she may take a position at the end of a row or in the center of the formation. Although some groups have one member dedicated to vocal percussion, in most cases differ-ent singers assume the role for different songs. Occasionally a song will feature multiple percussionists.

The music director usually stands either in the middle of the arc, directly behind the soloist, or on the end of the arc, where the other singers can see him or her for countoffs and other cues.[4] Although some directors conduct during performances, many singers criticized this practice. Anna and Jennifer, alum-nae of Amazin' Blue, found that conducting gestures pull the audience's atten-tion away from the soloist. They also saw conducting as counterproductive; a well-rehearsed group of singers, they believed, should not require such cues and might themselves be distracted by them. Finally, the presence of a conduc-tor carries choral or classical connotations that Anna and Jennifer considered antithetical to the ethos of a cappella. As Anna put it, "If I wanted to go see a choir, I'd go see a choir! I sang in choirs before where there was a conductor, and you need that. But that isn't why I joined an a cappella group. I wanted edge. I wanted different."

Thus, although in some a cappella performances the director is a marked position, many singers prefer that, however powerful he or she may be in re-hearsal, the director remain unmarked in public performance. In all cases, however, the soloist is marked. He or she stands apart from and in front of the rest of the group, the focus of the audience's attention and the lyrical and emo-tional leader of the performance.

Using Humor Between and Within Songs

Many collegiate a cappella groups perform short, humorous, semi-impro-visatory skits between songs, sometimes called "intros" if they segue to the next song. These sketches may relate to the theme of the concert, if one is specified. In the high-school-themed concert the Fallen Angels was planning in the pre-vious chapter, the women presented four brief scenes, developing a plot line based on two 2004 films about adolescent relationships: *Napoleon Dynamite*, which features one socially awkward boy's relationship with his family and friends; and *Mean Girls*, which follows a hierarchical social clique of young women. Several members of the group played roles that caricatured teenage and academic stereotypes: the popular kids, the nerds, and the math geeks, all of whom happily participated in a "prom" in the final scene. By parodying these films, the performers created a context familiar to many in their audience, who themselves had recently lived through adolescence and would likely be familiar with both films. They also enacted social relationships in academic settings, which would be highly relevant to themselves and their audience. Meanwhile, their adoption of such roles served to distance the women from the high school settings they portrayed. In essence, the singers in the Fallen Angels drew on knowledge that was already circulating in popular culture to create a humorous experience for their audience, embodied social forces they and their college-aged friends encountered in their everyday lives, and indicated their progress toward maturity and adulthood.

The Fallen Angels concert a semester earlier played on a different theme: crime television programs. The skits in "Angels: Most Wanted" featured several of the women as "criminals" (fig. 6.1). For example, Anne played a shoplifter whose primary motivation for theft was her own vanity, a recipe with endless comedic possibilities. Beneath the surface, however, we can read this character—indeed, this whole theme—as achieving ends similar to those of the high-school-themed concert. As the misdeeds of each "criminal" were, in fact, driven by petty character flaws, "Angels: Most Wanted" enabled the women to embody unsavory personality traits they encountered in their daily lives, as well as promote a more general cultural moral regarding proper behavior.

At other times, satirical humor may deliver more pointed political commentary. For the coffeehouse gig, VoiceMale concocted an elaborate sketch poking fun at then president George W. Bush's seemingly futile search for "weapons of mass destruction" and the "war on terror" but altered the plot and setting to correspond to the a cappella scene at its school. One member played the bumbling president of the "Brandeis States of A Cappella," who initiated a search for "arrangements of mass percussion." Through his "no singer left behind act," a parody of Bush's "No Child Left Behind" education initiative, he encouraged all students to form a cappella groups regardless of musical skill or talent—a swipe at the unusually high number of groups at Brandeis.[5] Finally, he celebrated the disbanding of VoiceMale's chief rivals on campus, Spur of the Moment, as evidence of success in his war on "aca-terrorism."[6] The densely packed student audience responded with uproarious laughter and applause.

Humor is a useful performative strategy, not just for its entertainment value. The construction of skits provides opportunities for collective, creative action in ways similar, but not identical, to the rehearsal process. Skits allow those whose leadership qualities may not stand out in musical situations to assume important roles and thus feel valued. They also provide opportunities for group members to earn social capital by demonstrating of their mastery of pop culture and politics, whether local, national, or international.

Choreographic gestures, even small ones, can also provide opportunities for humor. For example, when VoiceMale performed "All I Have To Do Is Dream," Drew would accentuate his part, which emulated a stand-up double bass, by treating Ben, who stands a head shorter, as that instrument. He would wrap his left around the front of Ben's left arm and chest, making plucking gestures, and raise his right above Ben's head, fingering imaginary strings on an imaginary fingerboard. The gesture included a spin in which Ben, the "body" of the instrument, would actually turn around. The humor behind this quick and simple movement depended on the emulative character of the music; the audience's consistent response further demonstrated their implicit understanding of the instrumental function of each VoiceMale member's vocal part.

A Cappella Performance and the Language of Gesture

Collegiate a cappella performers take many of their cues from popular music, especially, in the case of soloists, with regard to the physicality of performance. Standing apart from the rest of the group, an effective solo performance depends on two convincing displays: an embodiment of the persona of the song's protagonist and the gestural language of performance itself. This second kind of display locates a cappella performance most specifically in a post–rock 'n' roll context.

The idea that the soloist plays the role circumscribed by the song is certainly not new with a cappella. Indeed, it has long been the basis for performance in musical theater. Simon Frith, among other scholars of popular music, recognizes the importance of the acting involved in this kind of performance: "Pop singers don't just express emotion but also play it," he writes, "enacting the protagonist in the song," which means expressing appropriate emotions at appropriate times in appropriate ways.[7] The soloist in the Dear Abbeys' "Renegade" did this with his frantic scurrying about the stage, acting as if he was, indeed, on the run from the law. His embodiment of the song's protagonist is physical in the sense that he actually moves from place to place in particular ways, but he also communicates his character's emotional state through facial gestures and timbre. Moreover, the song's high melody forces him to strain his voice, introducing another kind of physical tension. The coiled energy required to sing the melody seems to stand in for the nervous anxiety of an outlaw knowing his capture is immanent. "The 'as if' of the song performance," as Frith puts it, "is foregrounded in order to naturalize the 'as if' of the musical performance."[8]

In addition to telling the story in the song, soloists also use a more general gestural language of performance, derived from late-twentieth-century popular music performance practice. It seems that, more than in earlier genres, rock 'n' roll (and subsequently rock) performance is premised on both the musical *and* the physical, the aural *and* the visual. Before Elvis's hips or Hendrix's guitar, perhaps the most important innovations in popular music performance (at least judging from the scholarly literature) were the electric microphone and radio, technologies that enabled a generation of popular singers beginning in the 1920s, known as "crooners," to sing in a more intimate way than was possible for the "shouters" of earlier eras. It could feel like Rudy Vallée and Bing Crosby were singing—perhaps even whispering—directly into the listener's ear.

Yet these technological innovations, and the changes in musical practice that immediately followed, were primarily aural. By contrast, rock 'n' roll's innovations were also visual. Reebee Garofalo illustrates the "outrageous stage antics" of Bill Haley and His Comets, whose "Rock Around the Clock" features prominently in rock histories,[9] with a photo of the band showing the saxophonist lying on his back on the stage floor while the stand-up bass player, also on his back, plays upside down, using his feet to support the weight of his instrument.[10] The visual spectacle often centered on the lead singer, whose gestures may derive from playing the song's protagonist's role. Doon Arbus described a James Brown performance in 1966: "He has all the classic mannerisms: snapping his elbows to his sides to hike up his pants, flinging out his arms for a fresh start at the beginning of each new phrase, pantomiming the lyrics." (That Arbus calls these gestures "classic" indicates that, by 1966, they were already commonly understood.) Toward the end of the performance, singing "Bay*bay*! Yahdone me*wrohng*," Brown seems to break down with despair. Two members of his band, the Flames, try twice to escort him off the stage, wrapped in a gold cape: "Danny and Bobby each put an arm around his shoulders, trying to tell him it's all right, it's all gonna be all right. He stamps his feet again. Again, he flings off the cape. He is back on his knees with the microphone, back where he belongs."[11] Was Brown really so upset he could not continue the show? Of course not. His shows often included numerous encores, a testament to his boundless energy. Instead, he was playing the role the song called for; then, in his refusal to leave and insistence on returning to the microphone, he was playing another rock star's role, the romantic artist—someone who needs to perform, whose very existence depends on doing so.

But beyond simply playing a role, a lead singer's gestures also draw on two more general expressions. The first is the overwhelming effort and energy required by the act of performance. As Frith observes, "[R]ock performers are expected to revel in their own physicality . . . to strain and sweat and collapse with tiredness."[12] The second is the pleasure of that performance, crucial to the experience of rock 'n' roll, which Barry Shank calls the "physical expression of having a good time."[13] That these two physical expressions are germane to rock 'n' roll, rock, and the popular styles that followed, indicates powerfully that, despite a cappella's deep historical roots, the gestural language of its contemporary practice is a more recent development.

Jason Toynbee offers a thorough analysis of popular music performance as a theatrical phenomenon, proposing several useful modes of performance: *expressionist,* which is "concerned with truth to the subject, a full issuing out of music from the inner being" (James Brown figures here); *transformative,* which refers backward to earlier styles and is particularly evident in diasporic genres; *direct,* the key value of which is sincerity, which Toynbee claims was the dominant performance mode before rock 'n' roll; and *reflexive,* in which performers are especially aware of the iterative nature of their own performance.[14] While Frith and Shank are thus not the only scholars to stress the importance of the visual or physical in rock performance, analyses of specific gestures are few and far between. The following analysis of a specific gesture in a specific a cappella performance is intended to begin to remedy this lacuna.

By the end of the 2004–5 academic year, the members of VoiceMale had gained months of performance experience, including two semester concerts, a few coffeehouse gigs, several guest appearances at other schools, many off-campus gigs, and their weeklong spring break tour. Even the new members had become seasoned performers, including Jon, a freshman, who spent most of the year singing the solo on the first verse of "Falling Over You." Figure 7.2 shows Jon (center), in midperformance, during a concert in April 2005.

This image, taken from a video of the performance, captures Jon invoking gestures common to rock imagery: a contorted face, closed eyes, bent body, extended arm, and pointed finger. The first three may be termed "gestures of effort," connoting great energy and exertion, as if to suggest that Jon is working incredibly hard in order to perform the song (fig. 7.3 offers another example, this time showing Lance, from Amazin' Blue, singing Marc Broussard's "The

Fig. 7.2. Soloist's "gestures of effort" and "gestures of engagement" (*center*). Brandeis University VoiceMale performing "Falling Over You." (Photo by the author.)

Wanderer" in March 2010). This is, after all, what is expected from such performers. "The popular audience wants to see how much has gone into its entertainment," Frith writes. The "performance of labor is a necessary part of the popular aesthetic."[15] Gestures of effort, and the other types of gestures that follow, may be considered "emblems," symbolic bodily actions with specific cultural meanings that usually send some kind of message.[16]

Gestures of effort may appear spontaneous even when they are actually repeated from performance to performance. (In reviewing videos of several performances over the course of the year, one sees Jon's gestures become increasingly pronounced, confident, and consistent.) Audiences expect a measure of spontaneity in live performance, even if, in popular music, recordings maintain what Theodore Gracyk calls "ontological priority."[17] As most a cappella arrangements are based on recordings, their ontological priority does not seem open to question. But if recordings are favored, David R. Shumway asks, "[W]hy do rock fans continue to go to concerts at all? What is the point of a 'live' repetition of something that can be repeated *ad infinitum* on the home stereo or portable listening device?"[18] In fact, in a genre like a cappella, it is likely that greater numbers of listeners experience the music at live performances than through recordings. So it comes as no surprise that a cappella groups value spontaneity in their performances. Paul, president of the Dear Abbeys, explained, "[Y]ou've got to engage the audience" by seeming spontaneous. "That excites people, because they get into it. They're like, 'alright, Joe's rockin' the solo on "Harder to Breathe." What's he going to do?' You've *got* to bring that spontaneity to your show, because otherwise nobody's going to give a shit—nobody's going to *come back*, and that's what we want people to do." In other words, there must be something *seemingly* new or unexpected in each performance or the audience will turn its attention elsewhere.

Fig. 7.3. University of Michigan Amazin' Blue singing "The Wanderer." (Photo by the author.)

Paul's mention of engaging the audience leads to the other gestures seen in Jon's performance, his outstretched arm and pointed finger. Some of the most heavily criticized a cappella performances I have witnessed were those in which the soloists just stood still, arms at their sides while singing. With these "gestures of engagement," Jon literally and physically reaches out to the audience, entreating them not only to pay attention, but also to invest in his performance. A cappella is, after all, an amateur practice in which professional competence is not expected; mistakes will be made. Jon's open stance and outstretched arm allow audience members to feel like they are part of his performance and link their satisfaction to his success. In an additional example, figure 7.4 shows Joe, from Amazin' Blue, reaching for the audience during a performance of "December 1963 (Oh, What A Night)" in March 2010. John Blacking writes of "fellow feeling," the phenomenon that occurs when people are so attuned to each other that they share a heightened sensitivity. Fellow feeling relies on nonverbal cues, "shared somatic states."[19] In a good a cappella performance, the audience's investment in the soloist may be understood as a manifestation of fellow feeling, and gestures of engagement facilitate this process.

Fig. 7.4. University of Michigan Amazin' Blue singing "December 1963 (Oh What A Night)." (Photo by the author.)

Members of the all-male Dear Abbeys, like many performers, combine gestures of engagement with gender roles, sometimes actively flirting with their audience. "If that means picking out somebody that you don't know that you might think is hot and pointing at her in the middle of the song," Paul told me, "we'll do it. Everybody should know that *we will do it!*" In this way, sexual appeal can become an important aspect of the Dear Abbeys' performance. Of course, that is nothing new to popular music. Crooners like Vallée were particularly popular with women radio listeners (a fact on which critics pounced).[20] Yet the visual element of that appeal, here exemplified by particular gestures of engagement, cannot be traced to crooners but instead to more visually oriented rock 'n' roll.

If a cappella singers reproduce the physicality of popular music performance, how do they learn this gestural language in the first place? One possible answer is the music video. Music Television (MTV), the cable network devoted to popular music programming, broadcast music videos following its 1981 inception (it has since diversified its lineup but retained teenagers as its primary audience). E. Ann Kaplan reports that, by the spring of 1986—around the same time as the a cappella explosion discussed in chapter 4—the channel reached twenty-eight million American households. While many of MTV's videos contained narrative structures, a significant portion also included concert footage or images of the performers making music in other settings.[21] Singers may also observe and internalize the gestural performance practice of their favorite artists by attending live concerts themselves or even seeing promotional posters, whose imagery frequently includes a band's lead singer seemingly captured in the act of intensely performing. Finally, as a cappella groups encounter each other, they may observe the gestures of other a cappella singers, especially soloists. Sometimes value is explicitly affixed to such gestures. One of those times is competition.

Performance as/in Competition

Competitions create a special environment in which groups encounter each other and are openly judged on all aspects of performance, including gestures, movements, choreography, use of humor, and musical qualities. The annual International Championship of Collegiate A Cappella is, for some groups, the centerpiece performance event of the academic year. It is unsurprising, then, that some take it seriously. "Competition was a religion," Julie Moffitt, the ICCA Midwest producer for the 2005–6 season, writes retrospectively of her experience as an undergraduate competitor.[22]

The ICCA, currently owned and operated by the executive director of Varsity Vocals, Amanda Newman, has become the major live performance competition of the collegiate a cappella world.[23] The Varsity Vocals staff chooses competitors from the pool of groups that submit a live recording and an application fee. There are usually three or four first-round concerts in each geographic region, with between five and eight groups competing in each concert. The top two advance to the regional semifinals, from which the top-ranked group advances to the finals to vie for the championship.

In many genres, competition structures and influences musical performance. It can serve as a basis for innovation or as a "keeper of the status quo."[24] Competitors often feel pressured to offer fare that jurists will find acceptable. Describing piano competitions, Joseph Horowitz observes that some competitors and critics fear an interpretive homogenization of the repertory out of concern that juries will view unusual or innovative interpretations unfavorably.[25] At the ICCA, unlike a piano competition, there are few song-specific interpretive norms; adjudicators are instructed not to compare a group's or soloist's performance to the song's original recording, only to judge whether the interpretation is appropriate and effective.[26]

The twelve-minute time limit is one of the first constraints competitors encounter at the ICCA. As a result, most groups' sets follow a three-song format. As if giving a miniconcert, they typically begin with an up-tempo number, follow with a slow song, and then close with another fast-paced, exciting song. Mixed groups usually feature both male and female soloists, and groups of all stripes may showcase as many individuals as possible, maximizing their chances to impress the judges with a standout soloist while avoiding the impression that they depend on a single star member.

Judging criteria also shape performances in competition.[27] The ICCA guidelines were developed with the conscious understanding that they should both define a "good a cappella performance" and allow for enough variation to accommodate the genre's many performance styles. Still, the categories pertaining to visual presentation are a frequent source of concern and debate. The 2004–5 ICCA Group Adjudication Sheet (still in use) divides visual presentation into several subcategories: visual cohesiveness, effectiveness of presentation, energy/stage presence, appropriateness of movement, creativity of movement, transitions/blocking, and professionalism.[28] The guidelines never mention "choreography," yet many groups feel compelled to include staging, movement, or dancing in their sets, which reveals a tension between the official intent of the competition and the beliefs of many of its participants. (In a cappella discourse, "choreography" includes preplanned gestures, movement, staging, and dancing.) Newman stresses that choreography is optional, declaring that "visual presentation" is more important than staging, movements, or dancing. Ultimately, it is a question of appropriateness, she says.

> It's not "are you good at dancing?" It's "is the movement appropriate? Does it detract from [the performance] or add to [it]?" A lot of people will have very synchronized movements, but it's distracting and it's causing them to sing poorly, so they are going to score lower in that category.

A cappella singers hold differing views of choreography in the ICCA and in a cappella performance generally. Although some groups routinely incorporate choreography and movements into their performances at the competition and elsewhere, other groups prefer not to. But the perception that choreography is pervasive or even required in the competition is widespread. One strongly opinionated contributor to the RARB discussion forum wrote:

Am I the only one who is scared for the future of a cappella[?] For all of us who have gone to any of the ICCA's in the past few years, I hope you are as worried as I am. This so called "choreography" that groups are doing these days is not only puzzling ... it is appalling and personally I am insulted not only by each of the groups that do it ... but mostly by the a cappella community for encouraging this behaviour.[29]

In response, another offered a more positive report.

My experience with choreography has been quite different. Our group does not regularly choreograph every song in our repertoire, however, I feel that learning the choreography for our ICCA set has been nothing but positive for the group ... The choreography starts as a challenge and perhaps a chore for some. By the end of the process, the choreography ends up bringing the group together (visually and emotionally) as the members of all backgrounds have been able to conquer such a challenge. We're all good musicians and few of us are dancers. The sense of accomplishment really adds to the experience and in the end makes us better performers when we're NOT doing any choreography. In addition, we've had great responses from later concerts and tours while performing our "ICCA set."[30]

It may be possible to trace the use of movement or choreography in a cappella performances to group members' experience in high school "show choirs," which similarly emphasize dance, gestures, and physicality. This attribution is complicated, however, by the fact that such ensembles are predominantly a midwestern choral phenomenon, while collegiate a cappella has mostly northeastern roots (see chapter 4).[31] The commercial success of the Fox television network's series *Glee*, which features a high school choral group performing popular songs complete with elaborate choreography and staging, has also been named as a contributing factor in the prevalence of choreography in a cappella.[32] The show cannot be considered a cause, however, since a cappella's choreography became prevalent years before the show's first season in 2009.

The Dear Abbeys: A Case Study in Resistance and Humor at the ICCA

The Dear Abbeys understood the situation: they might have to change their usual performance in order to succeed in the ICCA, and the result might alter the identity they projected through their performance. So in the 2004–5 season, they used the competition's alleged "choreography requirement" to critique—indeed, resist—that very requirement. To do so, they drew their best weapon: humor. During one musical interlude in "Renegade," the first song in their set, they leaned forward and hunched down, raising their hands to their brows as if to block the sun while scanning the horizon for signs of the sheriff. Meanwhile, the soloist scampered from side to side on the stage, evading authorities. Through their actions, both the soloist and background singers seemed aligned, their actions suggesting a similar subjectivity. At other moments, the background singers' gestures assumed a subjectivity opposing that of the soloist, for example, by each raising one arm and pointing the other hand at the soloist in an accusatory fashion.

Toward the end of the song, two members standing in the back row of the arc raised handwritten signs that read "We—Dance." The audience laughed, either appreciating the Dear Abbeys' self-deprecating humor or understanding that the butt of the joke was not just the group but the whole competition. But the Dear Abbeys was not quite finished. A moment later, just as the laughter was dying down, the singers raised a third sign between the first two, completing the phrase, "We—Don't—Dance." The new display highlighted the amateur quality of the group's choreography, as well as its feminizing potential. The audience erupted in laughter and cheers, drowning out the singing. The Dear Abbeys' resistance was complete.

Humor is a unique form of discourse, according to Joanne Gilbert, because it can be "antirhetoric, that is, a rhetoric that always simultaneously promotes and disavows itself—renouncing its intent even as it amuses audiences and advances agendas." This particular brand of comedy sends a double message, constructing a kind of Bakhtinian "double-voiced discourse" that incorporates the dominant discourse, thus guaranteeing impunity, while subverting it.[33] The members of the Dear Abbeys used self-deprecating humor strategically in their performance: they choreographed their movements while simultaneously drawing attention to that fact. Their joke may have been rooted in a wry sense of self-ridicule, but the additional layer of meaning, resisting the ICCA's "choreography requirement," was certainly not lost on the audience. The performance earned them a first-place finish and advanced them to the finals the following month, where they were crowned Grand Champions of the ICCA.

As the Dear Abbeys case shows, for some groups, competition performances are different from performances elsewhere. They are calculated, changed in ways the singers hope will improve their chances of success. Christina, of the University of Michigan Harmonettes, a women's ensemble, explained that her group added choreography to one of its songs specifically for the ICCA competition: "We thought that it would improve our score. We had never done the competition before, and we had heard from other groups that choreography is looked upon highly."

If, as previously argued, a group's identity, negotiated through the rehearsal process, is projected through its performances, then it is a small step to conclude that, if competition structures performance in ways that distinguish it from other performances, a group's projected identity may vary between competitive and noncompetitive settings. The choreography the Harmonettes added to its ICCA performance differed from its usual fare because it included suggestive hip movements and seductive facial expressions. "That is the only time we've ever done anything that sexual on stage," Christina said. These moves did not reflect the group's regular performance style, which she and other Harmonettes described as less sexual and more "genuine."

The Dear Abbeys' experience was similar. In noncompetition performances, the singers acted silly and goaded each other; spontaneity and unpredictability helped them keep their energy up and put on a better show. It was such an integral part of their performance routine that it became an essential element of what it meant to be a member of the group. Paul explained.

> We like to ham it up onstage and to do something that will probably directly affect our musicality in the name of doing something different and making somebody laugh. We've found that that's the most successful formula to bring to a performance. That's just what we do.

But that carefree, boundary-testing silliness was not what the Dear Abbeys presented at the ICCA. The judges might have considered such behavior unprofessional, especially since "professionalism" is one of the criteria. Meanwhile, the overt sexuality of the Harmonettes' performance was thought to be competitive, a fact that points as much to the gendered expectations of a cappella—indeed, popular music—performance as to the Harmonettes' efforts to comply with the ICCA's "choreography requirement."

Why go to all this trouble to reconfigure performance routines? Competitions are powerful because they attract public attention—perhaps to a greater degree than any single group can accomplish on its own.[34] Most ICCA events I attended filled the hall, no matter how large. The finals are routinely sold out. Moreover, the ICCA's effects are felt not just nationally but also on local campuses by groups not competing. Following its 2002 ICCA win, the University of Michigan Compulsive Lyres boasted its achievement as a new and powerful recruiting tool; an appearance on NBC's *Today* show on April 29 of that year certainly helped. When the fall semester began a few months later, the group stood at the forefront of the Michigan a cappella scene. Helping it along the way was the school's embrace: the University's news services promoted the victory as a positive reflection of the quality of the student body.[35] Thus, success in the competition brings prestige, altering the dynamics of power between a cappella groups.

Despite their power implications—or perhaps due to them—competitions (and other live performances) are venues for the transmission or exchange of ideas regarding musical practice. "I think it opened our eyes to see what we could potentially be," Christina said of the Harmonettes' experience at the ICCA. Many of the singers I spoke with would agree, acknowledging that observing other groups, whether in competitive or cooperative settings, sometimes inspired their own performances. But opportunities for such observation are limited to live performance contexts, rendering negotiations of group identity determined in rehearsal invisible to outsiders. What remains are the sounds and gestures of the stage act. As the cases of the Harmonettes and the Dear Abbeys suggest, what one group sees in another's live performance, the very observations that may affect its own subsequent performances, may not accurately reflect the identity the performers attribute to themselves or their performance style. The projection of identity through performance is thus not a simple, one-way act but rather one of considerable complexity for both performers and observers.

Conventions and Cultural Aspirations at the ICCA Finals

The ICCA finals are held in New York City, usually at Lincoln Center in Alice Tully Hall (earlier venues included Carnegie Hall and the City Hall auditorium). Some stress the importance of this venue for its legitimating power, as the performance of collegiate a cappella music there implies that the genre is of equal worth and deserves a place alongside the other musical traditions presented in the same space. Newman addressed this implication directly: "We like the idea of New York because it's the capital of the country for cultural reasons. If you think about singing and dancing and great shows, you think of New York

... [Even] the a cappella groups in Wyoming have heard of Lincoln Center!" Yet the nature of the venue for the ICCA finals can conflict with some of the performance conventions of the practice itself, especially its humor.

At the 2005 finals, two young men (the evening's emcees) presented short comedic sketches between each group's set to give the judges time to complete feedback forms. Things began to go awry when, following intermission, one of the emcees came onto the stage dressed in drag, intending to impersonate Alice Tully by adopting a high-society air.[36] The sketch tapped into the prominent role of alcohol in collegiate culture and, perhaps inadvertently, suggested that Tully herself had a drinking problem. This prompted boos, hisses, and shouts from the otherwise jovial and festive audience, which reprimanded the emcees for their apparent disrespect. Had the vignette been presented in a concert on a college campus, in which the actor in drag might have been impersonating a sorority girl instead of Ms. Tully, it would have been quite funny. But at Lincoln Center, it was embarrassing. It was behavior, the audience's response suggested, unbecoming of such a venue and counter to the aspirations of the competition, its participants, and its audience.

It therefore seems that, in the right venue, a cappella's audience will defend the genre from commentary that might be seen as damaging. This was no more true than when MTV showed up at the 2009 ICCA finals with a camera crew and an onscreen host, Adrienne Bailon, to record the event for possible broadcast. Newman had coordinated the effort with MTV in advance, but on the day of the show things did not go exactly as planned.

In discussions on the RARB forum following the performance, competitors complained about various effects of MTV's presence, which, in the words of Benjamin Stevens (one of the judges), "cheapened" the experience for all involved.

> I hated it when, at the very end of Finals, the collegiate groups were called on stage and then treated, by MTV and Ms. Bailon, in the manner of "reality television": a low-budget, no-concept cruelty intended to generate artificial suspense but in the end only sucking all the energy out of the room and draining all of the evening's *natural* drama.[37]

Part of the elimination of the "natural" drama (i.e., the musical competition itself) was the superimposition of stereotypes on each of the groups. Robert, writing from Ithaca College's Ithacappella, bemoaned the way his group was allegedly painted, time and again, in its MTV interview as a group of "frat boys."[38] Dave, another Ithacapella member, reported on the same interview. In Dave's words:

> *MTV:* What sets you apart from the other groups here?
> *Member of Ithacappella:* We're extremely close. It's really like having an eighteen-person family.
> *MTV:* So would you say it's like. Fraternal?
> *Everyone in Ithacappella:* No, absolutely not like a frat at all. (and so on with explanations of how we are not a frat)
> *MTV:* So are you guys going to have a big rager or kegger when you get back to Ithaca?
> *Member of Ithacappella:* Well we're probably going to get together and have a chess and checkers tournament.[39]

Robert corroborated Dave's report: "That's not a joke. That's actually almost word for word how the interview went down. Including the chess tournament line."[40] A member of the Duke's Men, from Yale University, complained that his group was also stereotyped, "boxed into being the 'Ivy League Group.'"[41] Multiple contributors to the discussion claimed that MTV seemed more interested in uncovering a ruthless, "cutthroat" competition than in what the groups actually had to say (which was usually something like "We're thrilled to be here and sing with these other outstanding groups"). Moreover, Bailon allegedly was not prepared to discuss basic musical concepts. Robert claims one of her interview questions to his group was, "So do you guys work on stuff with tempos?"[42] Stevens summed up the complaints.

> It was low-brow, bought at the lamentably high cost of amateurishly essentializing the groups and so ignoring an audience's capacity for nuance. MTV imagined, and so tried to impose, a cardboard psychodrama of laid-back (read: drunken and/or stoned) frat boys, snooty Ivy Leaguers, and poor dumb kids from some obscure community college all at each other's throats for . . . what? There's almost *literally* nothing at stake—per Varsity Vocals new certificate policy, not even pieces of paper until later, by mail!—but the slightest bragging rights . . . and the amazing opportunity to sing for and with amazing people.[43]

Even if MTV were there to promote a cappella, its presence was interpreted as interference—whether the deliberate essentializing of group identities or slow-

ing the naming of the winners to artificially inflate the tension of the moment—in the normal practice of competition. Thus, even if, as Stevens points
out, there is little "literally" at stake in the competition, both the performers
and the audience were aware that *something* they valued—their personal identities, their group identities, whatever qualities they ascribe to the music that
reflect on themselves—was threatened.

Gendered Conventions: Masculinity, Femininity, and the Homoerotics of A Cappella

Whether in competition or under other circumstances, collegiate a cappella
performances take place within the historical context of rock music and a contemporary social context, within which gender is an important force. The construction of rock music as male (see chapter 5), creates certain challenges for
women performers, including those in a cappella groups. For example, the association of vocal percussion with masculinity (see chapter 6) makes it a risky
practice for women living in a highly charged, heterosexual environment. During college, many young people pair off and explore romantic relationships,
some of which lead to lifelong partnerships or even marriage. The socializing
rituals of fraternities and sororities play a role here, while talk of male students
during the Fallen Angels' check-in further asserts a heterosexual norm.[44] This
can put particular pressure on college women, who may feel they must toe the
line between performing the opposing roles of "good girl" and appearing at-
tractive and fun. In this context, the masculinizing potential of vocal percussion is dangerous because it defeminizes the percussionist and offers a gendered performance entirely opposite the one desired.

Women are not totally trapped, however. The Fallen Angels demonstrates
one way women a cappella musicians can challenge conventional gender roles.
Success in the social arena of college life depends partly on an individual's ability to seem exciting and desirable. The "Angels: Most Wanted" concert poster
(fig. 6.1) allowed the women to assume seductive poses and socially deviant
roles, which would generate interest in the concert with its "sex sells" advertising philosophy and promise of dangerous flirtation. But it did so in a manner
that was carefully and clearly framed as role-play. "Things I'll Never Say," one of
the songs the group performed frequently, similarly teased men in the audience
with the possibility of sexual encounter. On the surface, the lyrics appear to
subscribe to male perceptions of feminine ideals while simultaneously express-

ing young women's anxiety about courtship: "If I could say what I want to say," Candace, on the solo, would sing, "I'd say I want to blow you [pause] away / Be with you every night. Am I holding you too tight? / If I could see what I want to see, I'd want to see you go down [pause] on one knee / Marry me today, or am I wishing my life away?"[45] In performance, the pauses in the lyrics, from which emerge allusions to oral sex, enabled Candace to step outside the "good girl" role she may have been expected to play (especially since she was an *Ivy League* woman) and instead embody a less conventional and more thrilling female persona. But by the conclusion of each phrase, she returned to her less sexualized persona, leaving male listeners to realize that they had been tricked.

The importance of gender in a cappella performance extends beyond heterosexual concerns to include relations between men. A cappella's roots in barbershop suggest a historical precedent for such behavior, a homoerotics of performance. Richard Mook describes how barbershop, as one of many increasingly popular leisure activities in the late nineteenth and early twentieth centuries, created a space within which men could practice and perform their masculinity, drawing on late Victorian concepts of manhood that included, and even valued, physical contact.[46] In contemporary American youth culture, and in American culture more broadly, physical contact between men, even coordinated movement among men, is sometimes viewed with suspicion, since it can carry homosexual connotations. However, while often perceived as threatening to one's masculinity, male interaction and the specter of homosexuality can also serve as effective comedic devices. This has been especially true in theater, where men dressed as women can make for particularly funny characters (e.g., Monty Python) and sometimes a means of cultural critique. Dressing in drag is not unknown in a cappella either. In the spring of 2005 the Treblemakers performed a lengthy skit that claimed to reveal the genesis of the group (genesis skits are common). Mixing *West Side Story*'s rival gangs and the crazy antics of the film *Zoolander*, many of the men wore women's clothing and wigs, creating a mythical distance between their group's "ancestors" and its current members.

Dance is a highly gendered expressive form in contemporary American youth culture, wherein women are the archetypal dancers. Ramsay Burt writes, "Professional dance during the last hundred and fifty years has not been considered an appropriate activity for white men to engage in," adding race to the burden dance carries. (Break-dancing, an exception, is primarily a soloistic genre of black males.) Most men who are "dancers" are considered exceptional "others" and commonly associated with homosexuality, which often entails no-

tions of femininity.[47] Indeed, some notable acts in late-twentieth-century popular music, from Madonna to David Bowie to Boy George, were famous for
their gender-bending imagery, often combined with physicality and/or dance.

At times, the association of male a cappella performance with homosexuality can go from comedic to problematic to dangerous: Early in the morning on
January 1, 2007, members of the Baker's Dozen, a men's group from Yale University, were attacked and physically beaten by local youths while departing a
New Year's Eve party in the San Francisco area. Based on insults reportedly
hurled at the singers by the alleged assailants, homophobia was among the motivations for the attack.[48] Yet, however dangerous they may be, many men's
groups, such as the Dear Abbeys, continue to use choreographed movements.

There are two ways men physically relate to each other in a cappella performances. In the first, men execute coordinated movements or gestures but show
little direct interaction. For instance, in the Dear Abbeys' "Renegade," the background singers performed finger-pointing gestures at the same time and in the
same direction but did not directly interact with one another. Their coordinated
movements amounted to a show of group unity. Strength in numbers could,
perhaps, offset the feminizing potential of men dancing, a tacit understanding of
which fueled the "We—Don't—Dance" joke. In their discussion of overly masculine "cock rock," Simon Frith and Angela McRobbie point to a similar "ag-
gressive, dominating, and boastful" physicality, through which performers constantly seek "to remind the audience of their prowess, their control."[49]

The second way men relate to each other in a cappella performance involves
more direct interaction, including flirtatious or marginally "inappropriate" behavior with great comedic potential. It never fails to get a laugh when one man
jumps into another man's arms or touches another in an innocent yet inappropriate manner. A brief example demonstrates this point. At the ICCA semifinals
at Yale University on March 26, 2005, the Duke's Men of Yale, a men's ensemble,
closed its set with a rendition of the Jackson 5's "I Want You Back." Clad in tuxedos with tails, they split into three groups. Most of the members remained in a
single arc upstage, providing the background singing for the song. One member stepped forward downstage left and delivered the solo, mostly avoiding the
young Michael Jackson's high falsetto and instead singing the melody an octave
lower. The remaining four members stepped forward downstage right to provide the song's humorous choreography. Sometimes they assumed multileveled
formations near the center of the stage, waving their arms in a Busby Berkeley-
like display of opened palms, but mostly they remained side by side, executing

subtle yet humorous Motown moves, like stylishly waving their fingers, which kept the audience chuckling. In certain parts of the number, however, these four dancers interacted more directly. During each of the song's refrains, the dancers turned to face stage right, kneeling slightly. Each one placed his hands on the hips of the dancer in front of him, timed to the music so that the movements were executed on successive beats. During one of the later refrains, however, the fourth dancer made a "mistake." When the moment arrived for him to put his hands in place on the man in front of him, he did not reach for the hips, but instead issued a gentle tap on the bottom. This provoked mock outrage from the third dancer, who then mimed a slap across the fourth dancer's face. The audience laughed hysterically.

In his ethnographic study of college life in the mid-1980s, Michael Moffatt observes the connection between the performance of friendship and playacted homosexuality: "Heterosexual males dealt with mainstream homophobia by putting their physical contacts in certain acceptable frames." Moffatt calls one frame "'homosexual ironic,' in which male friends implied that they were so manly that they could act 'gay,' for fun, because no one would ever believe that *they* were really homosexual."[50] Such behavior signifies close friendships between individuals. As social relationships are central to a cappella, "homosexual ironic" gestures are one way to embody them, while, as the choreography used by the Duke's Men shows, also adding comedic value to the performance. Moreover, as Sheryl Garratt notes, a "touch of homosexuality seems to *enhance* a male star's popularity with women, in fact—especially if it is carefully denied elsewhere."[51] When read as a whole, the Duke's Men's ICCA set might suggest just the sort of ambiguity, if not denial, that, according to Garratt, makes such homoerotic choreographic displays successful. "I Want You Back" was preceded by the Barenaked Ladies' "What A Good Boy," a ballad that deals explicitly with male-female relations (though not in an overtly sexual way), and the set opened with a spiritual, which eschewed such relations altogether.

Deeply embedded cultural codes such as "homosexual ironic" are useful for interpreting the Dear Abbeys' and Duke's Men's performances but less helpful when it comes to women's groups. Many female singers complained to me about what they perceived as a double standard in a cappella choreography. The same movements that men's groups perform with great comedic effect would fall flat if performed by women, they contended. During the 2004–5 ICCA season and earlier, I never once saw a women's group attempt the sort of humor, homoerotic or otherwise, that the men's groups performed. Divisi, a women's group from the University of Oregon, was the only women's group to advance to the 2005 ICCA finals. It presented a highly choreographed set, including a showstopping rendition of hip-hop artist Usher's "Yeah!," but attempted no humor. Instead, the women rotated around the stage in precise formations and enacted moderately sexualized hip-hop-inspired moves that, like the rock gestures previously discussed, suggested the seriousness, intensity, and effort with which they dedicated themselves to the performance.[52]

Choreographic and gestural choices, and even humor, appear more limited for female performers than for males. Christina lamented that men's groups could successfully "make fun of female attitudes and homosexual ideas, and that gets a laugh. But if females try to do the same thing in reverse, people would just think it was socially awkward. If you try and masculinize yourself, *it's not funny,* it's *weird.*" To cope with this handicap, she explained, the Harmonettes abandoned its attempts at humor through choreography and skits. Instead, the singers adopted a more "genuine" attitude: addressing the audience seriously and honestly, emoting and demonstrating their warmth and close personal ties through facial gestures and glances around their arc, and generally "looking together and composed," as Kira, the group's music director, explained. "Perhaps that's not as entertaining," Christina said. "Perhaps people don't get a kick out of hearing about ourselves. But we just try and be honest and try to relate what the experience is like to be in our group."

Women comedians have long been a problematic category. "As inhabitants of the private rather than public sphere, with little if any true political power," Gilbert writes, "women humorists, like all women, have often been denied access to the 'old boys' club.' In the arena of comedy, as in many other professions, women have long been considered supporting rather than leading players."[53] As Barbara Levy points out, historically men have feared witty and clever women, who were viewed as dangerous and portrayed by male writers as shrews, witches, and bitches.[54] Combined with the masculine quality associated with rock music, such historically situated and deeply ingrained conventions of gendered performance help to explain the challenges the Harmonettes and other women's groups face when attempting to incorporate humor into their performances.

There are strategies through which women's groups can bring humor into their concerts while relying less on gendered expectations of feminine behavior, however. Members of the Fallen Angels played roles in their skits that were clearly established as caricatures, creating a rhetorical distance necessary for their humor to be effective—since it clearly did not relate to the women themselves. Moreover, individuals could still achieve comedic success, Christina noted, by telling funny personal anecdotes or employing self-deprecating humor when addressing the audience between songs. But the more successful strategy her group used was to make the entertainment "external." The women had a male singer from another group on campus serve as emcee at one of their concerts. At a different, prom-themed Harmonettes concert, they invited audience members onto the stage as candidates for prom "king" and "queen" and then had the rest of the audience vote. The Fallen Angels' use of the Din & Tonics may also be seen as a version of this method. In these strategies, the humor no longer depends entirely on the women themselves or their comedic skills for success. By abnegating their own agency, they ensure the success of their humorous efforts while also revealing the (harsh) reality of gendered categories in a cappella and American youth culture more broadly.

Conclusion: Interaction and Identity

Collegiate a cappella singers present their music while making connections, often through humor, among themselves, their group, and the world around them. Their performances can reflect and comment on myriad aspects of their lives—their campus a cappella scene and its political landscape, national and international politics, relationships among college-age youth, and the boundaries of the conventional performance of gender—as they proceed through a profound period of transition toward adulthood. At the same time, performers employ particular gestures that locate a cappella in its post–rock 'n' roll historical moment.

Musical exchanges may be found anytime two groups meet, but at the ICCA competition, the levels of exchange, observation, and reflection are more pronounced. As Christina put it, her group's experience at the ICCA "opened their eyes" to more possibilities. Referring to performances outside the ICCA, Dave, of the Treblemakers, echoed the same idea, adding that he also got a sense of a group's identity from its performance.

> I like to look for any indication for how they put a song together. Like, does their director direct them onstage? How are they singing together—are they more focused on each other? Are they more focused on themselves as individual singers or are they more focused on the performance for the audience? I

don't know, all those things that, you know, that tell you sort of how they be-
have or participate in rehearsals. Stuff like that for me is valuable just because,
you know, it gives you new ideas.

This effect extends beyond a cappella, too. "Contest rankings provide barbershop with its elites," Liz Garnett writes. They hold "considerable power to affect
the behaviour of other barbershoppers, in that winners are seen as setting examples: repertoire, choreographic gestures and interpretive decisions are all
mimicked by aspirant ensembles."[55]

In Pierre Bourdieu's terms, performers' and groups' habitus are affected by
the exchange of ideas through encounters; performative options are expanded.
And, as Toynbee would put it, the "likelihood" of performers making particular choices or choosing particular performance strategies is increased.[56] Those
strategies contribute to the identity the performance conveys. Dave emphasized
the limited opportunities for groups on his campus to present themselves.
When one occurs, it was a crucial moment of competition and self-presenta-
tion: "[E]ven if you're singing at one big benefit concert, it's still a competition,
because you're representing your group and it's the one shot you get to represent your group to a large number of people." Moffitt would agree. "The ICCA
was one form [of rivalry], certainly, but there was also the rivalry between us
and other groups on campus. Keeping our distance from the other groups," she
writes of her experience, "having the tightest arrangements and the most capti-
vating choreography, even attracting the best newcomers from each fall's in-
coming freshmen: it was all in the name of being the best, the 'premiere' group
on campus."[57] It is therefore not unreasonable to conclude, as Christina does,
that through performance "you're *defining* yourself."

CHAPTER 8

Technology in Collegiate
A Cappella Performance and Recording

In collegiate a cappella, technology, especially the digital kind, is ubiquitous. When considering music and technology, much scholarship focuses on the recording studio.[1] Recording is indeed a key musical technology in a cappella and popular music more generally, but before turning to the studio this chapter explores the role of technology in other areas of a cappella music making. Songs are encountered in digital format online; arranged on, shared with, recorded to, and modified by computers; distributed on digital compact discs or as MP3 files; and dissected and discussed in publicly accessible Internet forums, producing a discourse that in turn affects others as they select, arrange, record, and distribute music digitally. Taken as a whole, this process traces a "digital circle," a concept that helps to elaborate the impact of digital technology on musicking, which Timothy Taylor describes as "the most fundamental change in the history of Western music since the invention of music notation in the ninth century."[2] In the recording process, examined in the chapter's second half, technology is also an important tool—and one with both social and musical effects.

Finding Songs, Arranging by Computer

Aside from singers, a collegiate a cappella group's most basic need is music for its repertory. Group members find songs through recorded media such as radio, CDs, MP3s on iPods and other digital music players; the iTunes Music

Store and similar music distribution sites on the Internet; direct communication through e-mail and "instant messaging"; and websites from which lyrics and guitar tablature notation can be downloaded. These technologies enable a cappella musicians to access the "raw materials" of musical practice—commercially produced recordings of popular songs—in order to assess and select pieces to arrange for their group.

During my fieldwork, the most common method for accessing music was through MP3s. As compressed files, MP3s are easy to share and, given the near ubiquity of computers on campuses and support for the MP3 format across computing platforms, the format is nearly universal. Moreover, as a "nonrivalrous resource," one person's use of an MP3 file does not preclude another's, as would be the case with physical media such as CDs.[3] A cappella singers and arrangers typically get MP3s by creating them from their own CD collections, purchasing them from online vendors, or acquiring them from other people in their group, friends outside their group, or file-sharing websites, the most famous—and perhaps notorious—of which is Napster.[4] After getting an MP3 file, the song it contains can be arranged.

When learning their repertories, most groups read from arrangements printed in standard Western music notation. But for an amateur practice like a cappella, notation is a double-edged sword. On one hand, it is an efficient means of communicating information about what and how people should sing (it is, as Taylor suggests, a technology in and of itself). On the other, the ability to encode and decode musical ideas in notation requires certain training and skills, which sometimes even the best singers do not possess. Amazin' Blue, from the University of Michigan, held several debates regarding such skills when candidates auditioned for the group with great vocal but poor music-reading abilities. The question became, should the candidate be admitted for his or her excellent voice even if it means slower-paced rehearsals (since he or she would have to be taught by rote, a slower method) and possibly a smaller repertory as a result?

Some groups, like Brandeis University VoiceMale, avoided the question—whether purposefully or not—by using notated arrangements sparingly. Lianna, from Company B at Brandeis, sometimes taught her group's arrangements orally too. She found that the process produced not only musical results but also a deeper connection between singers and the sounds they were being asked to make: "The nice thing about teaching it orally, I've found, is that you have a lot more connection to it, because it's not this thing on a piece of paper.

It's like this thing that somebody's teaching you mouth to mouth, you know? It's [a] very … *personal* thing." Lianna's comments reveal that the "personal" aspect of a cappella music may begin quite early in the rehearsal process, when the singers are literally learning note by note. They also suggest that copresence is fundamental to the establishment of this personal feeling and that learning from another person is more emotionally involved than when learning is mediated by a printed score. However, most groups I encountered preferred to use scores, so there is probably at least some degree of "fellow feeling" created by that method as well.[5]

In most cases, once a song is selected, it is arranged by computer using music notation software. Doing so demystifies and simplifies the arranging process, relieving arrangers of the burden of realization, since they can rely on a computer's capacity instead of their own sight-singing, keyboard, or instrumental skills to play back and listen to their work in progress. Additionally, when students do not have instruments at their disposal, the computer may be the most practical way to hear their arrangements.[6]

Arrangers may also use the Internet to find musical information, such as MIDI files or sheet music, to help them with their arrangements. In fact, in a brief instruction guide for first-time arrangers, Deke Sharon specifically suggests finding a MIDI version of the song being arranged.[7] For some arrangers, the greatest challenge is translating the sound of a recording into a series of chords (the song's harmonic progression) from which vocal parts can be drawn. While talking about her arranging method, Debra, from the Harvard University Fallen Angels, explained, "[W]hen I find a song I like, I cheat: I look up guitar chords." Setting aside the question of cheating, it becomes clear that the Internet serves as a tool Debra uses to overcome a musical obstacle. Additionally, she said, "[I]t helps to have some written sheet music. So if I can find a piano sheet music for a certain song, that's really helpful, too, because it has the chords."

Typically, notation software complements an arranger's preexisting musical knowledge. Laura, a senior at Kalamazoo College and a member of the school's women's a cappella group, brought some musical knowledge and experience from high school to her group. When discussing arranging methods, she admitted that she could usually imagine parts in her head before notating them on a computer, which would then be used to confirm that she had notated them correctly. But in a few instances her imagination was less specific. "Sometimes I would play around with rhythms without really hearing what it is that I wanted," she said. "I would just sort of put something in and play it back and be like, 'okay, that does not fit at all!' And then I'd go back and change the rhythm again." In these moments, Laura used the computer's notation software not simply to confirm preexisting ideas but to test new musical possibilities. Arrangers who have difficulty discerning a song's harmonic progression can use a similar trial-and-error approach. By arranging on a computer, new and experienced arrangers can thus quickly gain and build experience, skills, and confidence.

A cappella singers routinely distinguish between those who have arranging skills and those who do not, and some seek instruction in arranging technique. Candice described learning the basics of arranging during a "workshop" in which the Fallen Angels invited someone from outside the group to explain the process. This tends to be the exception, not the rule, however. And despite the publication of Anna Callahan's arranging manual, most arrangers learn their craft by observing the arrangements already in their group's repertory and by arranging with other group members.[8] Lianna and Julia, from Company B, explained that all new arrangers in their group must complete their first arrangement with an older, more experienced member: "[W]e don't allow anybody who's new, who's never arranged, to arrange by themselves. You always have to arrange with somebody who's done it before." This process creates a chain of instruction between the past and present. It is not always explicitly instructional, Julia said, but sometimes relies instead on observation. "And it's this intricate, you know, pairing up of people to pass on how we arrange without sitting down and [saying], 'This is how we do it, these are the steps, this is how it goes.'"

Technology of Performance

To audiences, technology is perhaps most evident in collegiate a cappella through the use of microphones and amplification systems in live performances. Not all groups use microphones for all performances, but most do so for at least some performances each year, usually at a semester's concert or other events and gigs whose venues require amplification. Typically, overhead "area" or condenser microphones pick up the background voices, while the soloist, featured harmonies, and sometimes also vocal percussion and bass use additional handheld microphones. Some groups have more elaborate systems. For example, Amazin' Blue uses individual, handheld, wireless microphones for each singer in its concerts (see fig. 7.1). Microphones are important for both acoustic and performative reasons, and their impact on the details and experi-ence of performance can be powerful.

A cappella is sometimes characterized as a particularly "pure" or "natural" genre, consisting of only voices, unmediated and unhindered by technology, in-cluding instruments. During the first season of *The Sing-Off*, a televised a cap-pella contest broadcast on NBC in December 2009, celebrity host Nick Lachey repeatedly emphasized the lack of instruments and the fact that the performers made their music "with just their voices." Speaking to the a cappella commu-nity more specifically, John wrote on the RARB forum, "A cappella music is that which should be performable with no added instruments." When technologies (John singled out "computer and electronics") become "*fundamental* to a per-formance, instead of an enhancement to the performance, then that seems to cross a line."[9] A cappella is not alone in this quandary. The idea (or, rather, ide-ology) that a musical genre "is" or "should be" something when the common practice suggests otherwise is also found, according to Liz Garnett, in barber-shop harmony (see chapter 1).[10]

The use of microphones and sound systems complicates the image of a cap-pella as a pure or natural musical practice. After all, even the highest-quality microphones can capture only a certain range of frequencies, albeit a wide one. Similarly, the ability to reproduce those frequencies depends greatly on the quality, construction, and placement of the speakers used to amplify them. In-deed, as Michael, an alumnus of the Massachusetts Institute of Technology Logarhythms, pointed out in a response to John, "[E]ven an acoustic space is technically a violation" since the particular shape of a room and the qualities of its reflective surfaces can affect sound. And if one accepts acoustic spaces as nat-ural, what about the (more or less) exact replication of such spaces using elec-tronic equipment during a live performance?[11]

Beyond its acoustical effects, technology can also have profound social ef-fects, especially when groups interact and find themselves using unfamiliar technologies. When they travel to sing at other schools, they are sometimes faced with circumstances radically different from those under which they are used to performing. Such exposure to different groups and contexts helps cir-culate ideas within the a cappella world, as the following example illustrates.

By late March 2005, the members of Starving Artists, a mixed group at Brandeis University, were getting excited. During the first weekend of April they were scheduled to drive south from Boston to Philadelphia to open for Off the Beat at the University of Pennsylvania. Aside from the excitement of a trip together, socially appealing in itself, opening for Off the Beat was an honor. That group, they all knew, was one of the foremost in the country, with repeated appearances on the annual *Best of College A Cappella* compilation album. I traveled to Philadelphia to observe the encounter.[12]

Two hours before the show, I caught up with a few members of Starving Artists in a coffee shop on the corner of 34th and Walnut Streets, a few blocks from the concert venue. They were talking about the microphones they had found during their sound check, their time to rehearse in the venue with its amplification system and adjust volume levels and microphone placements in advance of the actual performance. Much to their dismay, the setup differed markedly from their expectations.

Off the Beat had set up the microphones in its usual fashion, with many on the stage—almost one per singer—and most affixed to stationary stands positioned in two arcs. Unlike the usual arc formation, however, Off the Beat positioned the ends of its arcs close together, so the singers standing in those positions faced each other directly at a distance of only a few feet. The resulting shape was more of a *U* than an arc or crescent. It quickly became clear that Starving Artists would not be able to perform in its usual way. The new stage configuration was foreign to the singers and proving stressful. "When we got there it was really disconcerting and scary to have to deal with all of this equipment," recalled Becca, one of the group's singers. They were used to the more common setup described earlier, with overhead microphones on large "boom" stands to pick up most of the group, which kept the stage mostly empty, allowing the singers considerable freedom of movement, and a few handheld units for the soloist and featured harmonies. They now worried that their choreography would have to be cut. Ashley, the group's president, described their predicament as one of her "biggest fears," since she considered choreography an important way Starving Artists connected with the audience.

Beyond physical considerations, the members of Starving Artists wanted to convey a different message through their performance than they believed was possible with Off the Beat's setup. The *U* formation reflected Off the Beat's artistic priorities. It allowed only a small portion of the audience, those seated in the very center of the auditorium, to view all the singers' faces. Compared to the atmosphere of a wider arc formation, their performance seemed more exclusive. They sang energetically and loudly at each other rather than to the audience. During a song, the only direct communication between the group and the audience took place via the soloist. Unlike Starving Artists, Off the Beat had no staging or choreography. Whether intentional or not, Off the Beat's setup effectively contained the visitors' performance, limiting the possibility that their guests would upstage them.

The setup at the University of Pennsylvania also differed acoustically from the Brandeis singers' usual format. Singers in Starving Artists were not used to having their voices amplified individually, as would be the case with nearly one microphone per singer in the arc. Additionally, Off the Beat's vocal percussionist wore a microphone in the form of a throat patch. It picked up a deep, crisp percussion sound that was much more powerful than any the members of Starving Artists or I had ever heard outside a studio. Moreover, in a technique rarely heard outside a studio (at least for collegiate groups), the signal from one or both of the bass microphones was electronically doubled an octave lower.

Although actual dialogue between the two groups was minimal—aside from a few cursory greetings at the sound check, the members of Starving Artists and Off the Beat did not mingle before the performance—their encounter was rich with interactive meaning. The members of Starving Artists at first saw the situation as a foreboding challenge, a competition. "Not only were we *scared* by the microphones a little bit during our sound check," Becca said, but

> we were very... "We understand that you guys [Off the Beat] do your a cappella like this, but that's *not how we do it*." And so we were very [reactive] to everything that they did, because we were like, "they're trying to impose their style of a cappella on us, and we don't like it, and we don't want to do it."

As they continued to discuss the situation, however, their attitude changed. They decided to approach the concert not as a competition between two performance styles but instead as an opportunity to reaffirm what their group valued in a live a cappella performance. Ashley and Becca later recalled:

A: There were a lot of discussions in that period, and following the show, as to different forms of a cappella: the very mechanical, technological form versus our more organic form. And what's better? Or what's worse? And how are they different? And why would you choose?

B: Yeah, so we were talking about it. And we kept bringing up UPenn, like, what are we going to do tonight? And all of a sudden we all just have this epiphany, like, "Fuck that!"—excuse me—we can go there and be really good the way we are and not try to alter ourselves, and not worry about their microphones, and not try to think about what they're doing with relation to our a cappella. Because it doesn't even really matter. And so we were like, "We're just going to go have fun, and we don't even care if they like us or not."

A: We'll do what we do best, and we'll see how it works.

The force with which Becca described their rejection of Off the Beat's approach demonstrates the conviction that their way was better, at least for their group. The technological constraints they encountered limited the very aspects they considered crucial not only to a good performance but also to the faithful expression of their group's identity. In the end, the members of Starving Artists had to adapt their performance style to suit the physical circumstances. As they did, however, they strove to overcome them by adjusting their choreography and making a concerted effort to maintain visual contact with the audience. Ultimately, the experience reinforced their stylistic preferences. In later concerts and gigs back at Brandeis, they returned to their usual performance practices.[13]

Digital Distribution and Dissection

The distribution of collegiate a cappella music is closely related to digital technologies. Perhaps the most basic means is the CD, a medium on which audio is stored digitally (unlike a record's acoustic process or a cassette tape's magnetic one). The role of digital technologies becomes more obvious, however, when a cappella groups present themselves and their music online. Many groups maintain their own websites or pages on Facebook, which typically contain information about the group's current and upcoming activities and performances, members, and booking information. More elaborate sites feature group histories, as well as galleries of photos and recordings, most of which can be purchased directly from the site as MP3 files.[14]

Other online venues constitute virtual shopping malls of a cappella albums and tracks. Perhaps the most significant is A-Cappella.com (formerly Mainely A Cappella), which carries a wide range of a cappella recordings by collegiate, professional, barbershop, doo-wop, and other groups, as well as sheet music, instructional videos, pitch pipes, and other paraphernalia. Groups whose CDs are available through the site receive payment at regular intervals based on their sales. Another site is acaTunes, which is conceptually modeled on Apple's iTunes Music Store and distributes digital copies of a cappella tracks as MP3s.[15] Finally, some groups offer their albums directly through better-known sites such as the iTunes Music Store, where the *BOCA* albums are also available.

The benefits of digital distribution are clear: because nonrivalrous resources like MP3 files can be easily copied and transferred, their music is more accessible. And although the a cappella community has not always been on the forefront when it comes to the legal ramifications of its practice—witness repeated online discussions regarding mechanical licenses for a cappella recordings—it has begun to catch up.[16] For example, a recent visit to the acaTunes site's page devoted to the University of Pennsylvania Counterparts showed five albums listed. Although one can listen to a thirty-second excerpt of nearly all the songs, some were not actually available for purchase and download but instead listed as "unlicensed." One of them was "Daddy's All Gone," a ballad by James Taylor, which Counterparts recorded on *Afterglow* (1999). Whether by the group's request, acaTunes' decision, or the will of James Taylor's publisher, acaTunes did not have the legal right to sell it—or six other of *Afterglow*'s seventeen tracks.

Next to the listing for "Daddy's All Gone" was a string of numbers, "4/5/4/4/2," which indicated the scores that particular track received from the RARB's reviewers. The RARB's critical function differs from typical rock criticism, however, because it acknowledges the amateur nature of the musical practice. Reviews are aimed not only at a cappella consumers but also at the artists themselves in order to provide constructive criticism and offer ways to improve future arrangements and recordings. For example, Mark Manley's review of Starving Artists' album *Honestly* (2004) includes suggestions for improving both the group's vocal percussion and its choice of repertory.[17] Reviewers also make frequent recommendations regarding arranging technique, syllable choice, the order of tracks on an album, and the use of digital effects. A similar instructive function can be found in the columns published on the website of the Contemporary A Cappella Society of America (an outgrowth of the CASA's earlier *Contemporary A Cappella News*) and through the society's Contemporary A Cappella Recording Awards (CARAs), which are judged by individuals scattered across the globe through a password-protected website containing the candidates and nominees and then announced on the CASA site. Thus, through these digital media, a cappella musicians can observe which musical choices are received favorably and modify their own accordingly, shaping their aesthetic ideas and understanding of the musical practice. An element of competition, particularly strong in the CARAs, imbues these media with the power of prestige, the ability to distinguish between a cappella groups based on musical quality and distribute that information in the a cappella community.

Completing the Digital Circle

The digital circle is complete when information about or deriving from finished recordings, available online, feeds back into the selection and arrangement of songs. One instance of this feedback occurred at Kalamazoo College when a singer brought the song "Insomniac" to his men's a cappella group, the Kalamadudes, in the spring of 2010. He had first encountered the song through the all-male University of Virginia Gentlemen's recording of it, which appeared on *BOCA II* (1996) and on which he purposefully based his arrangement. Lacking a copy of the Gentlemen's score, however, he composed his arrangement through close listening to the Virginia group's recording.

This case illustrates how the selection of one group's recording for *BOCA* rendered it a model for others to follow in two ways. Its *BOCA* appearance increased the visibility of that particular song and suggested its exceptional suitability for a cappella performance, making it more likely to be selected by other groups for their repertories. Additionally, the *BOCA* selection attached particular value to the Gentlemen's *arrangement*, tempting other groups to follow it closely in their own renditions of the song (the effects of *BOCA* are explored more deeply in the next chapter). In fact, "Insomniac" has become one of the most influential collegiate arrangements and continues to be sung by groups across the country—not only men's groups like the Gentlemen but also mixed groups (e.g., McGill University Soulstice A Cappella) and women's groups (the Wheaton College Whims).

As one follows the digital circle of collegiate a cappella music making, it becomes clear that technology, in various forms, is at the heart of nearly every aspect of the musical practice. This fact challenges the perception of a cappella as a particularly pure or natural mode of music making and helps to locate today's a cappella firmly in its historical moment. Of course, a cappella's status as pure or natural is most clearly called into question—and, as the next chapter will show, most fiercely debated—when the technology of the recording studio is at issue. Although singers, engineers, and producers may employ various methods to make the recording process and its final product seem natural, just like a live performance, to some degree artificiality is inherent to both the process and the product. At the same time, the recording process also brings to the fore new aspects of a cappella's sociability.

The recording studio is unlike any other musical environment. As an a cappella group warmed up before a session in his studio, one recording engineer likened the experience to a tour on a submarine: quiet and dark, save the glow of computer screens, racks of electronic gear, and some soft overhead lighting. As Thomas Porcello observes, "[S]emiotic markers of acoustic difference from the everyday," like the thick, foam-lined walls, are everywhere, and the effect—of which an "unnatural quietness" is only one aspect—results in different kinds of social relations between musicians. as well as a different way of experiencing time.[18]

The studio is also a place where the musical and social aspects of a cappella music are vastly different from rehearsal and performance. In rehearsal and live performance, all the musicians usually sing concurrently and can directly see, hear, and interact with each other and their audience. In the studio, however, important visual cues, such as watching the shapes of other singers' lips and mouths in order to improve blend, are more difficult and sometimes impossible due to the physical and temporal impositions necessary to ensure sonic isolation and accuracy.

Like the rehearsal, recording can be a time of social performance and bonding. Due to certain pressures inherent in the process, however, its social effects can be as divisive as they are cohesive. In this rarefied space, perfection is sometimes believed to be possible, and the stakes, therefore, can seem higher than in live performance. Moreover, the tangible product, the recording itself, is a sounding record of a group, reverberating long after the final notes of a concert have fallen silent.

The Purposes of Recording

Although many artists use recordings to make artistic, philosophical, or political statements, they also record for financial reasons, a fact that scholars recognize.[19] To some degree, the same is true for collegiate a cappella. "It's how you market yourself when you're not always singing," said Dave, of the Boston University Treblemakers. Recordings can generate income through album sales and represent a group to future clients. Before Amazin' Blue was selected to sing backup for pop crooner Michael Bublé during his 2007 summer tour's stop at the Fox Theatre in Detroit, the group was asked to send the Detroit-based media company coordinating the local musicians one of its albums, the mere existence of which reinforced the group's professional qualifications. The economic aspect of the recording process should not be overstated, however, as the benefits individual group members see from CD sales are not monetary. This suggests that, aside from the economic aspects of recording, the process and product also serve social purposes, two of which are interpersonal bonding through shared experience and accomplishment and a tangible signifier that enables nostalgia and personal gratification.

The recording process is a project with a collective goal for a group's members. Dave explained:

> It becomes very important to you because it's a lot of hard work. And just like any big project, you want it to be good. It's a huge commitment. Fund-raising is a huge commitment . . . But on a personal level it's very important because it keeps morale up. And it's cool to have a CD. Like, "Hey, this is what I did in college." To have a CD and say, "This is what I *did*. Check this out. I'm proud of this," it's really important.

This common goal provides a foundation on which social relationships are built. Even disagreements can improve a group's sense of closeness and community, if suitable musical results emerge from them. Amazin' Blue alumna Anna reminisced that recording "was a time when we were together for hours and hours and hours on end, which of course makes you argue more. But on the other hand, you end up with something that's totally amazing . . . you work your ass off, fight, and in the end you're so much the better for it."

Although Anna describes arguments leading to positive results, the recording process also harbors divisive possibilities. In May 2001, I and the other leaders of Counterparts were concerned that the group had insufficient time to satisfactorily record all the songs for our upcoming album, *Ten*. We had limited funds for recording and limited time before the group's seniors graduated and left, so we announced that the studio's control room would be open to only the group's officers. We hoped that this policy would minimize the potential for time-consuming deliberations among group members who were not empowered to make final decisions, but instead it proved destructive. Most members were shunted to the studio's waiting room when they were not actually singing. They felt left out, disconnected from the project, and some grew resentful. The group's leaders soon faced an unhappy ensemble—and I thought they sometimes sounded unhappy when they sang.

Ultimately, the album contained complete recordings of all the songs we planned to include. But even years later it sounds to me uninspired. (RARB reviewer Matt Cohen agreed, calling the album "a letdown.")[20] While a more open and inclusive policy of studio access might not have resulted in a stronger-sounding album, subsequent experiences have suggested that such displays of power, even when conceived with the best intentions, can undermine an ensemble's social fabric. On the other hand, carefully including group members can have positive social effects. Having learned from my experience working on *Ten*, I attempted to involve the members of Amazin' Blue as they recorded tracks, six years later, for our album *Lost in Sound*. We all collaborated in artistically drawing a detailed flowchart of the recording process, to be hung on the studio's wall so all members could understand "where we were" at any time and how their actions fit into the larger project.

Once an album is completed, it serves as a lasting embodiment of a group's efforts. A recording's ability to transcend the passage of time and memory makes it a reminder of the liminal experience of college. "Recording's important; it's a more *permanent* thing, whereas performing is *immediate*," explained Emily, a Treblemaker. Recordings are "literally a record of what you've done the past four years."

A cappella recordings are replete with vivid memories carved from the experience of their creation. Nearly all the a cappella singers and alumni I interviewed smiled, laughed, and enjoyed telling stories of their groups' recording sessions, even in cases when alumni, like Anna, also recalled some of the tensions involved. Whereas in rehearsal and live performance a sense of "fellow feeling" may emerge among singers, Manley links a feeling of connectedness from live performance to recording and, specifically, to memory.

> In that spot, when that happens, you're sharing a moment with someone. And one of the things in my [RARB] reviews that I talk about all the time is *making musical moments*, making *memorable* moments. And that can happen onstage, locking eyes with someone or realizing that you're suddenly synced up with somebody. Or it can happen on a recording, too, when you hear everything just completely coalesce perfectly and crystallize beautifully for a moment. And then you keep hitting rewind to hear it over and over again, to hear that build, that hit, back at that one spot.

Manley's idea of "memorable moments" has a double meaning. In one sense, it refers to moments any listener might find memorable—a particularly good vocal percussion fill or solo take, for example. In another, it indicates memories made in the studio during the recording process, memories of the recording process and its social effects. For the singers, these are triggered, remembered, and reexperienced while listening. Engineer and producer Bill Hare touched on this same point in a RARB discussion about listening to one's own group's recordings.

> Having been there for the recording [session], you have the other 95% of the experience in your head to play back as you hear the track. The impossible-to-reproduce nervous/electric energy in the room, the smells, the fun things that were said or happened—the event in general outside the 3 minute snapshot that was taken. Because of that, the few lucky listeners who were in the room for any of these recordings hear (see) the final track differently.[21]

This kind of memorable moment hinges on the prior lived experience of that music's and that recording's creation. Thus, the singers I observed and spoke with showed considerably weaker emotional ties to albums their groups recorded before they joined.[22] During a recording session, one member of the University of Michigan Harmonettes said, "I want to be able to listen to our own recordings and enjoy them. So if nothing else, we're doing it for ourselves."[23] Christina, another Harmonette, remarked, "In a cappella, the people who prize the recording the most are the people who made the recording."

When years pass between a recording's completion and the release of the album, the issue of memorable moments becomes even more acute. The Treblemakers, for example, had started recording new tracks shortly after the release of its second album, . . . And We're Back, in 2002. At that time, the group committed to making a new album of the highest musical quality, so much so that Dave described the 2003–4 academic year as one in which they made it their top priority. But by the end of 2006, the new album still had not been released, and most of the members whose voices were featured on it had graduated. They were replaced by new singers who, though committed to the group, did not share the same enthusiasm for recording or desire to promote the album or raise the funds to complete it, largely because they were not on it. They had little stake in the project. (The album, titled Not Gonna Lie . . . , was finally released in 2007.)

Choosing and Cutting Tracks: Power, Economics, and Aesthetics

Most collegiate a cappella groups schedule their recording sessions in professional studios at the end of the fall or spring semesters, with more time typically spent in the studio during the spring sessions. Financially, by the end of a semester, groups have usually raised enough money to pay for studio time. Academically, if scheduled during or after an exam period, recording sessions will not conflict with classes and members are better able to attend. And musically, by the end of a semester, group members have been singing together long enough for music to be learned, an ideology of blend and group habitus to be shared and practiced, and other aspects of the group's musical identity to be internalized.

Some groups simply record their entire repertory from a given academic year. The main drawback of this inclusive approach is that each song receives limited studio time and attention, which may lessen the overall musical quality of the recordings. However, for many groups, musical excellence is not the only goal of recording. Documentation is also important; the more songs are included on the album, the more opportunities exist for memorable moments and maximizing their nostalgic potential. Reviewers for the RARB call an album recorded this way a "yearbook album," since it is a sounding document of a particular configuration of voices over a specific period of time, much like a visual yearbook of photos.[24]

Alternatively, the contents of an album may be chosen from a group's larger repertory by vote. The group determines the number of songs that can be recorded based on its budget; those songs earning the most votes are selected. A third approach is for songs to be selected by the group's leaders. This method concentrates the decision-making power in a few individuals, thus carrying the highest potential to sow discontent among the rest of the members. With these two approaches, only certain songs are selected from a group's repertory. The documentary aspect of recording is less pronounced, and the resulting tracks can no longer be taken as a representation of all the group's musical efforts for the year but rather privilege certain sounds or voices over others—a social distinction.

Once selected, groups must choose precisely how their songs will be recorded. A cappella arrangements are typically organized into *voice parts*, which are usually represented on separate staves on the musical score. For example, Christine, who sings alto with the Treblemakers, knows to follow the second staff in each system (or group of staves) as her ensemble moves through each page of its arrangements. In the recording studio, however, individual audio components are organized into *tracks,* which contain the sound of a voice. The term originally indicated specific parallel spaces on a reel of magnetic tape, but with the advent of digital recording those spaces are now virtual rather than physical. When the recording is played back, all the tracks can be heard at the same time. (Here *track* differs from the usage when the word refers to a discrete song on an album.)

The choices begin with how to organize the basic tracking of background voice parts. Just because arrangements are organized in parts does not mean that each part must correspond to a specific track. An individual singer might record his or her part two or three times ("doubling," "tripling," or "layering" them in studiospeak) onto separate tracks, a technique that can help the overall recording sound thicker, as if there are more voices singing than there are actual singers. An individual singer might also record separate tracks, each containing a different voice part, to fill in for absent singers or to bolster specific parts. Finally, different sections of a voice part may be recorded onto separate tracks in order to optimize the different functions each has in the arrangement. For example, the same part may "be" a rhythm guitar during one section of a song (e.g., the verses) but a background vocalist in another section (e.g., the choruses). By separating a part onto different tracks according to its function, the sounds on each can be treated and digitally enhanced separately to guide listeners toward an interpretation of the sounds that aligns with the intended function. The sections of the song where a singer's part imitates a guitar can be treated with a guitar distortion effect, for example, but the sections where his or her part is intended to sound like a vocalist will not. In the end, the resulting recording is a creation, an illusion of simultaneity or sound quality that never actually existed in reality.

A common method of tracking a song's background parts is to have all the singers record their voice parts concurrently onto separate individual tracks (multitracking), singing in the studio in a manner similar to a live concert or gig. Gimble, a mixed group at the University of Michigan, uses this technique to maximize the number of songs it can record on a limited budget. When I attended one of its sessions in December 2005, the group's leaders explained their procedure. First, they import a MIDI version of the song's arrangement from the computer notation program into the digital audio-recording software at the studio (in this case, ProTools) to serve as a "guide track," providing a simple click to keep the singers and vocal percussionists in time and some chordal harmony (or in this case, the exact parts from the arrangement) to keep the singers in tune. Second, the vocal percussionist records the percussion part according to the guide track. Next, all the background singers record their parts simultaneously onto individual tracks. Finally, the soloist and any featured harmonies are overdubbed, recorded while the previously recorded tracks are playing.

The main drawback to Gimble's approach is that mistakes may be left uncorrected due to lack of time. As Gimble's singers tracked the background parts to the Kelly Clarkson song "Addicted," I asked the music director what he was listening for. His goal, he replied, was for the background tracks to sound like the group's memory of its best concert performance. He did not focus on attaining musical perfection because small errors can sometimes be mitigated later by decreasing the offending individual's track's volume during a problematic passage. Moreover, there simply was not enough time to sing the song repeatedly in the hope that all sixteen singers would perform it perfectly on the same attempt. He allowed the group two attempts before moving on to the solo.

One advantage of Gimble's approach is its efficiency. In a setting where time is money, it maximizes the number of people whose voices can be recorded in a short period. Another advantage is social. Although much about the studio environment is unfamiliar and different from a live performance, when Gimble records its songs, most singers get to make their music in ways with which they are already comfortable. They stand near their fellow group members, sometimes even next to the other singers on their part. They watch their music director for important cues. And, because everybody is basically doing the same thing at the same time, they share in the fellow feeling of their music making.

Although Gimble's approach results partly from economic considerations, the same cannot said for the Yale University Whiffenpoofs, which I observed in a recording studio in New Haven in January 2005. The two groups' recording methods differed slightly: the Whiffenpoofs did not use guide tracks, it used fewer microphones to record the group, and its arrangements did not always include solo parts. But in other ways they were quite similar. The Whiffenpoofs singers sang each song only two or three times in a manner much like their live performances, and they largely avoided digital editing and effects. Unlike Gimble, however, the Whiffenpoofs did not face the same budgetary constraints—the regularity of the group's recording projects suggests a broad and dependable financial base.[25] Therefore, aesthetic choices, rather than financial necessity, motivated the choice of recording method.

In groups that adopt a recording aesthetic similar to that of Gimble and the Whiffenpoofs, a sense of authenticity often underscores beliefs regarding the recording process and its products. To these musicians and, presumably, their audience, there is value in recordings that sound like the group's concert performances. The creation of recordings that sound markedly different from live performance is, in this view, problematic because it challenges beliefs about authorship and the authentic sound of the human voice (see chapter 9).

This aesthetic stance is not universal among or even within a cappella groups, however. The recording process Amazin' Blue uses eschews group tracking in favor of isolating individual parts and singers through more liberal overdubbing. Singers enter the studio alone or in small groups (usually up to four), depending on how many people sing any particular part, and sing along with the guide track and the parts that have already been recorded. They are often separated within the studio space, sometimes even with movable sections of wall, in order to ensure that each person's voice is only picked up by his or her microphone (see fig. 8.1).

Unlike Gimble's approach, the singers in Amazin' Blue are typically allowed to correct mistakes by "punching in" and rerecording specific passages. Songs are recorded piecemeal: each four- or eight-measure phrase is attempted several times until an adequate "take" is recorded before moving on to the next phrase. The solo is usually tracked after the background parts, followed by any featured harmonies or additional overdubs, and then the vocal percussion is supplemented with additional rhythmic and sonic layers. The process takes much longer than recording singers simultaneously and is therefore more costly.

Amazin' Blue's method reveals an aesthetic shift: recordings are no longer taken to be idealized representations of live performance but artistic works in and of themselves whose components and overall sound are slowly and carefully crafted using all the technologies at the group's disposal. These recordings are less documentary, realistic, or "authentic" vis-à-vis live performance but instead exist outside the live performance context. They may still fulfill a nostalgic function but do so through an arrangement of sounds conceptually different from yearbook albums.

The approach to tracking that Amazin' Blue uses also highlights how the experience of recording music in a studio can differ greatly from live performance. The differences can seem especially striking to college-age amateur singers whose musical experience is limited to rehearsal and performance spaces. In the studio, the co-temporality (the sense of being in the same place as others at the same time) of performance is removed and singers can only respond to the sounds that were recorded before them. "Instead of *interacting* in

Fig. 8.1. Jessica, from Amazin' Blue, recording her tracks in a Michigan recording studio. (Photo by the author.)

the process of ensemble performance," Porcello writes, "all performers . . . are *reacting* to those tracks recorded before them."[26]

Musically, Amazin' Blue's approach improves the accuracy of each part through the isolation of singers and the encouragement of repeated takes, thereby producing what group members believe is a better final product. Socially, it alters the nature of the recording project as a collective or collaborative effort. "When music is recorded in this fashion," Porcello writes, "performance itself is no longer collaborative in the traditional sense of the word. Even though it is undeniably collective activity, it is no longer defined as such based on temporal simultaneity of performance."[27] That "temporal simultaneity" makes the experience of a Gimble or Whiffenpoofs recording session seem more like a live performance—an activity that all (or at least most) of the singers engage in *together*—than an Amazin' Blue session. Gimble or Whiffenpoofs sessions can serve a community-building purpose for the singers because of the temporal simultaneity of their efforts, but for an Amazin' Blue–style session to serve the same purpose requires that the singers understand and accept that their individual musical contributions will be combined at a later time. Indeed, when I sat in on recording sessions with Gimble and the Harmonettes (which generally adhered to a Gimble-like approach), most of the singers remained near the control room, listening to their takes and the soloist's attempts. When I recorded with Amazin' Blue, fewer group members usually remained in the control room; the rest tended to hang out in the waiting room, studying or socializing.

Temporal simultaneity is one of the features of a live performance that may be "lost"—for better or worse—in the recording process, particularly when groups isolate and overdub their singers during tracking. I occasionally heard a cappella singers criticize heavily overdubbed a cappella recordings for what they described as a lack of "energy" or "cohesiveness." While such criticism implies that they were judging recordings by criteria drawn from the experience of live performance, perhaps they could sense when this interaction was missing.

Paul Théberge suggests that overdubbing also creates social and musical hierarchies within ensembles. "Within that hierarchy," he writes, "those who are recorded last (usually the vocalist or featured soloist) have the greatest degree of expressive and improvisational freedom; those who are recorded first are generally the most constrained."[28] This temporal fragmentation creates what Porcello calls an "antidemocratic force," which, in Théberge's words, emphasizes "the individual contribution over that of the collective. It creates a 'simulation' of collective activity."[29] Such an "antidemocratic force" counters the great efforts many a cappella groups make to value the contributions of each of their members. Yet overdubbing is an effective and efficient way to increase musical accuracy and, for some, improve the quality of recordings. The tension between these two impulses, the democratic valuation of each member's voice and the unequal emphasis on certain voices vis-à-vis overdubbing, reveals one way technology and a cappella can stand at cross purposes.

Constructing and Correcting Parts

Studio technology offers tremendous abilities to digitally manipulate recorded sound. Of course, recorded sounds have been manipulated since the days of cutting and splicing magnetic tape, each containing a different take, to create the illusion of a seamless performance. Digital recording technology can take cutting and splicing to a new level, however, and can fashion combinations of sounds that never existed in reality. Sometimes collegiate a cappella groups (and their engineers and producers) may choose to do this in order to achieve certain artistic goals—combining the emulative qualities of certain syllables with particular studio technologies used on the actual instruments being emulated to create a more mimetically realistic sound, for example. At other times, digital manipulation may be employed to compensate for a lack of musicianship. Such sound construction is merely the means, then, where the end is a better final product.

Take the case of "Alex," a struggling vocal percussionist. He has had limited time to learn how to create the individual sounds of vocal percussion, how to combine them in realistic-sounding patterns, and how to keep from running out of breath while doing so. In fact, after eight or ten months of practicing he has become proficient at the sounds and patterns, but breathing is still a challenge. In live performance he is barely able to maintain a steady beat all the way through a four-minute song, and he often has to simplify the patterns to conserve energy. In the recording studio, Alex must fit his percussion into a song's musical texture established by the parts already recorded. He starts off well, mostly sticking to the beat and only flubbing a handful of snare drum sounds. But as the song enters its final chorus, just when the excitement should peak, he runs out of steam. He stops and places his hands on his knees, panting and trying to catch his breath.

In the control room, the group's music director reports that Alex had a few convincing kick, snare, hi-hat, and crash cymbal sounds but that most of the others were not good enough. In consultation with Alex and the engineer, she decides it will be easier to spend half an hour building a drum track by digitally copying and pasting particular, discrete sounds into the right pattern—a process known as "sampling" or "sequencing"—than to have Alex finish the song and then go back and punch in, attempting to replace each and every mediocre sound with a better one. They listen to what Alex recorded and select one good example of kick and snare drums and hi-hat and crash cymbals. After putting the selected sounds into the right sequence, they select a two-measure sample of the pattern and duplicate it throughout the rest of the song. The resulting track does not have the subtle variety of a live performance (or Alex's first attempt at tracking), since all the snare sounds are exactly identical. But the pattern is sonically and rhythmically perfect. The sounds are all Alex's, and the pattern was even his suggestion. But the specific sequence of sounds only exists because it has been digitally constructed.

A cappella groups may go through a similar process with background parts. If all of a song's four choruses are arranged identically (probably a result of copying and pasting in the arranger's music notation software), then some groups see little need to track them all. Why not improve efficiency by concentrating each singer on getting one or two choruses perfect and then copying those choruses to the right places later in the song? And if a group is willing to digitally copy musical phrases from one section of a song to another, why not also use digital tools to improve the quality of those phrases? Digital recording enables engineers to nudge individual words forward or backward in time to correct rhythmic mistakes, and software like Antares's AutoTune and Celemony's Melodyne can shift a voice's pitch up or down until it sounds perfectly in tune.

To make these digital alterations convincing, singers need to be physically and acoustically isolated during tracking. When they are too close together, a microphone may pick up multiple voices and record them on a single track. When those voices are not completely in sync, melodically or rhythmically, the differences are easy to hear but difficult to correct. Pitch correction software may raise the pitch of the louder voice if it was originally a little flat, but in the process it will also raise the pitch of the other, quieter voice. If that one was originally correct, it will become sharp. Solving one problem can thus create another. The same goes for rhythm, since shifting one singer's erroneous note earlier or later may inadvertently move another singer's correct one out of time.

Many of the a cappella singers I spoke with objected to digital rhythmic and melodic manipulation on the premise that what results is inauthentic ("that's not what was sung") or artificial. "Remember, perfect does not equal beautiful," writes Dylan Bell in a column on the CASA website. Instead, he recommends a more moderate approach in which groups aim for "plausible perfection."[30] But many singers might be equally appalled to hear a recording without any correction, since it probably would not match their idealized memory of a live performance. One contributor to the RARB forum hoped to resolve this paradox while avoiding recording vocal percussion that sounded "like a guy sittin['] around with a Casio keyboard." He asked for advice on the question "How do you get it to sound 'perfect' but still human?"[31] The query inspired numerous answers. One was to avoid cutting out the sounds of the vocal percussionist's breaths, which may communicate to listeners that the sounds were actually supplied by a human being.[32] Another answer was to alternate between two or three samples of each sound when building the sequenced percussion track. This alternation creates a sense of sonic variety similar to a live performance but maintains a more consistent rhythm.[33] Hare suggested combining a sequenced percussion track with another full "live" take, which would suggest a more "live" feel to listeners.[34] These suggestions restore or preserve the slight imperfections Charles Keil calls "participatory discrepancies," the small, mostly unnoticed differences between the ways ensemble musicians make music that create the "groove," invite participation, and ultimately constitute music as "personally involving and socially valuable." Rhythmic or temporal discrepancies are called "processural," while those concerning " 'timbre,' 'sound,' [and] 'tone qualities' " are considered "textural."[35]

Much follow-up research using Keil's theory focuses on rhythmic issues, which supports the term's application to vocal percussion.[36] But it can also be applied to tuning. When voices are transposed to precisely matching frequencies in order to correct for pitch, textural participatory discrepancies may be lost. A cappella musicians may interpret such a loss as either detrimental to blend or downright inhuman. One engineer described how, when using pitch correction software, he is careful to transpose pitches closer to the desired pitch but rarely precisely to it. Moreover, when transposing multiple singers' voices, he purposefully places them at miniscule but varying distances from the "correct" frequency in order to maintain a variety of pitch discrepancies. To alter timbre by correcting the pitches too perfectly, then, one may alienate the singers from their own recording and disappoint other listeners whose sense of well-blended a cappella depends on some pitch discrepancies.

The process of recording is filled with artificiality. From the physical attributes of the space to the digital options for musical correction and sonic enhancement, the studio is an environment worlds away from the everyday. Amazin' Blue's approach to recording enables the creation of musically "better" recordings at the cost of the simultaneity, the togetherness or fellow feeling, that makes a live performance seem real. The approach that Gimble and the Whiffenpoofs use limits the kinds of choices they can make during the recording process and may constrain how close their final recordings come to their idealized memory of live performance, but at the same time it may retain the temporal simultaneity of live performance and therefore seem to listeners (group members and non–group members alike) more like an accurate representation or documentation of the way the groups "actually" sing.

The idea that the recording process is inherently artificial is not a novel claim, yet that artificiality challenges musicians and listeners. A dilemma emerges wherein "better" recordings are created using tools and techniques that maximize artificiality, aesthetically and socially. The choices that a cappella groups make help to determine the products of the recording process, from the sound of an album to the memories of social relationships it encodes and triggers. The next chapter looks more closely at how those choices and products are received by listeners within the a cappella community.

CHAPTER 9

Listening to Recordings: *BOCA* and Discourse

Recordings are sounding records of musical events around which swirls a maelstrom of ideas, opinions, practices, and discourse. In collegiate a cappella, they can be vehicles for a group's wider recognition in local, regional, and (inter)national scenes, especially when they are included in compilation albums, such as the annual *Best of College A Cappella.* The competitive nature of *BOCA,* as well as the live competition, the International Championship of Collegiate A Cappella (ICCA), align a cappella with a history (sketched earlier in this book) of competitive choral music in the United States. Despite this historical connection, however, some of the issues surrounding *BOCA* could not have been raised in earlier musical competitions because they involve technologies that were unavailable or largely inaccessible throughout most of the twentieth century. Examining the ways people listen to a cappella recordings, especially the highly valued *BOCA,* can reveal the way (inter)national circles of prestige are interpreted and affect musical practice on a local level. Moreover, the stylistic changes evident in fifteen years of *BOCA* albums demonstrate the increasing importance of technology in the production of recorded a cappella music, an issue hotly debated on the RARB discussion forum. Ultimately, *BOCA* and other a cappella prizes (such as the Contemporary A Cappella Recording Awards, or CARAs) can be considered vehicles for the accumulation of cultural or social capital, whose effects include the perceived homogenization of the music and the maintenance of a network of informed musicians who perpetuate certain stylistic ideals.

This argument builds on that of the previous chapter: despite claims to a cappella's "natural" or "pure" qualities, in this practice people, their voices, and technology become closely entwined in the act of making music. Whereas the earlier discussion focused on the experience of the recording process, this one turns to the products of that process. Although artificiality is a central concern in the RARB discourse, it is more often attributed to recording technology, such as digital editing and effects, than to the experiential qualities of the recording process. These effects are usually applied during the editing and mixing stages, when recorded tracks are modified and manipulated to compose the overall sound of the song.[1] The amount of time and money spent on these tasks varies, depending both on the availability of resources and the group's goals. Some of the common studio tools include pitch correction, pitch shifting (dropping bass parts an octave or two, even for women's groups), compression, delay and reverb, distortion, sampling and sequencing, and copying and pasting of audio within or between songs. These can help to make an amateur recording sound better (or more professional) to some ears, but for many they raise troubling issues.

Listening to BOCA

One of *BOCA*'s purposes, claim Deke Sharon and Don Gooding, is to introduce the genre to audiences outside the a cappella community. (About 13 percent of album sales but 60 percent of legal downloads, they estimate, actually go to "outsiders.") Other purposes include exposing collegiate a cappella to noncollegiate vocal groups, encouraging excellence within collegiate a cappella, and serving as an "economical way for the collegiate a cappella community to learn about the 'state of the art' in arranging and production."[2] The albums' reception by and impact on the a cappella community suggest that it is a particularly powerful force for three reasons: many people within the community pay close attention to it, for many it serves as a model for or evidence of success, and it inspires much discourse about a cappella and recording practice.

The annual announcement of each new edition's track list is eagerly anticipated. The RARB forum is set aflutter with predictions regarding which new recordings will be selected.[3] Sometimes the predictions themselves turn into friendly competitions, complete with their own scoring systems.[4] (Other discussions have called for similar predictions and tournaments for the CARAs and the ICCA.)[5] Once announced, the *BOCA* selections are scrutinized in discussions that fill several web pages each.[6] This discourse continues in countless other discussions, which, while not explicitly about *BOCA*, nonetheless include commentary on the compilation's tracks. Why? Because their inclusion on

BOCA means they will be widely circulated and therefore convenient reference points. All this suggests that, on one hand, many people pay close attention to *BOCA* and are invested in its process and products (fulfilling one of its stated purposes) and, on the other, that—despite Sharon's assertions to the contrary—*BOCA* is perceived as a cappella's top prize.[7]

If a *BOCA* selection is a prize, then recordings featured on the album have some value. Thus, some a cappella singers see *BOCA* as evidence of excellence in musical innovation or execution (again, fulfilling one of its purposes). Sharon calls it a "primer," and Gooding calls some of its arrangements "base recipes" for arrangements that are then adopted and adapted by groups far and wide.[8] Christina, from the University of Michigan Harmonettes, described it as "a communication tool" groups can use to share their musical ideas with "the rest of the national groups [and demonstrate] what new things are happening in a cappella, what new things can be achieved using human voices." When I asked Andrea, a singer with Michigan State University Capital Green, about influences on her arranging technique, she specifically mentioned how *BOCA* guided her syllable choices. Debra, from the Harvard University Fallen Angels, remarked similarly, "I'll listen to *BOCA* and try to take the syllables they use, the sounds that they use for guitar or the sounds that they use for an organ or a piano, and try to imitate that whenever I hear the same instrument in the song that I'm trying to arrange." And Sharon writes, "Who knew 'Insomniac' [featured on *BOCA II* (1996) and discussed in the previous chapter] would become such a standard? That's due to *BOCA*." Tracks and albums that have been selected for *BOCA* or won other awards thus become models for myriad aspects of musical practice, from song choice (does this year's compilation feature more classic rock? hip-hop? original songs?) to arranging technique (e.g., syllable choice) to approaches to recording (e.g., multitracking or pitch shifting).

Having a track selected for *BOCA* is important to many a cappella singers, their groups, and even some recording studios. James Harrington, an ICCA judge and a cappella producer, described the aspirations of the members of Ursus Verses, a mixed group at Bowdoin College, whose album he was working on at the time of our interview: "We're really hoping to get a *BOCA* track. We're really hoping that that will propel their sales and get their group more popular and get them better gigs." Some groups, according to recording engineer and producer Bill Hare, even conceive their recording projects with the explicit aim of earning a spot on *BOCA*. Mickey Rapkin calls the competition for *BOCA* selections "fierce" and describes a "cottage industry of recording studios," extending as far as Singapore, devoted to its pursuit.[9] In their publicity materials, recording studios and engineers have been known to list the number of tracks they have worked on that were selected, assuming that such information will speak to the quality of their work and attract new clients. As of this writing, Hare's studio's website, for example, lists its forty *BOCA* selections, over one hundred CARA nominations and wins, eighteen albums that were RARB "picks of the year," and the collegiate album that received the highest score ever from the RARB (Stanford University Talisman's *Passage*, 2004).[10] A representative for VocalSource, a network of a cappella recording engineers, posted a public congratulatory note for the thirteen of its clients whose tracks were selected for *BOCA 2010*.[11] The *BOCA* series is also unique because of its prestige within the community. It is older and generates more discourse, laudatory and critical, than the other extant compilations: *Sing* (which began in 2003), *Top Shelf A Cappella* (three editions between 2004 and 2007), and *Voices Only* (begun in 2004).[12]

Yet some in the a cappella community have expressed concern over the trends they hear in the *BOCA* selections. "*BOCA* is too perfect," wrote an alumnus of the University of Illinois No Strings Attached on the RARB forum.

> There are not enough imperfections. There is less and less character in these compilations and more product . . . Yes, it's nice to have very well-executed songs—songs sometimes that are near-perfect technically—but when every single song gets to be this way, I find it enormously boring and homogenous.[13]

Another contributor pointed to the "production values" of the recordings as a homogenizing factor.

> I think the only thing getting better on each *BOCA* is the production values. The groups themselves aren't much different than they were in the '90s, but if all the tracks on *BOCA I* [1995] were produced for what they are today and if all the effects and auto-tuners were added, there wouldn't be much difference [between them].[14]

Some groups feel pressure to adopt recording strategies that include heavy doses of multitrack recording techniques, pitch correction, and other digital editing tools and effects in order to remain competitive with other a cappella groups (a point explored more deeply later), which has a homogenizing effect.

One widely held view is that such technologies are more frequently employed because they are becoming easier to access. Harrington explained:

> Until the next unbelievable cutting edge comes, I mean the next wave of "holy crap I had no idea that was possible," I fear that we're just going to keep hearing the same "alright, everyone got a ProTools rig, and everyone figured out Auto-Tune, and everyone figured out flange effects." And now who cares who's doing what? You can barely hear the difference between the recordings.

Although there may be a connection between increased access to technology (e.g., ProTools digital recording hardware and software) and the perception of a gradual homogenization of a cappella recordings, increased access to technology is just part of the story. Other factors include the way that technology is used (which may or may not be becoming standardized) and how that use is perceived. In particular, which uses are valued? Given the currency *BOCA* is afforded, as well as its relatively wide distribution, it seems the likely force—perhaps culprit?—in the dissemination of the practices that have become "standardized." Critics have thus charged the *BOCA* enterprise: its selections are "overproduced" and all sound the same. Yet the fact that the *BOCA* series is the target of such criticism indicates its importance and wide impact. Moreover, it suggests that any examination of these charges (or the impact of *BOCA* on a cappella practice more generally) should start by considering the music itself.

Fifteen Years of BOCA

The first sixteen editions of the *BOCA* series spanned 1995–2009, including fifteen annual "best of" compilations and one special edition devoted to humorous songs and parodies. The tracks were selected by a committee of two people with connections (personal and/or financial) to a cappella's other institutions, at various times including Deke Sharon and Adam Farb (who started the series together), Jessika Diamond, and Don Gooding. Amanda Newman, executive director of the ICCA, joined Sharon starting with *BOCA 2009*. The 301 total tracks include 123 by men's groups (41 percent), 120 by co-ed groups (40 percent), and 58 by women's groups (19 percent). Most selections come from groups at private institutions (207 or 69 percent), and while the greatest percentage of tracks comes from groups in the northeastern United States, several other American geographic areas are also represented (fig. 9.1). Musically,

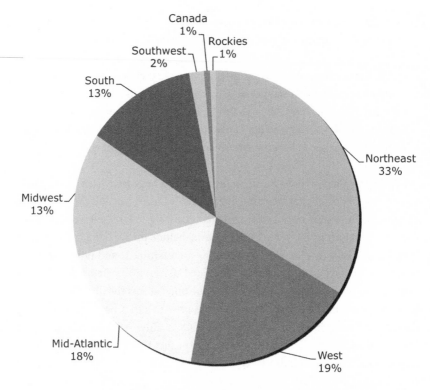

Fig. 9.1. Geographic origins of tracks selected for *BOCA*, 1995–2009.

these albums reveal several general trends in collegiate a cappella arranging and recording practices.

First, it is true that, as RARB forum contributors have alleged, "production" has increased when it comes to pitch correction and rhythmic precision. As Sharon has pointed out, amateur, college singers have not necessarily improved over the years, but the technology to make them sound better has improved.[15] Tuning issues, ragged entrances and cutoffs, and other imperfections on early *BOCA* tracks have been largely eradicated from most of the later selections thanks to careful digital editing.

For example, on the University of Michigan Amazin' Blue's 1992 recording of Sting's "An Englishman in New York," which appears on *BOCA I* (1995), most of the background parts during the verses consist of a brief "wop" syllable in three- or four-part harmony, occurring between each of the four beats in every measure. Such offbeat figures are difficult to coordinate precisely, and in several instances voices can be heard entering a split second early or holding their pitches just a bit too long. (When listeners concentrate on the melody line, such imprecision is hardly noticeable.) As the Ampex 499 analog tape masters in the group's archive indicate, this recording was not made digitally. A digital version would have enabled the audio engineer to easily edit each voice (assuming they were tracked individually) so that the group would begin and end each note at exactly the same time.

Second, syllabic variety increases as one advances chronologically. On *BOCA I* the syllables are mostly conventional: open vowels, "doo," "ba," etc. For example, the background parts of the University of Pennsylvania Counterparts' "I've Got Right" consist almost entirely of "doo," in both loud and quiet passages. A later arrangement of the same song might change from "ooo" to "ah" for louder portions. The Tufts University Beelzebubs' recording of "Hey You" is an exception, with unusually nasal and pinched "wow" and "now" syllables during the song's bridge.

The University of Virginia Gentlemen's rendition of "Insomniac," with its "jim-ba-dim, jim-ba-dim, jigga-jigga" introduction, marked a notable change on *BOCA II* (1996). It was the sole and standout syllabic innovation on that year's compilation, introducing a *j* sound to directly emulate a guitar strum. Within a few years, syllables with a *j* sound became standard fare. Just under half the tracks on *BOCA 2006*—a decade later—depend on *j* syllables. For example, in the cover of Michelle Branch's pop song, "Are You Happy Now?," recorded by Elon University Twisted Measure, *j* syllables permeate the texture, providing harmonic support behind the lead melody. Yet many are not happy with this development. Reviews by RARB bemoan recordings that rely too heavily on these now staid syllable choices.[16]

Third, as groups embraced multitracking and overdubbing, the number of voices that seem to be singing simultaneously has increased. While those tools were available when tracks appearing on the first few *BOCA*s were recorded in the early 1990s, the total number of voices seems rather low compared to those on later recordings. It is difficult to determine aurally the number of voices present in a recording since blend, equalization, stereo imaging, and other techniques can suggest more or fewer voices than were actually recorded. Perhaps the only way to know for sure is to look at the actual computer files pertaining to the recording sessions (if they were done digitally), an impractical task given the number of recordings under consideration. However, ethnographic evidence suggests ways to make such determinations. Amazin' Blue alumna Jennifer described the limited number of tracks available to her group during its recording sessions in 1991–92.[17] Based on the tapes in the group's archives, it is likely it used an analog twenty-four-track machine. Yet some of Hare's comments in the RARB forum show that digital recordings made in the mid-2000s consist of close to one hundred tracks after individual voices are doubled or tripled, percussion is layered in multiple tracks, and extra harmonies are added.

> I don't consider a "member" of the group as equal to a "part." For example, if for just the verse section, 8 people . . . are singing a "ja-na" sort of syllable, emulating a guitar, then in the chorus those same 8 are singing a horn section sort of sound, and in the bridge they are doing words, I consider those to be 3 different "events," each worthy of individual treatment . . . Having the events on their own channels allows the mixer to have much more control in shaping the individual sounds. So now, just single tracked, these 8 people (who are only half the group) have filled 24 channels—double tracked they would be 48, and triple tracked would be 72![18]

By applying the same process to vocal percussion, a simple pattern can fill fifteen to twenty tracks. Thus, the total number of tracks quickly rises, and the resulting recordings sound thicker and more complex. Doubling may not seem a revolutionary technique in some musical circles, but it indicates a shift in a cappella recording practice, as more groups and engineers conceive of recording projects less in terms of voices and more in terms of vocalized instruments and instrumental functions.

Fourth, the prevalence of distorted voices increases as the *BOCA* series continues. Early recordings, such as the Wesleyan University Spirits' version of "Everything She Wants" on *BOCA I*, feature stereo doubling, chorusing, and flanging techniques that were well established in rock recording by the mid–twentieth century (e.g., the music of the Beatles). Later *BOCAs* include recordings that apply guitar-based overdrive and distortion to voices, including the accompanying parts and the lead melody. Such distortion can become an important element in the recording's composition. For example, in "Beautiful," recorded by the University of Southern California Sirens and selected for *BOCA 2002*, the lead is distorted strategically at the climax of the song's refrain, suggesting that even an ugly (sounding) person can be beautiful: "But I'm not beautiful like you. *I'm beautiful like me!*" Although Joydrop uses this same technique in its original recording, it seems more pronounced in the a cappella version because there are no instruments, just voices.

If these increasingly technologized sounds are taken as the "best" of collegiate a cappella, we might ask how they are received, understood, and made meaningful in this musical community. The discourse on the RARB forum and publications on the CASA website indicate that issues such as the use of digital sampling, sequencing, and other effects are the focus of much debate. Often simplified as "purism versus production," they entail three major arguments: first, that these tools disrupt the clear and direct authorship of a cappella recordings; second, that they obscure the natural human quality of the voice; and, third, that they are necessary in order to keep up with the advancing field of a cappella recordings. As these discussions unfold, in person and on the Internet, they frequently expand in scope to question "good a cappella," a cappella's status as "art," and the definition of *a cappella* itself. And although the discourse on the RARB forum or the CASA website is that of a relatively small pool of a cappella's most enthusiastic practitioners, their views were echoed in countless conversations I had with singers throughout my fieldwork.

Editing, Mixing, Effects, and the Question of Authorship

"A cappella is a performance art," proposes one regular contributor to the RARB forum, writing under the alias "hyperdel": "Production work sounds great to me . . . but it loses the specialty and magic when overproduced like what we have as commonplace today." By "production work," hyperdel means the sampling and sequencing of vocal percussion sounds, the application of guitar distortion to vocal lines after they have initially been tracked, and the use of automated fades (in or out) and dynamic (volume) levels. Hyperdel's argument questions the authorship of "overproduced" recordings, suggesting that collegiate a cappella singers abnegate this highly valued quality through the application of production techniques: "Using sampled VP [vocal percussion], automated fades, automated dynamic anything, copy/paste splicing anything like that and etc. . . . None of those to me are the work of a skillful, supremely talented vocal group or band. It's the genius and skill of a great sound engineer/producer."[19]

In scholarship on popular music, authorship is often defined by the relationships among songwriter, song, and performer. Especially in cases in which preexisting material is used, however, it can become difficult to assign creative credit. Will Straw draws the distinction, tenuous though it may sometimes be, between songwriter and song.[20] Yet a cappella demonstrates one community's sensitivity to the distinction between performer and engineer/producer. This shift in terms, from songwriter/performer to performer/producer, may result partly from the fact that few collegiate a cappella groups perform original music, removing the songwriter from the equation. Hyperdel's comments also highlight the tensions arising from the electronic and human mediation of non–group members whose participation is vital to the recording process.

In response to positions like hyperdel's, others argue the ontological differences between live performance and studio recordings.

> Studio craft and live performance craft are not the same thing. This is a reality that in my experience is not widely accepted by the a cappella community . . . Most of us see the recording studio as an opportunity to create something larger, fuller, and more complex than what a live performance allows us. In some ways, complaining about multi-tracking, autotune, and other studio techniques is like complaining that a film director used any special effects that [he or she] couldn't have made work live on a theater stage.[21]

This position resonates with those of many scholars of popular music, although it is universally accepted in neither the a cappella world (as hyperdel's position demonstrates) nor in academic circles.[22] Importantly, it recognizes an a cappella aesthetic rooted in "an aesthetics of rock" wherein recordings have "ontological priority." As Theodore Gracyk writes, "[I]n rock the musical work is less typically a song than an arrangement of recorded sounds."[23]

The issue, then, is the extent to which a cappella singers are responsible or can take credit for the "arrangement of recorded sounds" that ultimately appears on their albums. During my fieldwork, singers often preferred recordings that approximated live concert performances over those that sounded more "produced," although those preferring more produced recordings were sizable minority.[24] But such a "purist" position may give too much agency to the singers. Even in live performance the singers do not have complete control over their sound; they are not the only authors of the musical experience. Venue acoustics, audio equipment, the skill of the live sound engineer, and the composition and behavior of the audience can profoundly affect a group's presentation and are never entirely under the group's control as they might be in a recording studio. The recording engineer is thus positioned as an aesthetically engaged moderator whose involvement raises concerns and prompts debate.

Authenticity and the (Lost?) Human "Spirit of A Cappella"

Another theme emerging from the RARB discourse is the complaint that production techniques yield recordings that no longer sound like natural human voices. This issue is somewhat ironic considering collegiate a cappella's stylistic goal of emulating popular recordings, nearly all of which involve nonvocal or instrumental sounds.[25] But the recording process enables groups to alter their vocal timbre in much more pronounced ways than in live performance, which raises the issue of authenticity: does the audio on the recording still sound like real people?

In March 2005, the music director of the Amalgamates, a mixed group at Tufts University, offered the following polemic on the subject.

> This seems to be an issue that arises so often in the a cappella community nowadays. With top-notch studio effects becoming more and more attainable through digital music recording and editing, it is becoming easier and easier to create a top[-]notch album, as long as you have top-notch soloists . . . and the time to put into editing and post-production. Backgrounds can be built, note by note if necessary, as opposed to sung.
>
> One could even argue that the studio has become an instrument. What exactly defines an instrument anyway? I listen to many [a cappella] albums and hear notes, not voices . . . whether the sound originated from a voice or not almost becomes irrelevant.
>
> Has the spirit of a cappella been lost?
>
> On a personal level, a cappella to me has always been about the blending of voices, not the tuning of notes. . . Sadly, much of the a cappella community seems to see things quite differently.[26]

The use of production techniques, the Tufts student concludes, detracts from blend, a foundation of a cappella aesthetics, and ultimately siphons the humanity from the music. This complaint echoes what Paul D. Greene calls an "anxiety of engineering fakery," which is founded on the premise—true for a cappella—that "for many listeners an originary presence of actual voices, bodies, instruments, or performances is very important; it functions, in some sense, as an anchor, a guarantor of the recording's meaning and value."[27] This position contrasts with an aesthetics of rock, in which such an "originary presence" is unnecessary to guarantee a recording's value.

The a cappella recording that perhaps best exemplifies this concern is "Mr. Roboto," originally by Styx, the opening track of the Beelzebubs' *Code Red* (2003), an album over which much critical ink has been spilled, including the charge that it singlehandedly "ruined collegiate a cappella."[28] Ironically, its lyrics claim that "the problem's plain to see / too much technology / machines save our lives / machines dehumanize." The Beelzebubs leverages all the technological tools of the studio to create a recording (indeed an album) in which sounds can hardly be identified as voices; they are simply much closer to those of instruments. For example, synthesizers are mimicked by having singers record individual pitches, then digitally removing the beginning and ends of the audio and combining them into chords.[29] The result is a sound that would never—and could never—come from the mouth of a human. Ed, one of the Beelzebubs behind *Code Red,* who has since begun a career in a cappella recording, revealed the album's explicit purpose: to challenge what the group saw as the overly conservative "academic framework" within which collegiate a cappella was viewed by its community. "*Code Red* was intended to challenge that academic framework," he wrote. "We had no interest in doing what was 'correct' or 'right.' We WANTED to cross the line."[30]

In the eyes (and ears) of many listeners, cross the line they did. One forum contributor, from a group at the State University of New York at Buffalo, exclaimed, "I know I'm not the only one who, upon first listen, thought 'What the heck? They're using a synthesizer? Doesn't that count as an instrument?' Distorting the voices to the point that they might as well have been played on a Korg keyboard defeats the purpose of a cappella."[31] Another contributor generalized for the whole genre, in capital letters for emphasis, "FUNDAMENTALLY, A CAPPELLA IS CHEATING," suggesting perhaps that the very definition of *a cappella* had changed.[32] (In response to such criticism, the Beelzebubs sought to craft later albums, such as *Shedding* [2005] and *Pandæmonium* [2007], to the same standard but without the same level of technological mediation.)[33]

The positions in the "purism versus production" debate thus emerge rather clearly where authorship and authenticity are at issue. Those favoring the purist side bristle at the idea of mediation, electronic or human, in the process of making and recording music. The concept of raw voices blending in harmony seems almost sacred. Meanwhile, the amateur nature of the musical practice benefits the arguments for production. Technology intervenes to make inadequate musical performances passable, as Hare explains.

> There are many groups out there that don't have even a passable vocal percussionist. They still try, because they are young and willing to learn, and it's just cool to be the beatboxer . . . If they can't hold a groove, hold the wrong groove, or don't have the stamina, saliva production, or know[-]how to breathe to do more than a couple measures at a time (and uninspiring measures at that), what are our options for the recording? They can get away with this live, even make it a part of their act (the "suffocating VP" schtick) . . . but what are our options in recording? Usually sequencing. Believe me, it's a HUGE lesser of two evils.[34]

This raises a question: what about groups who need technology to compensate for musical shortcomings but adopt a purist view toward that technology's application? Musical practicalities seem to trump ideological positioning.

"Mr. Roboto" demonstrates the digital manipulation not only of voices but also vocal percussion, and listeners reacted to those kinds of technologized sounds too. Reviewer Dave Trendler criticizes the University of Pennsylvania Off the Beat for the precision of its percussion: "Off the Beat has computerized the vocal percussion on many tracks using studio magic like snap-to and sample/sequence. While the drum kit sounds are realistic and clean," meaning that they closely mimic the sound of real (recorded) drums, "some samples are too long and overlap during snare rolls and double kicks. The percussion is too precise, too quick, and comes off sounding a little fake."[35]

In some cases, however, the artistic goal of the recording is specifically *not* to sound human. In "Mr. Roboto," for example, the Beelzebubs takes a cappella's emulative imperative to an extreme, presenting sounds that would be impossible to reproduce live. And the group is not alone in this effort. A professional a cappella group treated emulation with similar severity, recording the entire Pink Floyd album *Dark Side of the Moon* (1973) a cappella.[36] "In the end a human-made kick sound doesn't sound as 'kick'y as one that's been EQ'd and octave-dropped to perfection," a singer from the Northwestern University Purple Haze stated. "Humans can't make a kick noise and cymbal crash simultaneously, etc."[37]

The desire to make a recording that surpasses the human capacity for live musical performance is certainly not unique to a cappella, but it does reflect a cappella's broader historical context. The very possibility of such a recording depends on a postrock perspective and recording technologies such as multi-tracking and overdubbing. Although musical recordings were made as early as the late nineteenth century, only with the advent of rock was the *record* widely conceived as a musical work distinct from a performance or song. Robert B. Ray finds the effect of recording technologies in the removal of the recording from performance, resulting in the situation in which "in semiotic terms, a record, like a movie, has become a sign without a referent," a result of numerous nonsimultaneous musical acts reordered but not representing (or documenting) one act of musicking.[38] A classic example is *Sgt. Pepper's Lonely Hearts Club Band* (1967), in which the Beatles famously created a musical work—a recording—that purposefully eclipsed the possibility of live performance.[39] In rock, Albin Zak writes, "presenting a transparent representation of some natural acoustic reality was never the point. Records were meant to be distinctive worlds of musical sound with the power to make their way into the consciousness of a mass audience, and the record-making process was a matter of building those worlds."[40]

Negotiating the Field of Artistic Production

The third argument in the "purism versus production" debate claims that production techniques are essential for a group's recording to remain competitive with other new recordings. Inherent in this argument is the act of comparison, in which members of one group listen to the recordings of another and evaluate both the other group's music and their own. (The use of technology to compensate for shortcomings in musicality also factors here.) In this process, new recordings respond dialogically to existing ones.

Competitive comparison affects musical practice early. As a member of Amazin' Blue, I was less likely to arrange a song for the group's repertory, or even endorse its suggestion, if it had already been featured on a *BOCA* album. Although there is no strict prohibition of repeated selections in the annual series, to date no song has been selected twice. On this issue, Sharon has observed how the "inclusion of a song is almost to cement it as a past standard. Not all songs, but many become officially 'done' once they're on *BOCA*, and to that end I think *BOCA* serves a purpose in 'retiring' tunes (by not including duplicate songs on later albums), urging groups to find new rep[ertory]."[41]

Competitive comparison also affects musical practice while tracking.

Rather than having all the singers in a group record their parts simultaneously (approximating a live performance), Hare explains, each voice should be recorded individually, one at a time. This maximizes the mixing engineer's control at later stages of the process (see chapter 8). "If you're looking at doing a contemporary album that will compete with the other collegiate stuff out there," he writes, "you can't do it with decades-old techniques."[42] Again, comparison with *Sgt. Pepper's* is apt, since that work was largely composed by recording musical elements individually over the course of several months and assembling and mixing them later, a process similar to that of some contemporary a cappella records.[43]

Finally, vocal percussion is also subject to competitive comparison, particularly when it comes to deciding whether to use an unedited, "live" take of continuous percussion or to sequence individual recorded sounds digitally (as discussed in the previous chapter). The business manager of Purple Haze wrote that despite the "losses" incurred by sequencing, his vocal percussionists concluded that doing so would help their recording compare with others: "[W]e eventually decided that just recording straight VP, no matter how awesome we think it sounds live, wouldn't stack up sonically when compared with all the sampled and sequenced tracks out there."[44]

The term *competitive comparison* is appropriate, since *comparison* indicates a search for sameness. Indeed, it is the sense of sameness between *BOCA* tracks, or between one group's recordings and another's, that motivates many complaints regarding the homogenization of a cappella recordings or the standardization of the processes by which they are made. But a cappella is certainly not the first or only musical genre to feature competitive comparison. The waves of musically similar pieces bearing the words *Foxtrot, Waltz,* and a variety of ethnic references in their titles during the heyday of Tin Pan Alley indicate the degree to which songwriting firms kept one eye on their product and another on those of their neighbors.[45] The search for similarity also affected Elvis Presley's music after his move from Sun Studios to RCA. At Sun, Sam Phillips helped create Presley's signature "slap-back" echo, a musical feature RCA sought to copy but could not quite replicate.[46] Importantly, the postrock perspective situates a cappella's particular brand of competitive comparison historically: the focus on sameness in *musical* composition (strong in Tin Pan Alley and present in later generations of pop) shifts to sameness in *sonic* composition (new with rock 'n' roll and pop and strong in a cappella).

To some, multitracking and percussion sequencing are merely examples of a larger trend in a cappella recording practice. "The root issue here," one RARB forum contributor wrote, "is that the 'standards' of perceived 'greatness' in a cappella recording are being 'raised,' but the level of mean talent isn't." Since recordings are evaluated in relation to others made on the same campus and across the country, no one wants to "risk being one-'upped' by their peer groups, and so they ask for as close to 'perfection' as their engineer is able to deliver."[47] The perception of ever-elevating, or at least changing, standards is widespread.[48]

Reviews, Reception, Recognition, and the Economy of Prestige

Critics at RARB routinely compare a collegiate a cappella group's newest work with its earlier output, implying an assumption or expectation of continuity. For example, Elie Landau's review of an album by the University of North Carolina Loreleis begins by invoking the group's accomplishments going back nine years, during which time its membership would have turned over twice.

> Seemingly in everyone's top 10, or even top 5 all-female groups, the Loreleis have been associated with first-rate collegiate a cappella probably dating back to their win of the inaugural National Collegiate A Cappella Championship (back then, it was just National) in 1996. Bolstered by this reputation and having previously heard a few selected tracks off their CARA-nominated last album *One,* I was very much looking forward to sitting down with their most recent effort—their ninth album overall, entitled *Take a Big Whiff.*[49]

Similarly, Matt Cohen opens his review of the Counterparts' *Afterglow* (1999) by imploring the reader to revisit the group's earlier reviews.

> Before you read anything about *Afterglow,* you should look through the RARB archives and see what people had to say about past albums by the Counterparts. Go ahead and look. I'll wait.
>
> Did you look? Good. I just wanted you to see how in general the Counterparts are fairly well respected. Keep that in mind when I say that *Afterglow* is easily their best album. I'm basing this on only having heard their three prior CDs, but *Afterglow* is such a major step forward that I feel confident in saying that their new CD is superlative.[50]

As the analysis of the rehearsal process showed, some groups actively try to maintain such continuity (see chapter 6). But many, perhaps most, do not.

Yet the assumption of stylistic continuity operates even when critics acknowledge the transience inherent in the musical practice. Early in his review of Off the Beat's *Burn Like a Roman Candle* (2004), Jevan Soo writes, "Off the Beat fans will find more of the same they've always loved. High-octane arrangements of tough alternative songs that almost no [one] else will tackle, sung with grit and energy and produced within an inch of their lives." Phrases like "more of the same" and "always loved" imply stylistic stasis, an unchanging aesthetic to which the group clings. But Soo concludes his review by commenting on the group's music director's legacy and specifying the year the director will graduate, thus acknowledging the potential for stylistic change.[51]

Beyond the commercial promotion of certain musical products, reviews affix value to certain recordings, which in turn shapes perceptions within the a cappella world. Rhetoric like Landau's, Cohen's, and Soo's reinforces the idea that there exists an elite echelon of a cappella whose groups not only produce top-quality recordings but enjoy a tradition of doing so. As an institution that supports a cappella practice, the RARB thus contributes to its hierarchical organization.

The CARAs similarly designate value in a cappella recordings, but they do so more explicitly because they are actually termed "awards" and operate under the auspices of the CASA. For the 2006 CARAs, I served as one of fifty-seven nominators; a separate panel of fifty-six judges, which included only some of the nominators, then voted on the winners in each category.[52] Because of the large number of knowledgeable people involved, one could argue that the CARAs carry high prestige. But my fieldwork revealed that rather few collegiate groups were aware of the CARAs, or even the society. Instead, many more (though certainly not all) were familiar with *BOCA*.

In *The Economy of Prestige,* James F. English outlines a system of cultural capital—the stuff prestige is made of—based on cultural prizes and awards, such as the Nobel and Pulitzer. Prize discourse is predominantly negative in tone, especially toward the top prizes. Yet the larger symbolic economy of these prizes relies on such discourse (much of which comes from journalists or other prominent figures in the field) to maintain and continually reinforce its value and prestige, reinvigorating the system.[53]

The a cappella world supports English's findings. With the attention it receives, its status as a model for success, and the discourse it inspires, *BOCA* can
be seen as a source of cultural capital. Within its community it enjoys historical
primacy, much like the Nobel, the first of the modern cultural prizes. And like
most top-tier cultural prizes, *BOCA* benefits from the prestige of the individuals behind it, even if those individuals are occasionally involved in the creation
and selection of winning content.[54]

The other competitions may also be sources of cultural capital. For example, on the RARB forum, one respected a cappella singer strongly criticized the
results of the 2005 ICCA Finals, particularly the appropriateness of certain
judges for a collegiate a cappella competition and certain numerical aberra-
tions between the scores of the three judges.[55] The critic was associated with On
the Rocks, a men's group from the University of Oregon. Within three years of
its founding in 1999, On the Rocks had advanced to the ICCA Finals (placing
third) and in its fourth year returned, placed second, and was selected for
BOCA 2004. The group also appeared on the second season of *The Sing-Off*.
These achievements earned the group, and this individual, considerable capital.
In response to his criticism, the ICCA producers adopted some of his recommendations. Judging panels were expanded from three to five, with the highest
and lowest scores discarded. Moreover, he was asked to judge the following
year's finals. (The diverse backgrounds of the judges remained, however, including prominent figures from the fields of a cappella, choral music, and barbershop.) His criticism thus ultimately reinforced the prestige of the prize.

Prize criticism is usually aired in the media, with print and television the
most common venues. For a cappella, the Internet (including forums and
blogs) is the prominent medium, particularly the RARB forum, where numerous and continuing debates surrounding *BOCA*, the ICCA, and the a cappella
world's other competitions emphasize their importance. Even the appearance
of seemingly competing compilations (*Sing, Voices Only*), live competitions
(the National Championship of High School A Cappella),[56] and Internet discussion forums (the short-lived "A Cappella Uncensored") underpin the idea
that prizes make distinctions in the world of a cappella.[57] And, as *BOCA*'s wide
distribution and effect on a cappella practice, as well as this ICCA example,
show, the cultural capital associated with winning a cappella's top prizes yields
the power to define a good a cappella performance, a good a cappella recording, and ultimately what makes for good a cappella generally. Thus, a cappella's

economy of prestige creates an (inter)national field within which power is distributed in the a cappella world.

Despite the value of prizes such as *BOCA*, many singers played down their importance. "It's not like our group *exists* to make *BOCA*," said Jake, a singer with Shir Appeal, a mixed group from Tufts University that emphasizes Jewish themes and a Hebrew-language repertory. Singers commonly responded to questions about *BOCA*'s importance by professing indifference to whether their group was selected, by criticizing the compilation's previous selections, or by remarking that a group must spend thousands of dollars to make a recording good enough to be chosen.[58] These comments serve a defensive function and preemptively protect singers and their groups from disappointment. Such rhetorical strategies acknowledge the power of the prize, however, and enable individuals and groups to participate in the prize "game" while positioning themselves "above" it. If the prize had no political or social fallout, there would be no need to protect one's self or one's group from disappointment, to posture around it, or to adopt a "strategy of condescension" through which artists "help to maintain a discernible degree of separation between the scale of aesthetic value and that of public acclaim, between true genius and mere success on the awards circuit."[59]

Are We Aware? Do We Care?: The Value of a Prize

The existence of an economy of prestige in collegiate a cappella implies that singers attend to *BOCA*, the ICCA, the RARB, and other venues where distinction is made, discourse abounds, and ideas about a cappella aesthetics are shared. Many musicians, such as Harrington and members of Usrus Verses, attend to these matters closely. An Amazin' Blue alumna, Caroline, answered with an emphatic "Yes, yes, being selected for *BOCA* was important to the group!" when asked about its importance during her membership, 1997–99. But many singers do not know about these prizes or venues, or care about them. Of the five groups with which I worked most closely, familiarity and investment varied greatly. Counterparts and Amazin' Blue, both of which had appeared on *BOCA* before I joined, were greatly invested in the economy of prestige surrounding these prizes. The men in VoiceMale were aware of *BOCA* and had appeared on the 2004 edition a few months before I met them; their recent album, *Propeller*, had also earned them recognition through the CARAs. Some of the members of the Fallen Angels were aware of *BOCA*, and Debra told me that she hoped one day they would be selected, but most of the group did not seem to care. Finally, members of the Treblemakers were largely unaware of *BOCA*.[60]

If my ethnographic sample is any indication, we may conclude that many but not all groups buy into a cappella's economy of prestige. In such cases, usually only a few (sometimes only one or two) members spend time and effort familiarizing themselves with these prizes, their winners, their judges, and so on. These individuals constitute a loose network of informed musicians who maintain links to each other through venues like the RARB forum. Interaction is essential to maintaining the network and takes place on the local level within groups during rehearsals, the regional level when groups encounter each other in concert performances and the ICCA, and the (inter)national level through venues like recordings, the RARB, and *BOCA*. "Networks exist," writes Dorothy Noyes, "insofar as their ties are continually recreated and revitalized in interaction."[61] Re-creation and revitalization are always necessary because the network's nodes are constantly changing—students graduate and move on—and, as seen in a cappella's rehearsal practices, they are constantly in flux.

What are the benefits of being selected for *BOCA*, advancing in the ICCA, or winning a CARA? For one thing, groups can transform the prize's cultural capital into social, political, or economic forms.[62] Sharon explains, "[I]nclusion on *BOCA* can be transformative in a group's reputation as well as their ongoing motivation." Awards can be used as recruiting tools in the perpetual search for new members. They can wield political leverage within the campus a cappella scene. They can serve as promotional talking points when soliciting performance bookings from the college or university, private clients, or local, regional, and national invitational concerts, thus turning cultural into monetary capital—which can then be reinvested in a future recording that may earn the group more capital. Within groups, awards can bolster an individual's political and social status as a leader through the validation of prize-winning arranging, performance, and studio production skills. And, as the Fallen Angels were acutely aware, a lack of such credentials can place an individual or group at a strategic disadvantage in the competitive arena of campus, regional, and national a cappella.

Groups that invest in a cappella's competitive field often seek the recognition that results from an increase in cultural capital. Jake, from Shir Appeal, saw *BOCA* as a way to expand his group's reach beyond what he described as a built-in synagogue audience. "A synagogue planning an event will hire us with no prior knowledge of what we do because we're a Jewish singing group," he explained. But being selected for *BOCA* constitutes "a justification of the fact that we've actually done something really incredible—it's really an honor when we break through to an audience that isn't Jewish." Having been recognized on *BOCA* in 2000, 2003, 2005, and 2008, the latter three with Hebrew-language songs, Shir Appeal expanded its audience (increasing its bookings and album sales) and demonstrated its musical parity with the best of the secular groups. Moreover, Jake and the other members of the group gained a sense of validation through the recognition of their musical excellence within a broad field.

Harrington theorized that the effects of a *BOCA* selection are felt more strongly on a local level than a national one, but that local interest is based on *BOCA*'s national perspective: "[A]nytime you get *national* recognition, local people go *crazy!*" A contributor to the RARB forum sensed a more regional effect, claiming that groups at Michigan State University (in East Lansing, Michigan) gained in prestige and name recognition when groups like Amazin' Blue, the Dicks and Janes, and the Compulsive Lyres at the nearby University of Michigan (in Ann Arbor) achieved success on a national scale.[63]

Others focus on *BOCA*'s national effect. One RARB contributor argued that a school's "a cappella prestige" depends on the quality of its groups as determined by awards won rather than the number of groups at the school.

> The quality of the scene seems to me to determine national recognition more than the size of it. The U of Oregon is the obvious example. *BOCA* appearances and competition success can catapult you to national recognition pretty quickly. Even at the big a cappella schools, embracing the national a cappella community, putting out top-notch recordings, etc., seems to me to be what gets you recognized. I think 7 of the 9 groups at Stanford have appeared on *BOCA* at least once, and the Harmonics, Everyday People and Mixed Co[mpany] are there every other year or so. [At] U Penn and Tufts, [there is a] similar level of national recognition, if not greater. I know that a bunch of schools, like Yale, Princeton, [and] Wash U in St. Louis, are teeming with a cappella groups, but I can't name most of them, [']cause I haven't heard their recordings or heard about them winning in ICCAs or anything.[64]

Another contributor agreed that national recognition, especially through recordings, is most prestigious. She took her own school, Rutgers University, as an example. Two groups from the school had advanced to the ICCA Finals, another made it to the regional semifinals twice, and in all cases they won awards at the competition. Yet none of the school's groups had much name recognition because none had ever been selected for *BOCA:* "Seems to me the quickest/easiest way for a college a cappella scene to get national recognition? *BOCA,* and recordings in general. I'd even go so far as to say that's the only way your school's going to get any real, LASTING recognition. Emphasis on the word 'lasting.'"[65]

Thus, in the eyes of these a cappella participants, recordings (specifically *BOCA*) remain the coin of the realm. Their value exceeds even the best memory of an award-winning live performance. Yet they also shape and are shaped by the discourse about a cappella, which, through a network of informed individuals, brings certain concerns and aesthetic ideas to thousands of singers. Importantly, crucial aspects of the sound of a cappella recordings and the discourse surrounding them depend on the particular historical moment at which the musical practice blossomed, as well as on rock music and its ontological and aesthetic shifts, which allow a cappella practitioners to make, listen to, and think about music in the ways they do.

Conclusion

In his seminal work on American music, Richard Crawford distinguishes between "composer's music," which upholds the authority of the composer's score and aims for transcendence of time and place, and "performer's music," in which a notated score is merely an outline for musicians as they create as accessible a performance as possible.[1] This distinction is helpful for determining the purpose of a musical genre or practice, but how does it apply to collegiate a cappella? Although certain aspects of the composer's original musical work must be reproduced in an a cappella rendition, the fact that instruments are denied rules out any strict fidelity to a notated score (which may only be present due to an arranger's aural-analytical analysis). Moreover, as a music in which great liberties may be taken in performance and new layers of meaning added through humor, gesture, choreography, and recording technologies, it might seem as if a cappella fits more comfortably in the category of performer's music.

However, paying attention to the lived experience of a cappella—what it is like to be an a cappella musician—reveals a practice that might suggest a new dimension of performer's music, different perhaps from what Crawford originally intended. A cappella is a tradition that, while certainly aiming for accessibility among its audience(s), simultaneously serves purposes beyond those that may first come to mind when considering the popular musicians the category was originally intended to entail. When imagining "performer's music," one may initially think of personal financial gain, celebrity, or even social or political commentary, but those are largely lacking in a cappella. Group members generally do not keep any portion of their group's revenues, and any celebrity is primarily local (on one's campus) and, as graduation approaches, fleeting. And while groups like Brandeis University VoiceMale certainly used their music for social and political commentary, most groups I observed focus more exclusively on their music. So what additional purposes does a cappella serve?

For one thing, a cappella groups provide their members with social support at precisely the time in their lives when they are distancing themselves from the support systems offered by their families. The Harvard University Fallen Angels' practice of "check-in" illustrates the importance of talk (or "troubles talk") as a mode of sociability, particularly in women's groups. Men's groups, on the other hand, tend to socialize through activity. In all cases (including mixed groups), music and socialization foster trust, which enables musical and social risk taking, the demonstration of musical skill, the mastery of a habitus of singing, and the accumulation of social capital.

Several a cappella singers reported that, in order to balance the demands of their group with their academic obligations, they learned to better manage their time. Many also learn business skills by taking on their group's administrative tasks. Most develop their vocal technique, and many foster musical abilities in arranging, vocal percussion, performance, and recording. More broadly, a cappella singers learn to navigate and negotiate the social, political, and cultural terrains of the world in which they live while enjoying a certain "safety net" of support provided by the bonds of friendship forged through common musical pursuits.

The creation of community through participation in a cappella may be observed in the genre's rituals, such as the alumni song, and in the broader, Internet-based discussions where ideas are shared and constructive criticism and advice are on offer. But it is perhaps most strongly felt emotionally, through the act of musicking, effecting "fellow feeling."[2] Susan, from the Fallen Angels, explained:

> It's the feeling you get when you're singing your heart out in your block [i.e., background] part, and you look at the person next to you, and they're singing their heart out on the block part, and you smile at them because you know that they're feeling the exact same feeling that you have right now. Just singing your part and knowing that everyone around you is having that same feeling . . . And I think the power of that personal experience, combined with group experience, is what the music does to bring people together.

Thus, like many choral practices, a cappella not only meets the needs of its particular community, it creates community. The close connection between musical and social life may not be new to ethnomusicological studies, but the illumination of such a connection in this particular context—contemporary, Western, amateur, choral, academic—is.

Wrapped within the fellow feeling of community is a sense of identity, which is expressed in several ways. One is through distinction: members of the Fallen Angels described themselves as Harvard's only women's *contemporary pop* a cappella group, while VoiceMale singers poked fun at the demise of their rivals through their skits. Another is through routine musical affirmation: although the University of Michigan Amazin' Blue adopted multiple vocal styles through one of its warm-ups, the group always ended the exercise with one bearing the group's name.

The formation of identity through a cappella music is an area that a cappella scholarship can continue to explore. It is not difficult to find a cappella groups with specific religious or ethnic affiliations, such as the Tufts University Shir Appeal.[3] In what ways do these groups' musical selections shape, reinforce, and project a sense of identity? How do these groups' social processes do the same? Do these groups differ significantly, musically and socially, from groups (like the ones explored here) without such affiliations—and can those differences be traced to those affiliations specifically? These questions are left unanswered in part because the answers are rich enough for their own monograph.

As one considers the a cappella world going forward, it is useful to highlight two issues of particular concern to some members of its community. The first is that, at its core, the a cappella repertory consists of renditions of other people's recordings, a fact that has caused unease. For example, one participant in a RARB discussion on the topic, from a group at the University of Maryland, expressed his mixed feelings on the issue. He wrote, "[I]t's not particularly creative or impressive to put out an album full of imitative arrangements of top-40 hits—from an artistic standpoint, we always want to create something NEW and groundbreaking. If it's already been done (and done quite well), why spend your time trying to do it again?" Most of his group's albums—he estimated 80 percent or more—were sold to friends, family, and local students, despite the fact that RARB reviews and discussion participants complain of "overdone" songs: "If the people who buy our CDs really like these songs, why should we care about the fact that RARB reviewers think they're lame?" If his group focused on more original compositions, he feared the loss of many of those sales and with it the enthusiasm of the local audience. At the same time, he predicted that such a move toward original works would resonate well on the RARB forum.

> If we were to put out an awesome CD of only original songs, I'm sure that a lot of the people on this board would love it. It would probably get great reviews, maybe win some awards, maybe even get on . . . *BOCA*. But I'm yet to be convinced that we would actually sell any more (or even as many) copies than we would with a disc full of "Fix You's" [by Coldplay] and "Bring Me To Life's" [by Evanescence].[4]

Indeed, many in the community are supportive of original music composed for a cappella groups. Deke Sharon described this as "the biggest possible step for college a cappella," and the CASA would seem to agree—it added a new category for original songs to its CARA awards in 2006.[5]

In 2005, the Stanford University Fleet Street Singers released *Fleet Street*, the first collegiate a cappella album consisting entirely of original songs. It was well received by RARB reviewers: Jonathan Minkoff called it a "rare jewel in the world of collegiate a cappella," while Elie Landau remarked that it represented a "new and exciting direction for collegiate a cappella," which should encourage other groups to "follow the example of risk taking and originality."[6] Yet judging by subsequent concerts, competitions, albums, and *BOCA* compilations, other a cappella groups have not done so. The four *BOCAs* released after *Fleet Street* comprise seventy-six tracks, only one of which was composed by a member of the group that recorded it (*BOCA 2008*'s "Pehchaan," recorded by Penn Masala from the University of Pennsylvania).

An embrace of original composition may help a cappella navigate the other issue likely to follow it in the near future: the legality of its efforts. This topic has been largely avoided in this text because here my aims are musical, musicological, and ethnomusicological, not legal. But no treatment of a cappella would be complete without observing the increasing vigilance of the recording industry in protecting its intellectual property and its effects on the a cappella world. As participants in the RARB forum's discussions have been reminded, music publishers retain the right to arrange their works and subsequently hold the copyright on any arrangements.[7] This would seem to create problems for a musical community whose repertory is founded on vocal arrangements of (mostly) copyrighted works, that is, if arrangers sought legal ownership of their arrangements, which would be necessary in order to sell them unless a specific license is granted. Moreover, as my experience with Amazin' Blue showed me, CD manufacturers are increasingly concerned that the artists whose albums they reproduce have secured the necessary licenses to record and sell copyrighted material. Such licenses are compulsory, meaning they must be granted once requested, but their requirement creates an additional task a cappella groups must perform—and pay for—as they complete their recordings.

The recording industry, through the Recording Industry Association of America (RIAA) trade group, brought a "blizzard" of well-publicized lawsuits against individuals, including college students, for illegally obtaining copies of commercial recordings through file-sharing services in the early years of this century.[8] The American Society of Composers, Authors and Publishers (ASCAP) has also bragged about its litigious enforcement of licensing and copyright infringements.[9] Such actions raise the specter of a similar assault on a cappella groups. Up to this point, a cappella seems to have flown beneath the RIAA's and ASCAP's radar. Besides, most groups are loose associations of individuals with little in group assets—hardly worth the expense of litigation. But without legal business entities of their own, a cappella groups may in fact be placing the assets of their individual members at risk. Perhaps in some cases a group's college or university might step in and help mediate any legal disputes, but this is far from certain.[10]

As a cappella continues to appear in mainstream venues, from Mickey Rapkin's *Pitch Perfect* book to Ben Folds's *University A Cappella* album to NBC's *The Sing-Off* television competition, it seems increasingly likely that someone at the RIAA or one of its member companies will take notice.[11] Individual a cappella groups may remain on solid legal ground as long as their on-campus performances are covered by their college's or university's blanket license from a performance rights organization, such as ASCAP or Broadcast Music, Inc., which allows live performances in the institution's venues. And their recordings may be safe as long as they purchase the necessary mechanical licenses.[12] But the question of arrangements, one of the key devices in the process of making a cappella music, may seem murkier, even if a convincing case can be made under the fair use doctrine, which allows exceptions to copyrights "for purposes such as criticism, comment, news reporting, teaching (including multiple copies for classroom use), scholarship, or research."[13] Arranging therefore remains one issue with which scholars of law and music may continue to wrestle. It would be unfortunate, perhaps even an ethnomusicological failure, if an entire musical genre and practice were driven to extinction by litigious performance rights organizations. It is my hope that as a cappella gains acceptance and prominence in mainstream media, reasonable ways may be found to aid groups—particularly college groups, whose members do not individually profit and whose purposes are educational and social—in meeting their legal obligations without squelching entirely their ability to make music.

In the end, from the first collegiate vocal ensembles of the late nineteenth century to the Whiffenpoofs in the early twentieth, all the way through the a cappella explosion and the increasing visibility of the genre in the early twenty first, the pleasure of singing and the enactment of community have remained the root of collegiate a cappella's musical practice. I will never forget one rehearsal in the spring of 2005 when I joined the Boston University Treblemakers as they sang their rendition of Patty Griffin's "When It Don't Come Easy." We stood in a circle, holding hands, in the dark. Our sounds echoed in the room, enveloping us as we all contributed our vital voices to a song about the kind of devotion only deep, intimate connections with others can create. Nor will I forget the last time I sang with Amazin' Blue, in April 2007, in a stairwell, belting out the solo to Marvin Gaye's "How Sweet It Is (To Be Loved By You)" as we came to the bittersweet realization that, even through the group would continue the following fall, it was the final time we would all sing together as that particular group of voices, of individuals, of friends. These moments can be analyzed for their musical and social significance, but ultimately it is their lived experience that makes them powerful and motivates a cappella singers, including myself, to keep on singing.

Notes

Introduction

1. Mickey Rapkin, *Pitch Perfect: The Quest for Collegiate A Cappella Glory* (New York: Gotham, 2008), 5.

2. Mark Slobin, *Subcultural Sounds: Micromusics of the West* (Middletown, CT: Wesleyan University Press, 1993), 98.

3. Gregory Barz, "'We Are from Different Ethnic Groups, but We Live Here as One Family': The Musical Performance of Community in a Tanzanian *Kwaya*," in *Chorus and Community*, ed. Karen Ahlquist (Urbana: University of Illinois Press, 2006), 21.

4. Reebee Garofalo, *Rockin' Out: Popular Music in the USA* (Boston: Allyn and Bacon, 1997), 2.

5. Theodore Gracyk, *Rhythm and Noise: An Aesthetics of Rock* (Durham: Duke University Press, 1996); Albin Zak, *The Poetics of Rock: Cutting Tracks, Making Records* (Berkeley: University of California Press, 2001).

6. In addition to Rapkin's *Pitch Perfect* and various media publicizing its publication (e.g., Elysa Gardner, "'Pitch Perfect': Drama A Cappella," *USA Today,* June 19, 2008, D4; Aled Jones, "The Choir: A Cappella USA," BBC Radio 3, April 27, 2008; Sarah Kliff, "Songs in the Key of Cheese," *Newsweek,* May 26, 2008; Mickey Rapkin, "Perfect Tone, in a Key That's Mostly Minor," *New York Times,* March 23, 2008), see also Karen W. Arenson, "Songsters Off on a Spree: Campuses Echo with the Sound of Enthusiastic A Cappella Groups," *New York Times* April 25, 2002, E1, 4; Rachel Baker, "These Are the Biggest Studs on Campus?" *Boston,* February 2007; Kurt Eichewald, "'Doo-Wop-a-Doo' Will No Longer Do," *New York Times,* June 22, 1997, B32; Phil Kloer, "Who Needs a Band When College Students Discover the Power of the . . . Naked Voice," *Atlanta Journal-Constitution,* April 6, 2006, 1D; "Profile: Yale's A Cappella Groups Rush Current Crop of Freshmen," *Morning Edition,* National Public Radio, September 9, 2002; "A Cappella Frenzy," *Sunday Morning,* CBS News, January 11, 2004; Victor Sandman, "Boy Bands over Bach," *American Music Teacher* 54, no. 5 (2005): 40; Meg Tirrell, "A Cappella in the Digital Age," *Medill Reports* (Northwestern University Medill School of Journalism), February 15, 2007; Heidi Waleson, "College A Cappella!" *Voice of Chorus America* 27, no. 4 (summer

2004): 1, 16; and *Who Needs a Band?* New England Cable News (NECN) television network, March 15, 2010.

7. Anna Callahan, *Anna's Amazing A Cappella Arranging Advice: The Collegiate A Cappella Arranging Manual* (Southwest Harbor, ME: Contemporary A Cappella Publishing, 1995). Unpublished undergraduate and graduate papers and theses include Jason Chua, "Wolverine Vocals: Detailing the History, Function, and Racial Homogeneity of A Cappella Groups in the University of Michigan," undergraduate musicology paper, University of Michigan, 2005; Judah Cohen, "'Beautiful Stories, Told in Some Very Melodic Ways': An Ethnography of Under Construction, Harvard-Radcliffe's Christian A Cappella Singing Group," graduate ethnomusicology paper, Harvard University, 1997; Helen R. Comber, "We Are Still Singing: The Musical Backgrounds and Motivations of Participants in Collegiate A Cappella Groups at One University," BA thesis, Pennsylvania State University, 2008; Ben Jackson, "Vocal Percussion: A Phonetic Description," BA thesis, Harvard University, 2001; Mark Manley, "*ROOM ZERO:* The Dialectical Worlds of Live Performance and the Recording Studio in Collegiate A Cappella," BA thesis, University of Virginia, 2002; Jane Alexander McIntosh, "In Harmony: A Look at the Growth of Collegiate A Cappella Groups and the Future of the Movement," MA thesis, Teachers College, Columbia University, 1999; Rebecca Reiman, untitled undergraduate anthropology paper, Brandeis University, 2005; Veronica L. S. Robinson, "University of Michigan A Cappella Group Pre-concert Traditions," undergraduate folklore paper, University of Michigan, 2005; and Stacey Street, "Voices of Womanhood: Gender Ideology and Musical Practice in American Women's Vocal Groups," BA thesis, Harvard University, 1990.

8. See Gene Grier, "Choral Resources: A Heritage of Popular Styles," *Music Educators Journal* 77, no. 8 (1991): 35–39. Grier's article begins with a reference to the Music Educators National Conference (MENC) 1967 Tanglewood Symposium, which considered popular music in music education. Wiley L. Housewright, president of the MENC, declared in 1969 that the it "not only accepts rock and other present-day music as legitimate, but sanctions its use in education" (Wiley L. Housewright, Emmett R. Sarig, Thomas MacCluskey, and Allen Hughes, "Youth Music: A Special Report," *Music Educators Journal* 56, no. 3 [1969]: 45), but the response was strong and polarized, including charges that Housewright had "sold out music education" (see "Rock Reverberations," *Music Educators Journal* 56, no. 6 [1970]: 3–15). On choral music practice in particular, see David Itkin, "Dissolving the Myths of the Show Choir," *Music Educators Journal* 72, no. 8 (1986): 39–41; and the response from Tim J. Sharar, "Eyes of the Beholder," *Music Educators Journal* 73, no. 1 (1986): 16–17.

9. Ruth Finnegan, *The Hidden Musicians: Music-Making in an English Town* (Cambridge: Cambridge University Press, 1989). The Contemporary A Cappella Society of America, for example, is not listed among the numerous choral societies and other institutions in Percy Young and James G. Smith's article on choruses in *The New Grove Dictionary of Music and Musicians* (s.v. "chorus" §5) or its continually updated online version, *Grovemusic,* http://www.grovemusic.com (accessed July 23, 2008).

10. Ingrid Monson, *Saying Something: Jazz Improvisation and Interaction* (Chicago:

University of Chicago Press, 1996); Benjamin Brinner, *Knowing Music, Making Music: Javanese Gamelan and the Theory of Musical Competence and Interaction* (Chicago: University of Chicago Press, 1995).

11. See Karen Ahlquist, ed., *Chorus and Community* (Urbana: University of Illinois Press, 2006), particularly Melinda Russell, "'Putting Decatur on the Map': Choral Music and Community in an Illinois City," 45–69. See also Duncan Vinson, "An Ethnomusicological Study of the Chorus of Westerly, an Amateur/Volunteer Chorus in Rhode Island," PhD diss., Brown University, 2004; and "Liberal Religion, Artistic Autonomy, and the Culture of Secular Choral Societies," *Journal of the Society for American Music* 4, no. 3 (2010): 339–68.

12. On notions of "fieldwork," "homework," and the process and products of ethnography, see, for example, Gregory Barz and Timothy Cooley, eds., *Shadows in the Field: New Perspectives for Fieldwork in Ethnomusicology* (New York: Oxford University Press, 1997); James Clifford and George E. Marcus, eds., *Writing Culture: The Poetics and Politics of Ethnography* (Berkeley: University of California Press, 1986); Roger Sanjek, ed., *Fieldnotes: The Makings of Anthropology* (Ithaca, NY: Cornell University Press, 1990); and Kamala Visweswaran, *Fictions of Feminist Ethnography* (Minneapolis: University of Minnesota Press, 1994).

13. Ted Solis, ed., *Performing Ethnomusicology: Teaching and Representation in World Music Ensembles* (Berkeley: University of California Press, 2004).

14. Sometimes I participated more directly. With their permission, I sang with VoiceMale during their rehearsals and once filled in for a missing member during a gig in January 2005. My presence sometimes effected change, for example, by introducing some members of the Treblemakers to aspects of the wider national a cappella scene. See Kay Kaufman Shelemay, "The Ethnomusicologist, Ethnographic Method, and the Transmission of Tradition," in *Shadows in the Field: New Perspectives for Fieldwork in Ethnomusicology,* ed. Gregory Barz and Timothy Cooley (New York: Oxford University Press, 1997), 189–204.

Chapter 1

1. Two years earlier, one of Folds's friends had shown him a YouTube video of a collegiate a cappella group singing one of his songs. Intrigued, Folds held a contest, inviting groups to submit videos of their performances of his songs. The winners appeared on his new album. Folds likened himself to a folklorist, making "field recordings" of groups "in their campus habitats." See "Ben Folds Goes A Cappella, with Help," *All Things Considered,* National Public Radio, April 26, 2009; Jim Farber, "A Cappella Poised for a Serious Makeover," *New York Daily News,* April 27, 2009; and John Jurgensen, "Harmony 101: A Pop Pianist Recruits College Singers for a New Album of A Cappella Songs," *Wall Street Journal,* April 24, 2009, W2.

2. Quoted in Jenna Johnson, "The Nerd Turns: A Cappella Singers Suddenly the Popular Kids on Campus," *Washington Post,* October 18, 2010.

3. Alan Clark Buechner, *Yankee Singing Schools and the Golden Age of Choral Music in New England, 1760–1800* (Boston: Boston University Scholarly Publications, 2003), 96.

4. See Harold Earle Johnson, *Hallelujah, Amen! The Story of the Handel and Haydn Society of Boston*, reprint with an introduction by Richard Crawford (New York: Da Capo, 1981 [1965]); and Harold Earle Johnson, *History of the Handel and Haydn Society of Boston, Massachusetts* (New York: Da Capo, 1977 [1883, 1913]). George Frideric Handel and Franz Joseph Haydn dominate histories of choral music, sometimes to the exclusion or marginalization of American choral composers, works, and ensembles. Choral scholar Percy Young's *The Choral Tradition*, rev. ed. (New York: W. W. Norton, [1962] 1981), for instance, introduces American music in a three-page closing section in the second of two chapters on the nineteenth century, making only a few scattered references thereafter, and returns to it only at the close of the final chapter. See also Robert L. Garretson, *Choral Music: History, Style, and Performance Practice* (Upper Saddle River, NJ: Prentice Hall, 1993); John Potter, ed., *The Cambridge Companion to Singing* (New York: Cambridge University Press, 2000); and Homer Ulrich, *A Survey of Choral Music* (New York: Harcourt Brace Jovanovich, 1973).

5. Percy M. Young and James G. Smith, "Chorus," in *The New Grove Dictionary of Music and Musicians*, §i.4, http://www.grovemusic.com (accessed January 31, 2010).

6. Mark Clague, "Choral Music," in *The Encyclopedia of Chicago*, ed. James R. Grossman, Ann Durkin Keating, and Janice L. Reiff (Chicago: University of Chicago Press, 2004), 159.

7. J. Merrill Knapp, "Samuel Webbe and the Glee," *Music and Letters* 33, no. 4 (1952): 346–51. See also Emmanuel Rubin, *The English Glee in the Reign of George III: Participatory Art Music for an Urban Society* (Warren, MI: Harmonie Park Press, 2003).

8. Buechner, *Yankee Singing Schools*, 108–9.

9. Frederick Chase, *A History of Dartmouth College and the Town of Hanover, New Hampshire*, ed. John King Lord (Cambridge, MA: John Wilson and Son University Press, 1891), 231, quoted in Richard Kegerreis, "The Handel Society of Dartmouth," *American Music* 4, no. 2 (1986): 177.

10. Marshall Bartholomew, "The 1st 100 Years, 1861–1961: A Short History of the Yale Glee Club," unpublished manuscript at the Irving S. Gilmore Music Library, Yale University, Marshall Bartholomew Papers, MSS 24, Box 3, Folder 1.

11. Buechner, *Yankee Singing Schools*, 108–9.

12. Kegerreis, "The Handel Society of Dartmouth," 177–78, 187, 189.

13. Mary Sue Morrow, "Somewhere Between Beer and Wagner: The Cultural and Musical Impact of German Männerchöre in New York and New Orleans," *Music and Culture in America, 1861–1918*, ed. Michael Saffle (New York: Garland, 1998), 79–109; Suzanne G. Snyder, "The Indianapolis Männerchor: Contributions to a New Musicality in Midwestern Life," *Music and Culture in America, 1861–1918*, 111–40.

14. Michael Broyles, *"Music of the Highest Class": Elitism and Populism in Antebellum Boston* (New Haven: Yale University Press, 1992), 129–30. See also Walter Raymond Spalding, *Music at Harvard: A Historical Review of Men and Events* (New York: Coward-McCann, 1935), 39–109.

15. William Weber, "Universities," §II.2, in *The New Grove Dictionary of Music and Musicians*, http://www.grovemusic.com (accessed January 31, 2010). Weber's article also mentions a choral ensemble at Harvard called the Pierian Society, founded in 1808. Broyles's discussion of the Pierian Sodality at Harvard, in *"Music of the Highest Class"* (128–38), shows it to have been primarily an instrumental group. H. Wiley Hitchcock, in *Music In the United States*, 3rd ed. (Englewood Cliffs, NJ: Prentice Hall, 1988), 77, locates the founding of the Harvard Glee Club in 1828, but other sources do not confirm this claim. According to Spalding, the earliest record of the Pierian Sodality to reflect "actual singing by the Pierian Glee Club" is dated April 29, 1834, although earlier efforts at organizing such an ensemble occurred on November 12, 1833, and again in 1841, before the club founded on March 16, 1858, took root (*Music at Harvard*, 54, 120).

16. Spalding, *Music at Harvard*, 73–74.

17. "College Music," *Dwight's Journal of Music*, June 19, 1858, quoted in Spalding, *Music at Harvard*, 76–77.

18. *The History of the University of Michigan Men's Glee Club* (n.p., 2003), available on the club's website, http://www.umich.edu/~ummgc (accessed November 11, 2005). For a firsthand look at college glee club life, see Bruce Montgomery, *Brothers, Sing On! My Half-Century Around the World with the Penn Glee Club* (Philadelphia: University of Pennsylvania Press, 2005).

19. *The History of the University of Michigan Men's Glee Club*, 1.

20. Bartholomew, "A Short History of the Yale Glee Club."

21. Harvard Glee Club and Pierian Sodality concert program, June 8, 1859, Harvard Archives, HUD 3428.159, "Harvard Glee Club": "Programs, etc., 1871–1892."

22. Karen Linn, *That Half-Barbaric Twang: The Banjo in American Popular Culture* (Urbana: University of Illinois Press, 1991), 18, 24–27.

23. The University of Michigan Men's Glee Club merged with the university's banjo club in 1890 and with the mandolin club in 1897 (*The History of the University of Michigan Men's Glee Club*).

24. Harvard Glee Club and Pierian Sodality concert program, June 8, 1859, Harvard Archives, HUD 3428.159, "Harvard Glee Club": "Programs, etc., 1871–1892."

25. Spalding, *Music at Harvard*, 127–28. Bartholomew observes a similar debate between "serious music or light entertainment" at Yale in the mid-1930s ("A Short History of the Yale Glee Club").

26. The source of the review and the name of the critic are unknown. The clipping can be found accompanying the concert program of April 24, 1874, Harvard Archives, HUD 3428.159, "Harvard Glee Club": "Programs, etc., 1871–1892."

27. Broyles, *"Music of the Highest Class,"* 132–35.

28. Bartholomew, "A Short History of the Yale Glee Club."

29. Harvard Glee Club and Harvard Banjo Club concert program, April 23, 1891, Harvard Archives, HUD 3428.159, "Harvard Glee Club": "Programs, etc., 1871–1892."

30. Untitled pamphlet accompanying a performance at Carnegie Hall, December 31, 1923, Harvard Archives, HUD 3428.159, "Harvard Glee Club": "Programs, etc., 1871–1892."

31. Bartholomew, "A Short History of the Yale Glee Club." In "Origins," posted on the Yale Whiffenpoofs Alumni website (adapted from Richard Nash Gould, *Yale 1900–2001*, vol. 2: *The Whiffenpoofs: Twentieth Century* [New York: Twentieth Century Project, 2004]), http://www.whiffalumni.com/origins, n.d. (accessed February 16, 2010), dates are provided as follows: "Caterwaulers of 1870 (a quintet), the Singing Club of 1872 (a quartet), the Crows of 1872 (an octet), and the Offenbachanalians of 1874 (a quartet). The Beethoven Bummers lasted into the 1870s with as many as fifteen singers."

32. Marshall Bartholomew, "Singing for the Fun of It," typescript at the Irving S. Gilmore Music Library, Yale University, Marshall Bartholomew Papers, MSS 24, Box 3, Folder 1, p. 163A.

33. *The History of the University of Michigan Men's Glee Club*, 7–8, 21. Of the six small ensembles listed in the *History*, only the Friars survives today. This group was founded by Walter Collins, a one-year sabbatical replacement for famed director Philip Dewey, in 1955–56. It was "patterned after the Yale Whiffenpoofs," of which Collins had been a member.

34. Helen Lefkowitz Horowitz, *Campus Life: Undergraduate Cultures from the End of the Eighteenth Century to the Present* (New York: Alfred A. Knopf, 1987), 39, 41.

35. Helen Lefkowitz Horowitz, *Alma Mater: Design and Experience in the Women's Colleges from Their Nineteenth-Century Beginnings to the 1930s* (New York: Alfred A. Knopf, 1984), 152–166.

36. Sherrie Tucker, "The Prairie View Co-Eds: Black College Women Musicians and Class on the Road during World War II," *Black Music Research Journal* 19, no. 1 (1999): 95. Tucker cites Maude Cuney-Hare, *Negro Musicians and Their Music* (Washington, DC: Associated Publishers, 1936; reprint, New York: Simon and Schuster, 1996), 55–57, 248–52.

37. A detailed, laudatory account of the Jubilee Singers is J. B. T. Marsh, *The Story of the Jubilee Singers, with Their Songs*, rev. ed. (New York: Negro Universities Press, 1969; originally published Boston: Houghton, Mifflin, 1881). A more recent account, focused on the experiences of the singers themselves, is Andrew Ward, *Dark Midnight When I Rise: The Story of the Jubilee Singers, Who Introduced the World to the Music of Black America* (New York: Farrar, Straus and Giroux, 2000).

38. Sandra J. Graham, "Reframing Negro spirituals in the Nineteenth Century," in *Music, American Made: Essays in Honor of John Graziano*, ed. John Koegel (Warren, MI: Harmonie Park Press, 2011).

39. Mellonee V. Burnim, "Religious Music," In *African American Music: An Introduction*, ed. Mellonee V. Burnim and Portia K. Maultsby (New York: Routledge, 2006), 63.

40. Gage Averill, *Four Parts, No Waiting: A Social History of American Barbershop Harmony* (New York: Oxford University Press, 2003), 22–23.

41. See Lynn Abbott, " 'Play That Barber Shop Chord': A Case for the African-American Origin of Barbershop Harmony," *American Music* 10, no. 3 (1992): 289–325; Averill, *Four Parts, No Waiting*; and Richard Mook, "The Sounds of Liberty: Nostalgia, Masculinity, and Whiteness in Philadelphia Barbershop, 1900–2003," PhD diss., University of Pennsylvania, 2004.

42. Averill, *Four Parts, No Waiting,* 33, 48.

43. Ibid., 80–84.

44. As Averill discusses, certain publications helped to cement barbershop's stylistic features: Claude Trimble "Deac" Martin, *A Handbook for Adeline Addicts: A Starter For Cold Voices and a Survey of American Balladry* (Cleveland: Schonberg Press, 1932); George Shackley, *Close Harmony: Male Quartets, Ballads, and Funnies with Barber Shop Chords* (New York: Pioneer Music, 1925); and Sigmund Spaeth, ed., *Barbershop Ballads* (New York: Simon and Schuster, 1925); and Sigmund Spaeth, *Barbershop Ballads and How To Sing Them* (New York: Prentice Hall, 1940). See also Liz Garnett, "Ethics and Aesthetics: The Social Theory of Barbershop Harmony," *Popular Music* 18, no. 1 (1999): 47–48.

45. Garnett, "Ethics and Aesthetics," 56. See also SPEBSQSA, Inc., *Barbershop Arranging Manual* (Kenosha, WI: SPEBSQSA, 1980).

46. Garnett, "Ethics and Aesthetics," 48.

47. Liz Garnett, *The British Barbershopper: A Study in Socio-musical Values* (Burlington, VT: Ashgate, 2005), 33, italics in the original.

48. Garnett, "Ethics and Aesthetics," 53.

49. For more information on the Barbershop Harmony Society's Collegiate Barbershop Quartet Contest, see the society's website, http://www.barbershop.org (accessed June 16, 2009).

Chapter 2

1. See, for example, "A Century of A Cappella," A-Cappella.com, n.d., http://www .a-cappella.com/category/century_of_acappella (accessed September 30, 2009); Mike Chin, "Friday Factoid: The Site of the First Collegiate A Cappella Show," posted on the A Cappella Blog, February 12, 2010, http://www.acappellablog.com/2010/02/12 (accessed February 16, 2010); and davidcharliebrown, "The Yale Whiffenpoofs, the first collegiate a cappella group, were formed in 1909. Modern a cappella is 100 years old!," posted on the Contemporary A Cappella Society of America website, January 28, 2009, http:// www.casa.org/node/1571 (accessed August 13, 2010).

2. The Whiffenpoofs appeared on *The West Wing* episode entitled "Holy Night," during the show's fourth season, December 11, 2002. Questions referring to the Whiffenpoofs have appeared on the game show *Jeopardy!* in episodes airing October 4, 1985; January 9, 1997; May 21, 2003; November 17, 2005; April 23, 2007; and July 23, 2009. The group appeared on NBC's *Today Show* on the episode airing December 8, 2002 and on NBC's *Saturday Night Live* on December 12, 1981. The *Gilmore Girls* episode, "Let the Games Begin," which aired November 19, 2002, also featured the group. Finally, the Whiffenpoofs was a competitor during *The Sing-Off*'s second season in December 2010.

3. Despite an endowment of over two million dollars, Mory's Temple Bar did not survive the market crash of 2008 and closed on December 19 of that year. A renovation and reopening effort was soon launched. See Brian Reed, "After 160 Years, Fabled Yale

Club Shuts Doors," *Weekend Edition,* National Public Radio, January 11, 2009. For more information on the history of Mory's, see George D. Vaill, *Mory's: A Brief History* (New Haven: Mory's Association, 1977).

4. Edward Waters, *Victor Herbert: A Life in Music* (New York: Macmillan, 1995), 324.

5. Marshall Bartholomew, "The Whiffenpoofs," unpublished typescript at the Irving S. Gilmore Music Library, Yale University, Marshall Bartholomew Papers, MSS 24, Box 4, Folder 1, 172.

6. Rev. James M. Howard ('09), "An Authentic Account of the Founding of the Whiffenpoofs," The Whiffenpoofs of Yale, Inc., website, http://www.yale.edu/whiffenpoofs (accessed October 3, 2005). This document was written for the Whiffenpoofs' fiftieth anniversary in 1959. It is reprinted in the booklet "A History of the Whiffenpoofs of Yale University and a Roster of the Membership: Prepared for the 85th Anniversary Celebration, April 29–May 1, 1994, New Haven, Connecticut," in Manuscripts and Archives, Yale University, RU 156, Ascension 2000-A-044, Box 1.

7. See, all by Marshall Bartholomew, "The 1st 100 Years, 1861–1961: A Short History of the Yale Glee Club," unpublished manuscript at the Irving S. Gilmore Music Library, Yale University, Marshall Bartholomew Papers, MSS 24, Box 3, Folder 1; "Singing for the Fun of It," unpublished manuscript at the Irving S. Gilmore Music Library, Yale University, Marshall Bartholomew Papers, MSS 24, Box 4, Folder 1; and "The Whiffenpoofs," 169–70.

8. "Gentlemen-Rankers" comes from the first series of Kipling's collection of ballads, *Barrack-Room Ballads and Other Verses,* which was initially published in 1892. See Rudyard Kipling, *Rudyard Kipling's Verse: Definitive Edition* (London: Hodder and Stoughton, 1940), 424–25.

9. The members were: Buff "The Colonel" Kimball, Theron "The Regular" Strong, Austin "The Major" Bruff, Skut "The Commissary" Ellsworth, Simy "The Captain" Chittenden, and Rusty "The Volunteer" Van Vechten.

10. Richard Nash Gould, *Yale, 1900–2001,* vol. 2: *The Whiffenpoofs: Twentieth Century* (New York: Twentieth Century Project, 2004), 2–4, 83–128.

11. Howard, "An Authentic Account of the Founding of the Whiffenpoofs."

12. Whim 'N Rhythm, a women's a cappella group founded at Yale in 1981, also limits its membership to seniors. The group positions itself as a female counterpart to the Whiffenpoofs, calling itself "the premier undergraduate female a cappella singing group in the nation" (Yale University Whim 'N Rhythm website, http://www.yale.edu/whim/about.html [accessed July 9, 2009]). See also Stacey Street, "Voices of Womanhood: Gender Ideology and Musical Practice in American Women's Vocal Groups," BA thesis, Harvard University, 1990.

13. Excerpt. The full poem is reprinted in Kipling, *Rudyard Kipling's Verse,* 424–25.

14. Charles J. Wrong, "The Officiers de Fortune in the French Infantry," *French Historical Studies* 9, no. 3 (1976): 408.

15. John Whitehead, ed., *The Barrack-Room Ballads of Rudyard Kipling* (Shropshire: Hearthstone, 1995), 143.

16. Howard, "An Authentic Account of the Founding of the Whiffenpoofs." It is reported to have been sung at Yale's Class Day exercises in 1908 ("Origins," posted on the Yale Whiffenpoofs Alumni website, n.d. [adapted from Gould, *Yale*], http://www.whiff alumni.com/origins [accessed February 16, 2010]).

17. Gould, *Yale*, 2–4.

18. Sigmund Spaeth, *A History of Popular Music in America* (New York: Random House, 1948), 513. Correspondence in the Bartholomew papers supports this claim, as does anecdotal evidence in Howard's history. See Marshall Bartholomew Papers, Box 4, Folder 9; and Howard, "An Authentic Account of the Founding of the Whiffenpoofs."

19. Marshall Bartholomew, ed., *Songs of Yale* (New York: Miller Music, 1935).

20. Whiffenpoofs Constitution, Marshall Bartholomew Papers, Box 4, Folder 1. The "Whiffenpoof Anthem" refers to what became known as the "Whiffenpoof Song."

21. Vallée recorded the "Whiffenpoof Song" no less than nine times between 1936 and 1966 according to Larry F. Kiner, *The Rudy Vallée Discography* (Westport, CT: Greenwood Press, 1985). According to *Billboard*, Bing Crosby's recording on Decca reached number 42 on the Hot 100 charts the week of December 31, 1947, and Bob Crewe's recording on Warwick reached number 96 the week of February 8, 1960. Perry Como recorded it in 1958 on RCA Victor, Louis Armstrong recorded it in 1959 on Decca, and the Statler Brothers recorded it in 1966 on Columbia. Elvis Presley recorded it in October 1968, but it was released on the 1995 collection, *Live a Little, Love a Little/Charro!/The Trouble With Girls/Change of Habit*. Count Basie's recording, which also features the Mills Brothers, was released on a 1974 MCA album. The "Whiffenpoof Song" was also adopted by the US Air Corps as an unofficial theme song under the title "Gentlemen-Flyers" (Gould, *Yale*, 58).

22. Howard, "An Authentic Account of the Founding of the Whiffenpoofs."

23. Helen Lefkowitz Horowitz, *Campus Life: Undergraduate Cultures from the End of the Eighteenth Century to the Present* (New York: Alfred A. Knopf, 1987), 12–13, 150.

24. One possible exception appears in measure 55 of the refrain, where the bass voice descends chromatically from G to $F^{\sharp}$, eventually leading to E on the downbeat of the following measure. Significantly, no new lyrics or syllables are enunciated during this passage, which serves harmonically to create a dominant seventh chord (D^7). Moreover, the next chord on the downbeat of measure 56, an E^7, does not resolve the tension this passage created, negating any extramusical value that might be derived from it, other than its purpose as voice leading.

25. The only exceptions are two secondary dominants in inversion, both of which function as passing chords driving toward moments of relative harmonic stability, and a half-diminished seventh chord built on the supertonic, which functions as a predominant preparation for the cadence that concludes the verse in the following phrase.

26. Sandra J. Graham, "Reframing Negro Spirituals in the Nineteenth Century," in *Music, American Made: Essays in Honor of John Graziano,* ed. John Koegel (Warren, MI: Harmonie Park Press, 2011).

27. Quoted in Gould, *Yale*, 48–49.

28. Bartholomew, "Singing for the Fun of It," 161–63A.

29. Bartholomew, *Songs of Yale,* 50–52; the spiritual "I've been a-List'ning all de Night Long" (also known as "I've Been Listening All Night Long" was first published in T. F. Seward, *Jubilee Songs* (Chicago: Bigelow and Main, 1872), and then in M. F. Armstrong, Helen W. Ludlow, and Thomas P. Fenner, *Hampton and Its Students, by Two of Its Teachers, Mrs. M. F. Armstrong and Helen W. Ludlow, with Fifty Cabin and Plantation Songs, Arranged by Thomas P. Fenner* (New York: G. P. Putnam's Sons, 1874), 247. See also the compilation by Kathleen A. Abromeit, *An Index to African American Spirituals for the Solo Voice* (Westport, CT: Greenwood, 1999), accessible online via the Academic Affairs Library at the University of North Carolina at Chapel Hill, http://docsouth.unc.edu/church/armstrong/armstrong.html (accessed May 21, 2007).

30. Bartholomew, "The Barbershop Quartet," quoted in Gould, *Yale,* 63.

31. Gould, *Yale,* 50–65, 125. "Velia" is also known as "The Vilja Song." See also "Early Repertoire," posted on the Yale Whiffenpoofs Alumni website (adapted from Gould, *Yale*), n.d., http://www.whiffalumni.com/early_repertoire (accessed February 16, 2010).

32. Gould, *Yale,* 65–66.

33. Ibid., 67–80.

34. Ibid., 48.

35. Author's field notes, November 20, 2004. While "Waiting In Vain" was originally written and performed by Bob Marley, Annie Lennox's later recording, from *Medusa* (Arista 25717, 1995), may have served as a model for the Whiffenpoofs' arrangement.

Chapter 3

1. Gage Averill, *Four Parts, No Waiting: A Social History of American Barbershop Harmony* (New York: Oxford University Press, 2003), 60–77; H. Wiley Hitchcock, *Music in the United States: A Historical Introduction,* 3rd ed. (Englewood Cliffs, NJ: Prentice Hall, 1988), 77; William Howland Kenney, *Recorded Music in American Life: The Phonograph and Popular Memory, 1890–1945* (New York: Oxford University Press, 1999), 8.

2. They recorded "Dinah" with Crosby in 1931, recorded "Dedicated to You" with Fitzgerald in 1937, and made numerous recordings (e.g., "Darling Nelly Gray") with Armstrong between 1937 and 1940.

3. Eileen Southern, *The Music of Black Americans: A History,* 3rd ed. (New York: W. W. Norton, 1997), 513.

4. Mitch Rosalsky, *Encyclopedia of Rhythm and Blues and Doo-Wop Vocal Groups* (Lanham, MD: Scarecrow Press, 2000), 397. The Mills Brothers switched to the Decca label in 1934.

5. Geoff Milne, liner notes to *The Mills Brothers: Chronological Volume 1,* London, JSP Records, JSPCD 301, 1988.

6. Richard Nash Gould, *Yale, 1900–2001,* vol. 2: *The Whiffenpoofs: Twentieth Century* (New York: Twentieth Century Project, 2004), 65.

7. Robert Pruter, *Doowop: The Chicago Scene* (Urbana: University of Illinois Press, 1996), xii.

8. Pruter's chronicle of Chicago doo-wop (ibid.) consists almost entirely of black performers, and Philip Groia's history of "rhythm and blues vocal groups" in New York tells a similar story (*They All Sang on the Corner: New York City's Rhythm and Blues Vocal Groups of the 1950's* [Setauket, NY: Edmond Publishing, 1974], revised and republished as *They All Sang on the Corner: A Second Look at New York City's Rhythm and Blues Vocal Groups* [West Hempstead, NY: P. Dee Enterprises, 1983]). Anthony J. Gribin and Matthew M. Schiff contrast early doo-wop with rockabilly, writing that "the performers of the first wave of doo-wop music were overwhelmingly black, and their audience, as measured by the meager penetration of their music onto the white pop charts, was mostly black as well" (*Doo-Wop: The Forgotten Third of Rock 'n Roll* [Iola, WI: Krause, 1992], 25).

9. Gribin and Schiff, *Doo-Wop*, 17–22.

10. This technique was usually applied to songs in AABA form. "A" sections would be sung in call-and-response, with a lead singer calling and the background singers responding and supporting harmonically. The "B" section would often shift to "concerted harmony" (Stuart L. Goosman, "The Black Atlantic: Structure, Style, and Values in Group Harmony," *Black Music Research Journal* 17, no. 1 [1997]: 86).

11. Gribin and Schiff identify this harmonic sequence typical of the doo-wop genre (*Doo-Wop*, 30).

12. For example, the song was recorded by Dion DiMucci (who would later lead Dion and the Belmonts) on *Wish Upon a Star* (Laurie P-2006, 1959), integrated doo-wop quartet the Crests on *The Crests Sing All Biggies* (CoEd 901, 1960), integrated doo-wop group the Del Vikings on *Come Go With Me* (Dot DP-35695, 1966), and Paul Anka on *Goodnight My Love* (RCA 4142, 1969).

13. Stephen Holden, "Neil Young and Billy Joel Revisit the Roots of Rock," *New York Times* August 7, 1983, H19. Holden suggests the Tymes as the song's model.

14. Gribin and Schiff, *Doo-Wop*, 54–57.

15. The album won awards for Best Pop Performance by a Duo or Group with Vocal (for "Boy From New York City"), Best Jazz Performance, Duo or Group (for "Until I Met You [Corner Pocket]"), and Best Vocal Arrangement for Two or More Voices (to Gene Puerling for "A Nightingale Sang in Berkeley Square"). It reached number 6 on *Billboard*'s Jazz chart and 22 on the Billboard 200. The track "Boy From New York City," also reached number 7 on the Billboard Hot 100 chart and number 4 on the Adult Contemporary chart.

16. Reggae is about more than just relaxation and tranquility, however. It has been a vehicle for Jamaican and black expressions of discontent. See Dick Hebdige, *Cut 'n' Mix: Culture, Identity, and Caribbean Music* (New York: Methuen, 1987).

17. There is little scholarship on beatboxing; most discussions of rap emphasize turntables, mixers, and samplers rather than percussive or nonsensical sounds. See, for

example, Tricia Rose, *Black Noise: Rap Music and Black Culture in Contemporary America* (Hanover, NH: Wesleyan University Press, 1994). A notable exception is David Toop, *The Rap Attack: African Jive to New York Hip Hop* (London: Pluto Press, 1984).

18. Deborah Wong calls this practice a "cipher," drawing her definition of the term from correspondence with the Asian American hip-hop artist Peril-L of the Mountain Brothers (*Speak It Louder: Asian Americans Making Music* [New York: Routledge, 2004], 250). Rose, in *Black Noise*, 74–80, discusses the drum machines hip-hop artists would use and beatboxers would emulate. Although vocal percussion and beatboxing are discussed here only in a Western context, it is worth noting that other traditions of vocalized percussion exist around the world, for example, in Indian vocalized drum sounds, or *bols*.

19. Marcus Reeves, *Somebody Scream! Rap Music's Rise to Prominence in the Aftershock of Black Power* (New York: Faber and Faber, 2008), 58. Reeves also mentions that successful rapper DMX began his career in the late 1990s as a beatboxer (225–26). See also TyTe and White Noise, "The Real History of Beatboxing, Part 2: The Old Skool," http://www.humanbeatbox.com (accessed July 17, 2009).

20. Michael Feldman, posted on the RARB forum, May 30, 2005, http://forum.rarb .org/forum/viewtopic.php?t=1639 (accessed February 1, 2010).

21. "LilVPboy," posted on the Contemporary A Cappella Society forum (topic: "Vocal Percussion"–"Naïve Question"), September 26, 2005, http://www.casa.org (accessed September 26, 2005).

22. "eksingpuccusser," posted on the RARB forum, June 10, 2005, http://forum.rarb .org/forum/viewtopic.php?t=1639 (accessed February 1, 2010).

23. TyTe and White Noise, "The Real History of Beatboxing, Part 2."

24. While the a cappella and beatboxing communities agree that in many cases (or at least as it pertains to a cappella groups) vocal percussion sounds mimic "real drum sounds," academic research does not always make the same distinction. One linguistic study, which calls beatboxing "a tradition of vocal percussion," places any attempt "to create *convincing impersonations* of drum tracks" under the category of beatboxing without specifying the authenticity of the drum sounds on those tracks. It also points to inhaled sounds as a crucial element of beatboxing, a claim my own observations of a cappella vocal percussionists do not substantiate. But, like many of the a cappella singers contributing to discussions on the RARB forum, the study's authors do consider the microphone a distinguishing characteristic of beatboxing (Dan Stowell and Mark D. Plumbley, "Characteristics of the Beatboxing Vocal Style," Queen Mary, University of London, Department of Electronic Engineering, Centre for Digital Music, Technical Report C4DM-TR-08-01, February 19, 2008, 1–3).

25. TyTe and Definicial, "The Real History of Beatboxing, Part 1: The Prehistory of Beatboxing," http://www.humanbeatbox.com/history (accessed July 17, 2009).

26. Wong, *Speak It Louder*, 250.

27. Jane Alexander McIntosh, "In Harmony: A Look at the Growth of Collegiate A

Cappella Groups and the Future of the Movement," MA thesis, Teachers College, Columbia University, 1999.

Chapter 4

1. Mickey Rapkin, *Pitch Perfect: The Quest for Collegiate A Cappella Glory* (New York: Gotham, 2008), 5.

2. This survey included mostly American groups but also a few in Canada and the United Kingdom. Data were collected primarily through groups' websites and supplemented with personal communications, ethnographic observations, and anecdotal evidence (it would have been impractical to contact every group individually to verify its data). Although numerous efforts have been undertaken to create a directory of a cappella groups, it is difficult, as new groups are constantly appearing and others disband. I began with an old directory supplied to me by Don Gooding, which itself was based on the original contact lists compiled by Deke Sharon and the Tufts University Beelzebubs in the early 1990s. I then consulted one of the largest online directories at the time, http://www.collegeacappella.com, and the "Acapedia" administered by the Contemporary A Cappella Society of America on its website, http://www.casa.org, to verify as much of the information as possible. When provided, I followed links to groups' websites, which often contained useful historical information, such as a founding date. In cases in which a group's existence could not be verified, it was not included in my list. Another, more recent, database of groups is hosted by the A Cappella Blog, http://www.acappellablog.com (accessed February 1, 2010).

3. The charts presented in figures 4.1 and 4.2 extend only to 2005 because my data for the years 2006 and 2007 remain especially scarce.

4. Andy Poe, "Amazin' Blue" history, available on Poe's personal website, http://euclid.nmu.edu/~apoe/acappella/AmazinBlue/index.html (accessed August 26, 2009).

5. Adam Bower, "Sons of Adam: An A Cappella Experience," undergraduate thesis, Kalamazoo College, 1995, 3.

6. Deke Sharon, personal communication, February 26, 2010.

7. James A. Keene, *A History of Music Education in the United States* (Hanover, NH: University Press of New England, 1982), 319–28. See also Leonard Van Camp, "The Rise of American Choral Music and the A Cappella 'Bandwagon,'" *Music Educators Journal* 66, no. 3 (1980): 36–40.

8. Keene, *A History of Music Education in the United States,* 329–30. The quote is attributed to Harry Carlson, director of the Chicago Swedish Choral Society, quoted from Harry Carlson, "The Interest in Youth in Ontario," *Proceedings MSNC for 1936,* 182.

9. Keene, *A History of Music Education in the United States,* 308–14.

10. Van Camp, "The Rise of American Choral Music," 36.

11. "Music: Russia's Songs in the Ukraine," *New York Times,* October 1, 1922, 91. See also Keene, *A History of Music Education in the United States,* 305–8.

12. Keene, *A History of Music Education in the United States*, 353–63. See also Michael L. Mark and Charles L. Gary, *A History of American Music Education* (New York: Schirmer, 1992), 364–65.

13. Christopher J. Lucas, *American Higher Education: A History* (New York: St. Martin's Press, 1994), 127–30. Lucas also draws on John S. Brubacher and Willis Rudy, *Higher Education in Transition: A History of American Colleges and Universities, 1636–1976*, 3rd ed. rev. (New York: Harper and Row, 1976), 85–86; and W. H. Cowley and Don Williams, *International and Historical Roots of American Higher Education* (New York: Garland, 1991), 85–87, 104–9.

14. John R. Thelin, *A History of American Higher Education* (Baltimore: Johns Hopkins University Press, 2004), 65. See also Lucas, *American Higher Education*, 200–201.

15. Thelin, *A History of American Higher Education*, 157–61. See also James C. Stone and Donald P. DeNevi, eds., *Portraits of the American University, 1890 to 1910* (San Francisco: Jossey-Bass, 1971).

16. Helen Lefkowitz Horowitz, *Alma Mater: Design and Experience in the Women's Colleges from Their Nineteenth-Century Beginnings to the 1930s* (New York: Alfred A. Knopf, 1984), 84.

17. Harriet Ruth Fox, "Student Life at Barnard," *Columbia University Quarterly* 12 (1910): 183, quoted in Horowitz, *Alma Mater*, 252.

18. Horowitz, *Alma Mater*, 172.

19. Brown University Chattertocks website, http://www.brown.edu/Students/Chattertocks (accessed July 24, 2009).

20. Lucas, *American Higher Education*, 156.

21. Thelin, *A History of American Higher Education*, 98.

22. Lucas, *American Higher Education*, 156. Lucas draws on Mabel Newcomer, *A Century of Higher Education for American Women* (New York: Harper and Brothers, 1959), 46–49. Slightly different figures—0.7 percent in 1870 and 2.2 percent in 1890—are supplied in Barbara Miller Solomon, *In the Company of Educated Women: A History of Women and Higher Education in America* (New Haven: Yale University Press, 1985), 64.

23. Lucas, *American Higher Education*, 228–31. See also Andersen and Snyder, *1989–90 Fact Book on Higher Education* (New York: Macmillan, 1989), 5–9, 133–45; and Thomas D. Snyder et al., *Digest of Educational Statistics, 1993* (Washington, DC: National Center for Educational Statistics, 1993), 172–223.

24. The two remaining Ivy League schools were coeducational much earlier. Cornell University was coed from its founding in 1865 (although female students did not enroll until 1872), while the University of Pennsylvania, founded in 1740, began receiving funds for the education of women in 1883. See Solomon, *In the Company of Educated Women*, 51–54.

25. Ibid., 44. Solomon draws her statistics from Newcomer, *A Century of Higher Education*, 37, and the US Department of Health, Education, and Welfare, National Center for Education Statistics, *Digest of Education Statistics*, 1976 and 1982.

26. The College Board website, http://www.collegeboard.com (accessed January 8, 2010).

27. Also notable is Todd Rundgren's 1985 album, *A Capella*, which, like McFerrin's work, was recorded entirely *a cappella* using extensive multitracking. Unlike McFerrin's recordings, however, *A Capella* makes more liberal use of signal processing devices, which draw attention to the studio-produced quality of the sound. The album reached number 128 on the Billboard Top 200, far below the others mentioned here.

28. Karen W. Arenson, "Songsters Off on a Spree: Campuses Echo with the Sound of Enthusiastic A Cappella Groups," *New York Times*, April 25, 2002, E1, 4.

29. Rapkin, *Pitch Perfect*, 35, 131.

30. Quoted in ibid., 82.

31. Bower, "Sons of Adam," 3.

32. *Contemporary A Cappella Newsletter* 2, no. 2 (December 1991): 15.

33. Richard Nash Gould, *Yale, 1900–2001*, vol. 2: *The Whiffenpoofs: Twentieth Century* (New York: Twentieth Century Project, 2004), 70.

34. *Contemporary A Cappella Newsletter* 2, no. 4 (April 1992): 1.

35. Rockapella, a five-man professional a cappella group, was originally formed by Brown University alumni Elliott Kerman, David Stix (who was soon replaced by Charlie Evett), Sean Altman, and Steve Keyes. The group sings original songs and pop covers, and aside from the *Where In the World Is Carmen Sandiego?* theme, is also known for its jingle for Folger's Coffee. Its first recording, *Primer*, was released independently in 1995.

36. *Contemporary A Cappella Newsletter* 2, no. 4 (April 1992): 13.

37. Anne Raugh and Deke Sharon, *Contemporary A Cappella Songbook*, 2 vols. (Milwaukee, WI: Hal Leonard, 1997). After Voices Music Publishing went out of business, it was published by Contemporary A Cappella Publishing (beginning in 1997) and distributed by Hal Leonard.

38. See Benedict Anderson, *Imagined Communities: Reflections on the Origins and Spread of Nationalism* (London: Verso, 1993).

39. Recorded A Cappella Review Board information page, http://www.rarb.org/what_is_rarb.html (accessed January 30, 2006).

40. Deke Sharon, posted on the RARB forum, March 1, 2004, http://forum.rarb.org/forum/viewtopic.php?t=513 (accessed November 17, 2004); Deke Sharon, posted on the RARB forum, November 16, 2004, http://forum.rarb.org/forum/viewtopic.php?t=1091 (accessed March 1, 2005).

41. The ICCA is not the only a cappella competition. Others include the annual barbershop competitions (such as the Barbershop Harmony Society's Collegiate Barbershop Quartet Contest), as well as the Harmony Sweepstakes, which allows a greater stylistic range from its competitors (unlike the barbershop contests) and therefore attracts professional and semiprofessional contemporary a cappella groups at its shows. The Collegiate Barbershop Quartet Contest was established in 1990, while the Harmony Sweepstakes was first held in Marin County, California, in 1985. Both competitions con-

tinue on a national and, in the case of the barbershop contest, international scale to this day.

42. Arjun Appadurai theorized certain cultural aspects of globalization, proposing that "the imagination has become an organized field of social practices . . . and a form of negotiation between sites of agency (individuals) and globally defined fields of possibility." One way the "field of possibility" may be defined for a cappella musicians, in Appadurai's terms, is through a combination the "technoscape" and the "mediascape." See Appadurai's *Modernity at Large: Cultural Dimensions of Globalization* (Minneapolis: University of Minnesota Press, 1996), 34–35. The Internet lies at this junction, and it is here we find virtual gathering places like the RARB (and others, discussed in chapter 8). "Imagined world" is a play on Anderson's "imagined community" in *Imagined Communities*. The idea of a "virtual community" is also explored in Howard Rheingold, *The Virtual Community: Homesteading on the Electronic Frontier* (Reading, MA: Addison-Wesley, 1993).

43. See Dick Hebdige, *Subculture: The Meaning of Style* (London: Methuen, 1979).

44. Liz Garnett, *The British Barbershopper: A Study in Socio-musical Values* (Burlington, VT: Ashgate, 2005), 58.

45. Gage Averill, *Four Parts, No Waiting: A Social History of American Barberhsop Harmony* (New York: Oxford University Press, 2003), 153–58.

46. Garnett, *The British Barbershopper*, 58.

47. Ibid., 59–62.

Chapter 5

1. The Musical Instrument Digital Interface (MIDI) is a standardized format in which computers and other digital instruments can share musical information.

2. In a cascade, all voices begin in unison, and while the highest voice maintains its pitch, the others descend in succession to their chord tones. A pyramid is a bell chord that builds up from the lowest voice/pitch. See Gage Averill, *Four Parts, No Waiting: A Social History of American Barbershop Harmony* (New York: Oxford University Press, 2003), glossary, 205–10.

3. Personal observation, Harvard University Fallen Angels rehearsal, December 16, 2004.

4. John Potter, *Vocal Authority: Singing Style and Ideology* (New York: Cambridge University Press, 1998), 169.

5. Averill, *Four Parts, No Waiting*, 165.

6. One instance when singers actively sought vibrato was when trying to effect a gospel style. Moreover, soloists do not necessarily need to avoid vibrato when singing a song's lead because it could function as a marker of emotional intensity.

7. Liz Garnett, "Ethics and Aesthetics: The Social Theory of Barbershop Harmony," *Popular Music* 18, no. 1 (1999): 41–61; Stuart L. Goosman, "The Black Atlantic: Structure,

Style, and Values in Group Harmony," *Black Music Research Journal* 17, no. 1 (1997): 81–99; James A. Keene, *A History of Music Education in the United States* (Hanover, NH: University Press of New England, 1982), 308–14.

8. Simon Frith, *Performing Rites: On the Value of Popular Music* (Cambridge: Harvard University Press, 1996), 191.

9. Personal observation, vocal percussion workshop at the Michigan A Cappella Conference, September 9, 2006. Carroll was one of the founding members of Five O'Clock Shadow and later joined the House Jacks. He has produced an instructional video that some groups use: *Mouthdrumming,* vol. 1: *Introduction to Vocal Percussion,* videocassette and DVD, Southwest Harbor, ME, Mainely A Cappella, 1988.

10. Personal observation at Bill Hare's studio (Bill Hare Productions), August 10, 2005.

11. Wes Carroll, "Can Women Do Mouthdrumming?," posted on the CASA website, May 19, 2005, http://www.casa.org (accessed May 19, 2005).

12. Kurt Walker (aka "playdeep"), posted on the RARB forum, November 16, 2005, http://forum.rarb.org/forum/viewtopic.php?t=1634 (accessed May 25, 2005).

13. Personal observation, Brandeis University VoiceMale rehearsal, March 3, 2005.

14. Personal communication (name withheld by request), April 15, 2006.

15. Sara Cohen, "Men Making a Scene: Rock Music and the Production of Gender," in *Sexing the Groove: Popular Music and Gender,* ed. Sheila Whiteley (New York: Routledge, 1997), 17–36.

16. See Steve Chapple and Reebee Garofalo, *Rock 'n' Roll Is Here to Pay* (Chicago: Nelson Hall, 1977), 269; Simon Frith, *Sound Effects: Youth, Leisure, and the Politics of Rock 'n' Roll* (London: Constable, 1983); Susan McClary, *Feminine Endings: Music, Gender, and Sexuality* (Minneapolis: University of Minnesota Press, 1991); Angela McRobbie, "Settling Accounts with Subcultures: A Feminist Critique," *Screen Education* 34 (1980), reprinted in *On Record: Rock, Pop, and the Written Word,* ed. Simon Frith and Andrew Goodwin (New York: Pantheon, 1990), 66–80; and Sue Steward and Sheryl Garratt, *Signed, Sealed, Delivered: True Life Stories of Women in Pop* (Boston: South End Press, 1984).

17. See Mavis Bayton, "Women and the Electric Guitar," in Whiteley, *Sexing the Groove,* 37–49 and others in the same volume; and Sheila Whiteley, *Women and Popular Music: Sexuality, Identity, and Subjectivity* (London: Routledge, 2000).

18. Simon Frith and Angela McRobbie, "Rock and Sexuality," *Screen Education* 29 (1978), reprinted in *On Record: Rock, Pop, and the Written Word,* ed. Simon Frith and Andrew Goodwin (New York: Pantheon, 1990), 371–89 (quote is from p. 375).

19. Social capital may be considered the value necessary to accomplish something within a social group or system, in this case, to become desirable. Pierre Bourdieu defines it as "the aggregate of the actual or potential resources which are linked to . . . membership in a group, which provides each of its members with the backing of the collectively-owned capital" ("The Forms of Capital," in *Handbook of Theory and Research for the Sociology of Education,* ed. John G. Richardson [Westport, CT: Greenwood Press,

1986], 248–49). See also Pierre Bourdieu, *Outline of a Theory of Practice*, trans. Richard Nice (New York: Cambridge University Press, 1977).

20. Mary Ann Clawson, "Masculinity and Skill Acquisition in the Adolescent Rock Band," *Popular Music* 18, no. 1 (1999): 108.

21. David Whitson, "Sport and the Social Construction of Masculinity," in *Sport, Men, and the Gender Order: Critical Feminist Perspectives*, ed. Michael A. Messner and Donald F. Sabo (Champaign, IL: Human Kinetics Books, 1990), 21, 23.

22. See, for example, David Brackett, *Interpreting Popular Music* (Berkeley: University of California Press, 1995), 75–107; Sara Cohen, "Identity, Place, and the 'Liverpool Sound,'" in *Ethnicity, Identity, and Music: The Musical Construction of Place*, ed. Martin Stokes (Oxford: Oxford University Press, 1994), 117–34; Aaron Fox, *Real Country: Music and Language in Working Class Culture* (Durham: Duke University Press, 2004); Simon Frith, "'The Magic That Can Set You Free': The Ideology of Folk and the Myth of the Rock Community," *Popular Music* 1 (1981): 159–68; Allan F. Moore, *Rock: The Primary Text—Developing a Musicology of Rock*, 2nd ed. (Burlington, VT: Ashgate, 2001); Steve Redhead and John Street, "Have I the Right? Legitimacy, Authenticity, and Community in Folk's Politics," *Popular Music* 8, no. 2 (1989): 177–84; and Motti Regev, "Israeli Rock, or a Study in the Politics of 'Local Authenticity,'" *Popular Music* 11, no. 1 (1992): 1–14.

23. Anna Callahan, *Anna's Amazing A Cappella Arranging Advice: The Collegiate A Cappella Arranging Manual* (Southwest Harbor, ME: Contemporary A Cappella Publishing, 1995), 1, 20, 39. *Transanging* is Callahan's term; only once in my fieldwork did an a cappella participant use it.

24. James Harrington, posted on the RARB forum, September 27, 2004, http://forum.rarb.org/forum/viewtopic.php?t=954 (accessed January 29, 2010).

25. For a case study of a cappella's emulative imperative, see Joshua S. Duchan, "'Hide and Seek': A Case of Collegiate A Cappella 'Microcovering,'" in *Play It Again: Cover Songs in Popular Music*, ed. George Plasketes (Burlington, VT: Ashgate, 2010), 191–204.

26. This technique also affects the song's narrative force, as the lead no longer carries the lyrical content alone. Instead, his or her voice is now, in effect, as powerful as the group's combined voices. A powerful example would be "Slumber," by Gabriel Mann, originally performed by the Gabriel Mann Situation, arranged by Stacey Burcham for the coed University of Southern California SoCal VoCals and recorded on *The SoCal Vo-Cals* (2004, also featured on *BOCA 2004*). At approximately 4:07 into the recording, the driving percussion stops just as all the voices join the soloist in singing the song's refrain. This climactic moment leads directly into the final chorus, during which disparate motives from earlier in the song weave in and out of the texture while the overall dynamic relaxes in the approach to the final chord.

27. George Plasketes, "Re-flections on the Cover Age: A Collage of Continuous Coverage in Popular Music," *Popular Music and Society* 28, no. 2 (2005): 150.

28. Robert A. Stebbins, *The Barbershop Singer: Inside the Social World of a Musical Hobby* (Toronto: University of Toronto Press, 1996), 62–72.

29. Ibid.

30. Simon Frith, "Towards an Aesthetic of Popular Music," in *Music and Society: The Politics of Composition, Performance, and Reception,* ed. Richard Leppert and Susan McClary (New York: Cambridge University Press, 1987), 140, 142; R. J. Warren Zanes, "A Fan's Notes: Identification, Desire, and the Haunted Sound Barrier," in *Rock over the Edge: Transformations in Popular Music Culture,* ed. Roger Beebe, Denise Fulbrook, and Ben Saunders (Durham: Duke University Press, 2002), 297.

31. *Oxford English Dictionary,* 2nd ed. (New York: Oxford University Press, 1989–96), s.v. "emulation."

32. David Horn, "Some Thoughts on the Work in Popular Music," in *The Musical Work: Reality or Invention?,* ed. Michael Talbot (Liverpool: Liverpool University Press, 2000), 30; Serge Lacasse, "Intertextuality and Hypertextuality in Recorded Popular Music," in *The Musical Work: Reality or Invention?,* 46.

33. Deena Weinstein, "The History of Rock's Pasts through Rock Covers," in *Mapping the Beat: Popular Music and Contemporary Theory,* ed. Thomas Swiss, John Sloop, and Andrew Herman (Malden, MA: Blackwell, 1988), 138.

34. One exception may be Michael Coyle's work on "hijacking hits," which attends to the racial implications of musical recontextualization ("Hijacked Hits and Antic Authenticity: Cover Songs, Race, and Postwar Marketing," in *Rock over the Edge: Transformations in Popular Music Culture,* ed. Roger Beebe, Denise Fulbrook, and Ben Saunders [Durham: Duke University Press, 2002], 133–57).

Chapter 6

1. See F. Melius Christiansen, *Choir Director's Guide* (Boston: Charles W. Homeyer, 1932; reprint, Minneapolis: Augsburg, 1940); Archibald T. Davison, *Choral Conducting* (Cambridge: Harvard University Press, 1940); Harold A. Decker and Julius Herford, *Choral Conducting: A Symposium* (Englewood Cliffs, NJ: Prentice Hall, 1973); Colin Durrant, *Choral Conducting: Philosophy and Practice* (New York: Routledge, 2003); Robert Garretson, *Conducting Choral Music* (Boston: Allyn and Bacon, 1961; reprinted in 1965, 1970, 1975, and 1981; reprinted by Prentice Hall in 1986, 1988, 1993, and 1998); Imogen Holst, *Conducting a Choir: A Guide for Amateurs* (New York: Oxford University Press, 1973; reprinted in 1990, 1993, 1995, 2000, and 2002); Daniel Moe, *Basic Choral Concepts* (Minneapolis: Augsburg, 1972); Donald Neuen, *Choral Concepts* (Bellmont, CA: Wadsworth, 2002); Brenda Smith and Robert T. Sataloff, *Choral Pedagogy* (San Diego: Singular, 1999; reprint, San Diego: Plural, 2006); and Frederick William Wodell, *Choir and Chorus Conducting: A Treatise on the Organization, Management, Training, and Conducting of Choirs, Choral Societies, and Other Vocal Ensembles* (Philadelphia: Theodore Presser, 1901; reprinted in 1905, 1909, 1919, and 1931).

2. Richard Schechner, "Toward a Poetics of Performance," in *Performance Theory* (New York: Routledge, 1988), 183. Ellen Koskoff observes that "in the Western classical tradition, a rehearsal is understood to be a structured event . . . in preparation for performance" and distinguishes rehearsal, which is "often controlled by relationships be-

tween and among people with varying degrees of ability, power, and status," from practice, which is done alone and during which all action is controlled by the individual musician ("Cognitive Strategies in Rehearsal," in *Selected Reports in Ethnomusicology*, vol. 7
[Los Angeles: Department of Ethnomusicology, University of California, Los Angeles,
1988], 59). See also H. Stith Bennett, *On Becoming a Rock Musician* (Amherst: University
of Massachusetts Press, 1980); Ruth Finnegan, *The Hidden Musicians: Music-Making in
an English Town* (Cambridge: Cambridge University Press, 1989); and Leslie C. Gay,
"Commitment, Cohesion, and Creative Process: A Study of New York City Rock Bands,"
PhD diss., Columbia University, 1991.

3. Carol E. Robertson, "Power and Gender in the Musical Experiences of Women," in
Women and Music in Cross-Cultural Perspective, ed. Ellen Koskoff (Westport, CT: Greenwood Press, 1987), 225–44. See also Johannes Fabian, *Power and Performance: Ethnographic Explorations through Proverbial Wisdom and Theater in Shaba, Zaire* (Madison:
University of Wisconsin Press, 1990); and Henry Kingsbury, *Music, Talent, and Performance: A Conservatory Cultural System* (Philadelphia: Temple University Press, 1988), 48,
85–110.

4. While Koskoff's study of rehearsals also examines an educational setting, it considers a percussion ensemble composed of adolescent males in a summer music camp,
as opposed to collegiate a cappella's context of higher education during the regular academic year ("Cognitive Strategies in Rehearsal").

5. The description provided here is a synthesis of Fallen Angels rehearsals meant to
represent some of the typical events that would occur in such a rehearsal. The material
is drawn from ethnographic observations and field recordings throughout the 2004–5
academic year, so certain inconsistencies do arise, such as the conflation of two separate
terms of group leadership. Details of most specific events come from rehearsals held on
February 28 and March 5, 2005.

6. Seventeen percent of Harvard College students were of Asian decent (in the Fallen
Angels, 16 percent), 8 percent were black (in the Fallen Angels, 8 percent), and 9 percent
were classified as "unknown/other" (in the Fallen Angels, 8 percent). Data on Harvard
College enrollment comes from the *Harvard University Fact Book, 2004–2005* (Cambridge: Office of Budgets, Financial Planning, and Institutional Research, Harvard University, 2005), 9.

7. Danielle, Fallen Angels president in the fall of 2005, was hesitant to describe the
Radcliffe Pitches as her group's rival and suggested that, due to their different repertories and a wide enough campus audience, there was room for both groups at Harvard.
"We're not trying to compete with the Pitches," she maintained, "or fill their niche." Yet
I also got the distinct impression that some of the Fallen Angels saw their group's relationship with the Pitches in competitive terms, a view that was exacerbated at the beginning of the academic year, when new members were auditioned and inducted.

8. The Sanders Theatre at Harvard University, modeled on the Sheldonian Theatre in
Oxford, England, is a historically significant venue, having hosted distinguished speakers such as Winston Churchill, Theodore Roosevelt, and Martin Luther King. In addi-

tion to being home to numerous undergraduate performance ensembles at Harvard, it is also occasionally used by professional ensembles, including the Boston Philharmonic. It is considered the most prestigious performance space on the Harvard campus. By limiting access to this venue, campus officials ensure its efficient use.

9. Group priorities have been a matter of debate within the Fallen Angels. Alyson, a founding member, told me, "It was really hard sometimes for people to be like, 'the whole point of this group is *not* to be like those other groups. The reason why we *love* what we do is because we're *not* killing ourselves and we're *not* slaving away, and we *like* each other. That's what's cool about our group!' And then there were people saying, 'yeah, but I want to sing in [the] Sanders [Theatre]. And that is my goal. And if that means that not every rehearsal is fun for you, then tough luck.' And that was this very big pull, and I think that still exists."

10. Directors Debra and Anne also echoed the Fallen Angels' perceived lack of accomplishment. Both said they would like to see this circumstance changed through the group's future application to the International Championship of Collegiate A Cappella and submission of tracks to the *Best of College A Cappella.*

11. Victor Turner, *The Ritual Process: Structure and Anti-Structure* (Chicago: Aldine, 1969).

12. Helen Lefkowitz Horowitz, *Campus Life: Undergraduate Cultures from the End of the Eighteenth Century to the Present* (New York: Alfred A. Knopf, 1987); Anne Matthews, *Bright College Years: Inside the American Campus Today* (New York: Simon and Schuster, 1997); Michael Moffatt, *Coming of Age in New Jersey: College and American Culture* (New Brunswick, NJ: Rutgers University Press, 1989).

13. David A. Karp, Lynda Lytle Holmstrom, and Paul S. Gray, "Leaving Home for College: Expectations for Selective Reconstruction of Self," *Symbolic Interaction* 21, no. 3 (1998): 253–76.

14. I mean here to invoke an understanding of "performance" that covers not only concerts, gigs, and other marked occasions of public music making but also the actions of individuals in less formalized and everyday environments. As Erving Goffman defines it, performance is "all the activity of a given participant on a given occasion which serves to influence in any way any of the other participants" (*The Presentation of Self in Everyday Life* [Woodstock, NY: Overlook Press, 1973], 15). It effects and affects social relationships, constituting "a forum for reconfiguring social relations" on any level, from the local to the national (Kelly Askew, *Performing the Nation: Swahili Music and Cultural Politics in Tanzania* [Chicago: University of Chicago Press, 2002], 23).

15. Anthony Giddens, *The Constitution of Society: Outline of the Theory of Structuration* (Cambridge: Polity, 1984), 64.

16. Deborah Tannen, *You Just Don't Understand: Women and Men in Conversation* (New York: William Morrow, 1990), 25, 53.

17. Mary Ann Clawson, "Masculinity and Skill Acquisition in the Adolescent Rock Band," *Popular Music* 18, no. 1 (1999): 108.

18. Gay, "Commitment, Cohesion, and Creative Process."

19. Gregory Barz, "'We Are from Different Ethnic Groups, but We Live Here as One Family': The Musical Performance of Community in a Tanzanian *Kwaya*," in *Chorus and Community*, ed. Karen Alhquist (Urbana: University of Illinois Press, 2006), 27.

20. Tannen, *You Just Don't Understand*, 85.

21. Ingrid Monson, *Saying Something: Jazz Improvisation and Interaction* (Chicago: University of Chicago Press, 1996), 174.

22. While my observations and Tannen's research suggest a connection between explicit, verbalized social support and women's a cappella, it is also clear that certain musical aspects of a cappella practice are closely linked to masculinity. The history of higher education is male dominated, at least until the twentieth century, so historical and cultural concepts of close harmony already contain a strong male character through ideas of "college men" (see Horowitz, *Campus Life*) and men's glee clubs (see chapter 1). Barbershop quartets were similar loci of masculinity, participating in a "search for lost male community" in the early twentieth century through the elimination of "musical practices that had previously allowed singers to separate physically" and the association of the singing style "with social spaces that had come to symbolize physical closeness and camaraderie between men: the saloon, the barbershop, and the gang" (Richard Mook, "The Sounds of Liberty: Nostalgia, Masculinity, and Whiteness in Philadelphia Barbershop, 1900–2003," PhD diss., University of Pennsylvania, 2004, 111). The continuing power and potency of such history persist in the prevalence of men's collegiate groups, which are usually the first to be formed on a campus (followed by women's and mixed ensembles) and which, based on my observations, continue to receive adoration from many undergraduate women.

23. Clawson, "Masculinity and Skill Acquisition," 104. See also Finnegan, *The Hidden Musicians*, 260.

24. Personal observation, Dicks and Janes rehearsal, April 2, 2003.

25. Koskoff, "Cognitive Strategies in Rehearsal," 62.

26. For theories and definitions of blend, see Stuart L. Goosman, "The Black Atlantic: Structure, Style, and Values in Group Harmony," *Black Music Research Journal* 17, no. 1 (1997): 88; and Neuen, *Choral Concepts*, 27. On blend in barbershop, see Gage Averill, *Four Parts, No Waiting: A Social History of American Barbershop Harmony* (New York: Oxford University Press, 2003); and Liz Garnett, *The British Barbershopper: A Study in Socio-musical Values* (Burlington, VT: Ashgate, 2005).

27. Charles Keil, "Participatory Discrepancies and the Power of Music," *Cultural Anthropology* 2, no. 3 (1987): 275–83.

28. Pierre Bourdieu, *Outline of a Theory of Practice*, trans. Richard Nice (New York: Cambridge University Press, 1977), 78–82; *Distinction: A Social Critique of the Judgment of Taste*, trans. Richard Nice (Cambridge: Harvard University Press, 1984), 2.

29. Judith Becker, *Deep Listeners: Music, Emotion, and Trancing* (Bloomington: Indiana University Press, 2004), 71.

30. Benjamin Brinner's definition of *experience* is useful here: "the product of age, education, and association. In other words, a musician has the potential to enlarge his or her

musical knowledge and ability through contact with others over time and the exact 'shape' of that competence will be influenced by the other musicians with whom he or she has contact . . . It will also be affected by the musician's ability and desire to hear and respond to what others do" (*Knowing Music, Making Music: Javanese Gamelan and the Theory of Musical Competence and Interaction* [Chicago: University of Chicago Press, 1995], 75).

31. Jason Toynbee introduces the concept of "likelihood" to accompany Bourdieu's ideas. This new parameter indicates the selection of artistic possibilities, noting that "creators" are more likely to choose certain possibilities over others. Possibilities in accord with style and genre conventions are more likely to be chosen in any creative act than those less strongly suggested by the creator's habitus (*Making Popular Music: Musicians, Creativity, and Institutions* [London: Arnold, 2000], 39).

32. Brinner, *Knowing Music, Making Music,* 3–4, 28, 35.

33. See Bourdieu, *Distinction;* Pierre Bourdieu and Loïc J. D. Wacquant, *An Invitation to Reflexive Sociology* (Chicago: University of Chicago Press, 1992), 97; and David Swartz, *Culture and Power: The Sociology of Pierre Bourdieu* (Chicago: University of Chicago Press, 1997), 117–42.

34. For example, in his review of the University of Pennsylvania Off the Beat's album *Burn Like a Roman Candle* (2004), Jevan Soo writes, "Off the Beat fans will find more of the same they've always loved. High-octane arrangements of tough alternative songs that almost no [one] else will tackle, sung with grit and energy and produced within an inch of their lives." Yet Soo concludes by commenting on the group's music director's legacy, even indicating the year when the director will graduate, thus acknowledging the potential for stylistic change: "I have a lot of respect for Ethan Fixell '04, who I understand has shaped the musical direction of OTB quite a bit over the past few years. But keep in mind this respect is tempered by the fact that I don't actually like said direction so much. This reviewer (and the listening world more broadly) will wait with interest to see where OTB heads next" (Review of the University of Pennsylvania Off the Beat, *Burn Like a Roman Candle* [2004], February 6, 2005, Recorded A Cappella Review Board, http://www.rarb.org/reviews/513.html, accessed January 9, 2007).

35. At the time of this writing, Off the Beat has been selected for all but two of the fifteen annual *Best of College A Cappella* compilations and also won Contemporary A Cappella Recording awards in at least one category every year between 1996 and 2006 (except 2001 and 2004). Data for the winners in 1993–96 are not available.

36. Monson, *Saying Something,* 97, 127–28.

37. Fabian, *Power and Performance,* 13.

38. Koskoff, "Cognitive Strategies in Rehearsal," 64.

Chapter 7

1. Description based on author's field notes, November 10, 2004.

2. On ceremonial gigs, see H. Stith Bennett, *On Becoming a Rock Musician* (Amherst: University of Massachusetts Press, 1980), 84–97.

3. On social gigs, see ibid.

4. These cues might be considered in terms of what Benjamin Brinner calls an "interactive system" (*Knowing Music, Making Music: Javanese Gamelan and the Theory of Musical Competence and Interaction* [Chicago: University of Chicago Press, 1995], 183–85).

5. At the time of my fieldwork, Brandeis University hosted thirteen a cappella groups for a total student population of about three thousand. By comparison, at the same time, the University of Michigan's Ann Arbor campus had the same number of groups for approximately ten times the undergraduate student body. One member of the Brandeis a cappella scene, who also served as a campus tour guide, claimed that Brandeis had the highest percentage of a cappella groups per capita of any college or university.

6. Personal observation, VoiceMale performance, November 10, 2004. *Aca-terrorism* is a conflation of *a cappella* and *terrorism*.

7. Simon Frith, *Performing Rites: On the Value of Popular Music* (Cambridge: Harvard University Press, 1996), 212.

8. Ibid., 211.

9. See Charlie Gillett, *The Sound of the City: The Rise of Rock and Roll* (New York: Da Capo, 1970), 14, 17, 51, 254; and Jim Miller, ed., *The Rolling Stone Illustrated History of Rock & Roll* (New York: Random House and Rolling Stone Press, 1980), 11, 12, 19, 61, 177, 329, 390–91, 456. See also Richard Crawford, *America's Musical Life: A History* (New York: W. W. Norton, 2001), 733–34; Roy Shuker, *Understanding Popular Music*, 2nd ed. (New York: Routledge, 2001), 177, 220; and Peter Wicke, *Rock Music: Culture, Aesthetics, and Sociology*, trans. Rachel Fogg (New York: Cambridge University Press, 1987), 44–45.

10. Reebee Garofalo, *Rockin' Out: Popular Music in the USA* (Boston: Allyn and Bacon, 1997), 132.

11. Doon Arbus, "James Brown Is Out of Sight," *New York Herald Tribune*, March 20, 1966, reprinted in *The James Brown Reader: Fifty Years of Writing about the Godfather of Soul*, ed. Nelson George and Alan Leeds (New York: Plume, 2008), 27, 30.

12. Frith, *Performing Rites*, 124.

13. Barry Shank, *Dissonant Identities: The Rock 'n' Roll Scene in Austin, Texas* (Hanover, NH: Wesleyan University Press, 1994), 125.

14. Jason Toynbee, *Making Popular Music: Musicians, Creativity, and Institutions* (London: Arnold, 2000), 56–65.

15. Frith, *Performing Rites*, 207.

16. Paul Ekman, "Biological and Cultural Contributions to Body and Facial Movement," in *The Anthropology of the Body*, ed. John Blacking (London: Academic Press, 1977), 40. Ekman draws the term from David Efron, *Gesture and Environment: A Tentative Study of Some of the Spacio-temporal and "Linguistic" Aspects of Gestural Behavior of Eastern Jews and Southern Italians in New York City Living under Similar as Well as Different Environmental Conditions* (New York: King's Crown, 1941).

17. Theodore Gracyk, *Rhythm and Noise: An Aesthetics of Rock* (Durham: Duke University Press, 1996), 38.

18. David R. Shumway, "Performance," in *Key Terms in Popular Music and Culture*, ed. Bruce Horner and Thomas Swiss (Malden, MA: Blackwell, 1999), 193.

19. John Blacking, "Towards an Anthropology of the Body," in *The Anthropology of the Body*, ed. John Blacking (London: Academic Press, 1977), 7–13.

20. Allison McCracken, " 'God's Gift to Us Girls': Crooning, Gender, and the Re-creation of American Popular Song, 1928–1933," *American Music* 17, no. 4 (1999): 365–95.

21. E. Ann Kaplan, *Rocking around the Clock: Music Television, Postmodernism, and Consumer Culture* (New York: Methuen, 1987), 1, 58–88.

22. Julie Moffitt, "Competition Ethics (What We Can Learn from Pick-Up Artists)," posted on the Contemporary A Cappella Society of America website, July 12, 2006, http://www.casa.org (accessed July 13, 2006).

23. Despite the visibility of *The Sing-Off* on NBC, the ICCA involves a greater number of singers over a longer season.

24. Sylvia Nannyonga-Tamusuza, "Competitions in School Festivals: A Process of Reinventing *Baakisimba* Music and Dance of the Baganda (Uganda)," *The World of Music* 45, no. 1 (2003): 97–118; Frank Gunderson, "Preface," *The World of Music* 45, no. 1 (2003): 7; Sean Williams, "Competing against 'Tradition' in the Sudanese Performing Arts," *The World of Music* 45, no. 1 (2003): 79–96.

25. Joseph Horowitz, *The Ivory Trade: Music and the Business of Music at the Van Cliburn International Piano Competition* (New York: Summit Books, 1990), 131.

26. According to the guidelines, under the heading "Interpretation," judges should ask themselves, "Is the performance true to the style of the arrangement? . . . Is the interpretation of the arrangement musically, lyrically and rhythmically interesting? Does it work in a live a cappella format? Does it convey appropriate emotion? (Please note: Do not compare the group against the professional groups they cover. Avoid preconceived ideas of how the music 'should' be performed.)" (ICCA Group Adjudication Sheet, 2004–5 season, p. 3).

27. The influence of judging criteria is also explored in Shannon Dudley, "Creativity and Control in Trinidad Carnival Competitions," *The World of Music* 45, no. 1 (2003): 34; and Liz Garnett, *The British Barbershopper: A Study in Socio-musical Values* (Burlington, VT: Ashgate, 2005), 59–64.

28. ICCA Group Adjudication Sheet, 2004–5 season, p. 4.

29. saveit, posted on the RARB forum, January 30, 2005, http://forum.rarb.org/forum/viewtopic.php?t=1282 (accessed February 1, 2005).

30. Brendan Jennings, posted on RARB forum, February 1, 2005, http://forum.rarb.org/forum/viewtopic.php?t=1282 (accessed February 1, 2005).

31. See Melinda Russell, " 'Putting Decatur on the Map': Choral Music and Community in an Illinois City," in *Chorus and Community*, ed. Karen Ahlquist (Urbana: University of Illinois Press, 2006), 50, 59–62.

32. Jim Diego, "To showchoir . . . or not to showchoir. Well, a cappella ain't showchoir . . . K?," posted on the Contemporary A Cappella Society of America website, April 15, 2010, http://www.casa.org (accessed June 1, 2010).

33. Joanne Gilbert, *Performing Marginality: Humor, Gender, and Cultural Critique* (Detroit: Wayne State University Press, 2004), 12, 158–9.

34. Dudley, "Creativity and Control in Trinidad Carnival Competitions," 21. A brief survey of scholarship on music competitions indicates that most, though not all, are adjudicated affairs. Genres whose adjudicated competitions have received major attention from scholars include piano competitions (e.g., Horowitz, *The Ivory Trade*), various African traditions (e.g., Veit Erlmann, *Nightsong: Performance, Power, and Practice in South Africa* [Chicago: University of Chicago Press, 1996], and Frank Gunderson and Gregory Barz, eds., *Mashindano! Competitive Music Performance in Tanzania* [Dar es Salaam: Mkuki wa Nyota Press, 2000]), Koranic recitation in the Muslim world (e.g., Lois al Faruqi, "Qur'an Reciters in Competition in Kuala Lumpur," *Ethnomusicology* 31, no. 2 [1987]: 221–28, and Anne K. Rasmussen, "The Qur'an in Indonesian Daily Life: The Public Project of Musical Oratory," *Ethnomusicology* 45, no. 1 [2001]: 30–57), and, in the United States, fiddle contests (e.g., Chris Goertzen, "George Cecil McLeod, Mississippi's Fiddling Senator, and the Modern History of American Fiddling," *American Music* 22, no. 3 [2004]: 339–379), and brass band competitions (e.g., Trevor Herbert, *Bands: The Brass Band Movement in the 19th and 20th Centuries* [Philadelphia: Open University Press, 1991]). Barbershop harmony competitions receive some attention in Gage Averill, *Four Parts, No Waiting: A Social History of American Barbershop Harmony* (New York: Oxford University Press, 2003); and Garnett, *The British Barbershopper.* An example of nonadjudicated competition can be found in the *despiques* of Portuguese *bandas filharmonicas* (e.g., Kate Brucher, "A Banda da Terra: Bandas Filarmónicas and the Performance of Place in Portugal," PhD diss., University of Michigan, 2005).

35. "A Cappella Group Wins Championship," *University Record* (University of Michigan), May 6, 2002.

36. For more on Alice Tully, see Albert Fuller, *Alice Tully: An Intimate Portrait* (Urbana: University of Illinois Press, 1999).

37. Benjamin Stevens, posted on the RARB forum, April 19, 2009, http://forum.rarb.org/forum/viewtopic.php?t=5285 (accessed April 19, 2009).

38. Adune, posted on the RARB forum, April 19, 2009, http://forum.rarb.org/forum/viewtopic.php?t=5285 (accessed April 19, 2009).

39. Dave Grossman, posted on the RARB forum, April 19, 2009, http://forum.rarb.org/forum/viewtopic.php?t=5285 (accessed April 19, 2009).

40. Adune, posted on the RARB forum, April 19, 2009, http://forum.rarb.org/forum/viewtopic.php?t=5285 (accessed April 19, 2009).

41. bsw24, posted on the RARB forum, April 19, 2009, http://forum.rarb.org/forum/viewtopic.php?t=5285 (accessed April 19, 2009).

42. Adune, posted on the RARB forum, April 19, 2009, http://forum.rarb.org/forum/viewtopic.php?t=5285 (accessed April 19, 2009).

43. Benjamin Stevens, posted on the RARB forum, April 19, 2009, http://forum.rarb
.org/forum/viewtopic.php?t=5285 (accessed April 19, 2009).

44. See, for example, Dorothy C. Holland and Margaret A. Eisenhart, *Educated in Romance: Women, Achievement, and College Culture* (Chicago: University of Chicago Press,
1990).

45. "Things I'll Never Say," by Avril Lavigne and Matrix, originally recorded by Avril
Lavigne on *Let Go*, Arista 14740, 2002.

46. Richard Mook, "The Sounds of Liberty: Nostalgia, Masculinity, and Whiteness in
Philadelphia Barbershop, 1900–2003," PhD diss., University of Pennsylvania, 2004,
91–135. Mook draws on George Chauncey, *Gay New York* (New York: Basic Books, 1994).

47. Ramsay Burt, *The Male Dancer: Bodies, Spectacle, Sexualities* (London: Routledge,
1995), 1, 22–23. While Burt maintains a distinction between "theatre" and "social" dance
(2), I would argue that the choreography in a cappella qualifies as theater dance because
of the purposeful, staged nature of its performance.

48. Philip Matier and Andrew Ross, "New Year's Nightmare for Visiting Yale Singers,"
San Francisco Chronicle, January 10, 2007, B1; Philip Matier and Andrew Ross,
"Firestorm over Yale Attack," *San Francisco Chronicle*, January 14, 2007, A1.

49. Simon Frith and Angela McRobbie, "Rock and Sexuality," in *On Record: Rock,
Pop, and the Written Word*, ed. Simon Frith and Andrew Goodwin (New York: Pantheon,
1998), 374.

50. Michael Moffatt, *Coming of Age in New Jersey: College and American Culture* (New
Brunswick, NJ: Rutgers University Press, 1989), 46. The concept of frames comes from
Erving Goffman, *Frame Analysis: An Essay on the Organization of Experience* (Cam-
bridge: Harvard University Press, 1974).

51. Sheryl Garratt, "Teenage Dreams," in *On Record: Rock, Pop, and the Written Word*,
ed. Simon Frith and Andrew Goodwin (New York: Pantheon, 1998), 402.

52. Author's field notes, 2005 ICCA finals, April 30, 2005.

53. Gilbert, *Performing Marginality*, 26.

54. Barbara Levy, *Ladies Laughing: Wit as Control in Contemporary American Women
Writers* (Amsterdam: Gordon and Breach, 1997), cited in Gilbert, *Performing Marginality*, 34.

55. Garnett, *The British Barbershopper*, 50.

56. Toynbee, *Making Popular Music*, 39.

57. Moffitt, "Competition Ethics."

Chapter 8

1. See Paul D. Greene and Thomas Porcello, *Wired for Sound: Engineering and Technologies in Sonic Cultures* (Middletown, CT: Wesleyan University Press, 2005); Mark
Katz, *Capturing Sound: How Technology Has Changed Music* (Berkeley: University of
California Press, 2005); René T. A. Lysloff and Leslie C. Gay Jr., eds., *Music and Technoculture* (Middletown, CT: Wesleyan University Press, 2003); and Louise Meintjes, *Sound*

of Africa! Making Music Zulu in a South African Studio (Durham: Duke University Press, 2003).

2. Timothy D. Taylor, *Strange Sounds: Music, Technology, and Culture* (New York: Routledge, 2001), 3.

3. Katz, *Capturing Sound,* 160–64.

4. The legality of such "P2P" (peer-to-peer) file-sharing services is the subject of much discussion; see ibid., 175–87. For other scholarship on Napster and file sharing, see Randal Doane, "Digital Desire in the Daydream Machine," *Sociological Theory* 24, no. 2 (2006): 150–69; and Markus Giesley, "Cybernetic Gift Giving and Social Drama: A Netnography of the Napster File-Sharing Community," in *Cybersounds: Essays on Virtual Music Culture,* ed. Michael D. Ayers (New York: Peter Lang Publishing, 2006), 21–56.

5. John Blacking, "Towards an Anthropology of the Body," in *The Anthropology of the Body,* ed. John Blacking (London: Academic Press, 1977), 7–13.

6. In this sense, computers are used as tools, which, in Marshall McLuhan's formulation, are technologies that extend human capacity. See Marshall McLuhan, *Understanding Media: The Extensions of Man* (London: Sphere Books, 1964). See also Andrew R. Brown, *Computers in Music Education: Amplifying Musicality* (New York: Routledge, 2007), 60–62.

7. Deke Sharon, "Contemporary A Cappella Arranging in 10 Steps" (n.p., 2000).

8. Anna Callahan, *Anna's Amazing A Cappella Arranging Advice: The Collegiate A Cappella Arranging Manual* (Southwest Harbor, ME: Contemporary A Cappella Publishing), 1995.

9. John Colton, posted on the RARB forum, August 29, 2009, http://forum.rarb.org/forum/viewtopic.php?t=5523 (accessed September 2, 2009).

10. Liz Garnett, *The British Barbershopper: A Study in Socio-musical Values* (Burlington, VT: Ashgate, 2005), 33.

11. Michael R. Miller, posted on the RARB forum, August 29, 2009, http:// forum.rarb .org/forum/viewtopic.php?t=5523 (accessed September 2, 2009).

12. This account is drawn from my field notes, April 2, 2005.

13. This episode points to the campus-based a cappella subcultures, inasmuch as similar norms exist across multiple groups on particular college and university campuses (see Dick Hebdige, *Subculture: The Meaning of Style* [London: Methuen, 1979]). At the University of Pennsylvania, for example, the use of microphones and stands might be considered an important part of performance norms within that subculture, although this is clearly not the case at Brandeis. A case might be made for physical formations onstage, although my experience with groups from across the country suggests that the arc formation is standard. Some of the singers I spoke with also believed that particular schools had distinctive styles of a cappella singing and arranging, particularly with regard to syllable choices.

14. See, for example, the Tufts University Beelzebubs' website, http://www.bubs.com, and the Yale University Whiffenpoofs' website, http://www.whiffenpoofs.com.

15. A-Cappella.com can be accessed at http://www.a-cappella.com, and AcaTunes can be found at http://www.acatunes.com.

16. For examples of these discussions, see Bill Hare, posted on the RARB forum, April 30, 2004, http://forum.rarb.org/forum/viewtopic.php?t=697 (accessed December 30, 2009); Mahka, posted on the RARB forum, January 17, 2005, http://forum.rarb.org/forum/viewtopic.php?t=1241 (accessed December 30, 2009); Sahjah-pah, posted on the RARB forum, July 28, 2005, http://forum.rarb.org/ forum/viewtopic.php?t=1789 (accessed December 30, 2009); Cooper Cerulo, posted on the RARB forum, December 10, 2005, http://forum.rarb.org/ forum/ viewtopic .php?t=2038 (accessed December 30, 2009); Daniel Herriges, posted on the RARB forum, June 4, 2006, http://forum .rarb.org/forum/ viewtopic .php?t=2519 (accessed December 30, 2009); Chris Ng, posted on the RARB forum, January 25, 2008, http://forum.rarb.org/ forum/viewtopic.php?t= 4181 (accessed December 30, 2009); James Cannon, posted on the RARB forum, April 18, 2008, http://forum.rarb.org/forum/ viewtopic .php?t=4455 (accessed December 30, 2009); and Daniel Herriges, posted on the RARB forum, August 13, 2009, http://forum.rarb.org/forum/viewtopic.php?t =5511 (accessed December 30, 2009).

17. Mark Manley, RARB review of Brandeis University Starving Artists, *Honestly* (2004), October 26, 2004, http://www.rarb.org/reviews/487.html (accessed January 9, 2007).

18. Thomas Porcello, "Sonic Artistry: Music, Discourse, and Technology in the Sound Recording Studio," PhD diss., University of Texas at Austin, 1996, 129–31.

19. See, for example, Robert Burnett, *The Global Jukebox: The International Music Industry* (New York: Routledge, 1996); Steve Chapple and Reebee Garofalo, *Rock 'n' Roll Is Here to Pay: The History and Politics of the Music Industry* (Chicago: Nelson-Hall, 1977); Simon Frith, *Sound Effects: Youth, Leisure, and the Politics of Rock 'n' Roll* (London: Constable, 1983); Charlie Gillett, *Making Tracks: Atlantic Records and the Growth of a Multi-Billion-Dollar Industry* (New York: E. P. Dutton, 1974); Charlie Gillett, *The Sound of the City: The Rise of Rock and Roll* (New York: Da Capo, 1996); Keith Negus, *Producing Pop: Culture and Conflict in the Popular Music Industry* (New York: E. Arnold, 1992); and Timothy D. Taylor, *Global Pop: World Music, World Markets* (New York: Routledge, 1997).

20. Matt Cohen, RARB review of the University of Pennsylvania Counterparts, *Ten* (2001), December 14, 2001, http://www.rarb.org/reviews/268.html (accessed December 31, 2009).

21. Bill Hare, posted on the RARB, December 29, 2009, http://forum.rarb.org/ forum/viewtopic.php?t=5831 (accessed December 30, 2009).

22. At times, singers would go so far as to verbally devalue their group's prior albums. In some cases, even if he or she was part of the album's creation, a singer would devalue albums in an apparent effort to promote current or future recording projects. This may be read as a reproduction of a familiar narrative trope in popular music: "My new material is much better than that old stuff!"

23. Personal observation, University of Michigan Harmonettes recording session, July 25, 2006.

24. See, for example, Dave Trendler, RARB review of University of Wisconsin–Madison MadHatters, *Friday After Class* (2005), September 10, 2005, http://www.rarb.org/reviews/563.html (accessed January 25, 2007). Trendler writes, "[T]he rhythmic clunkiness, awkward moments, and largely uninspiring arrangements, combined with the live recording of *Ave Maria* (yes, the same one you sang with your mediocre college men's group), smacks of a young group recording a yearbook album. As is usually the case with yearbook albums, relegate *Friday After Class* to family, friends—oh, and the Queen of Hearts' guillotine."

25. According Richard Nash Gould (*Yale, 1900–2001*, vol. 2: *The Whiffenpoofs: Twentieth Century* [New York: Twentieth Century Project, 2004], 83–128), and the Whiffenpoofs website, http://www.whiffenpoofs.com (accessed February 3, 2010), the group has recorded eighty albums, dating from 1915 to 2010. It has recorded an album each year since 1949.

26. Porcello, "Sonic Artistry," 60, emphasis in the original.

27. Ibid.

28. Paul Théberge, "The 'Sound' of Music: Technological Rationalization and the Production of Popular Music," *New Formations* 8 (summer 1989): 107.

29. Porcello, "Sonic Artistry," 61; Théberge, "The 'Sound' of Music," 105.

30. Dylan Bell, "Dylan Bell Blog: Shiny, Happy Robots," posted on the CASA website, June 11, 2010, http://www.casa.org (accessed June 12, 2010).

31. GangstaisCold, posted on the RARB forum, April 16, 2006, http://forum.rarb.org/viewtopic.php?t=2373 (accessed April 20, 2006).

32. WareHauser, posted on the RARB forum, April 16, 2006, http://forum.rarb.org/viewtopic.php?t=2373 (accessed April 20, 2006).

33. Mike DeLaura [Doc], posted on the RARB forum, April 16, 2006, http://forum.rarb.org/viewtopic.php?t=2373 (accessed April 20, 2006).

34. Bill Hare, posted on the RARB forum, April 16, 2006, http://forum.rarb.org/viewtopic.php?t=2373 (accessed April 20, 2006). He also referred to an article he wrote for the CASA, "Recording VP? You'll Be Sorry You Asked!," Contemporary A Cappella Society website, December 12, 2005, http://www.casa.org (accessed December 28, 2006), in which he suggested excerpting the best two- or four-measure portion out of a full take of vocal percussion and simply copying and pasting, or looping, that excerpt throughout the song.

35. Charles Keil, "Participatory Discrepancies and the Power of Music," *Cultural Anthropology* 2, no. 3 (1987): 275–83.

36. See Olavo Alén, "Rhythm as Duration of Sounds in Tumba Francesa," and J. A. Prögler, "Searching for Swing: Participatory Discrepancies in the Jazz Rhythm Section," both in a special issue of *Ethnomusicology* (39, no. 1 [1995]: 55–71 and 21–54, respectively) devoted to the theory.

Chapter 9

1. Thomas Porcello defines *mixing* as "the process of taking the individual tracks that comprise the multitrack master, performing any desired signal processing on them, assigning them spatial properties within the sound stage of the recording, and combining them with the sounds on the other tracks to form a composite stereo image" ("Sonic Artistry: Music, Discourse, and Technology in the Sound Recording Studio," PhD diss., University of Texas at Austin, 1996, 316).

2. Deke Sharon, posted on the RARB forum, November 16, 2004, http:// forum.rarb .org/forum/viewtopic.php?t=1091 (accessed March 1, 2005): "Truth is, we don't pick *BOCA* tracks for the people on [the RARB forum]. You guys already have many of the CDs, and frankly have quite strong opinions as to what you value." See also the discussion thread: "CARA's, BOCA, etc. . . ," May 2008, http://forum.rarb.org/forum/view-topic.php?t=4532 (accessed February 3, 2010); and Deke Sharon and Don Gooding, personal correspondence, July 14, 2008. "As a back-of-the-envelope estimate, let's say each *BOCA* CD has sold 5,000 copies," Gooding writes. About 5 percent, or 50, of the 1,000 of those that are sold through the groups whose tracks appear on the album go to "outsiders"; 70 percent, or 420, of the 600 that are sold through online retailers like Amazon.com and CD Baby go to outsiders; and approximately 5 percent, or 160, of the 3,200 sold through the a-cappella.com catalog and website (until recently owned by Gooding) go to outsiders, for a total of 630—about 13 percent of 5,000. About 3,000 full *BOCA* albums (with 19 tracks each) and 32,000 individual tracks were legally downloaded in 2007, for a total of 89,000 tracks, according to Gooding. About 60 percent of those, or about 53,400 tracks, went to outsiders.

3. See the RARB forum discussion threads "BOCA 2006 thoughts?" October–November 2005, http://forum.rarb.org/forum/viewtopic.php?t=1925 (accessed February 3, 2010); "BOCA '07?," October–November 2006, http://forum.rarb.org/forum/view-topic.php?t=2777 (accessed February 3, 2010); and "BOCA 2008 submissions," September–November, 2007, http://forum.rarb.org/forum/viewtopic.php?t=3829 (accessed February 3, 2010).

4. For example, see Deke Sharon, posted on the RARB forum, November 8, 2006, http://forum.rarb.org/forum/viewtopic.php?t=2777 (accessed February 3, 2010). In an earlier posting, Sharon alludes to an official *BOCA* prediction contest on the A-Cappella.com website, http://www.a-cappella.com, November 28, 2003, http://forum.rarb .org/forum/viewtopic.php?t=321 (accessed February 3, 2010).

5. See the RARB forum, discussion thread "ICCA Tournament Pool," January 2004, http://forum.rarb.org/forum/viewtopic.php?t=426 (accessed February 3, 2010); and "Speculation on CARA winners anyone??," March 2008, http://forum.rarb.org/ fo-rum/viewtopic.php?t=4383 (accessed February 3, 2010).

6. See, for example, RARB forum discussion threads "BOCA 2008 Tracklist," November 2007–January 2008, http://forum.rarb.org/forum/viewtopic.php?t=3957 (accessed

February 3, 2010); "BOCA 07—Reactions?," January–February 2007, http://forum
.rarb.org/forum/viewtopic.php?t=3123 (accessed February 3, 2010); and "BOCA 2006
Thoughts?," January–March 2006, http://forum.rarb.org/forum/viewtopic.php?t=2140
(accessed February 3, 2010).

7. Deke Sharon, posted on the RARB forum, October 19, 2006, http://forum.rarb
.org/forum/viewtopic.php?t=2777 (accessed February 3, 2010): "*BOCA* is not for acap-
pellaheads"; and the RARB forum, May 15, 2008, http://forum.rarb.org/forum/view-
topic.php?t=4532 (accessed February 3, 2010): "Remember, *BOCA*'s no award. It's a promotional tool for collegiate a cappella, and we'd be fools not to put (what we think is)
each year's best tracks on it."

8. Deke Sharon and Don Gooding, personal correspondence.

9. Mickey Rapkin, *Pitch Perfect: The Quest for Collegiate A Cappella Glory* (New
York: Gotham, 2008), 86.

10. Bill Hare Productions website, Awards page, http://www.dyz.com/bhp/awards
.html (accessed July 8, 2008).

11. VocalSource, posted on the RARB forum, November 23, 2009, http://forum.rarb
.org/viewtopic.php?t=5723 (accessed December 30, 2009).

12. The *Sing* series is produced by the Alliance for A Cappella Initiatives (http://
www.allforacappella.org), which also sponsors an annual a cappella festival in the
Raleigh-Durham area in North Carolina, SoJam (Southern Jam). *Top Shelf A Cappella*
was produced by the short-lived Collegiate A Cappella Music Organization, which
closed in 2007 after approximately three years. *Voices Only* was founded by Corey Slut-
sky and Brock Harris in 2004 and produced the first of its annual compilations the following year (http://www.voicesonlyacappella.com).

13. Ben Ferguson, posted on the RARB forum, April 12, 2005, http://forum.rarb.org/
viewtopic.php?t=1517 (accessed April 13, 2005).

14. CuriousGeorge, posted on the RARB forum, February 24, 2004, http://forum.rarb
.org/forum/viewtopic.php?t=513 (accessed November 17, 2004).

15. Deke Sharon, posted on the RARB forum, April 29, 2006, http://forum.rarb.org/
viewtopic.php?t=2393 (accessed February 3, 2010): "Whereas there have been some fan-
tastic advances in technology, as well as some wonderful forward motion in the use of
voices in collegiate a cappella, I don't think singers today are considerably better than
they were 20 years ago."

16. Dave Trendler writes in his RARB review of the University of Pennsylvania Penny
Loafers' album *Prophets & Pawns* (2007), "[M]ost of the rock/pop syllables on *Prophets
& Pawns* will be very familiar: 'ahh's, 'ohh's, their 'j' variations, 'jen's, 'juh's, etc.," May 14,
2008, http://www.rarb.org/reviews/801.html (accessed May 14, 2008).

17. A recording engineer could open up additional tracks in an analog session by
"bouncing" completed tracks, combining them into a single track and freeing up those
formerly occupied. But Jenny made no mention of bouncing, and given the level of
complexity of the songs on Amazin' Blue's 1992 album *Amazin' Blue's Compact Disc,* it
seems unlikely that much, if any, bouncing was done.

18. Bill Hare, posted on the RARB forum, October 16, 2005, http://forum.rarb.org/viewtopic.php?t=1891 (accessed January 27, 2006).

19. Hyperdel, posted on the RARB forum, May 22, 2005, http://forum.rarb.org/forum/viewtopic.php?t=1627 (accessed May 31, 2005).

20. Will Straw, "Authorship," in *Key Terms in Popular Music and Culture,* ed. Bruce Horner and Thomas Swiss (Malden, MA: Blackwell, 1999), 199–208.

21. Davidfourshadow, posted on the CASA forum, July 29, 2005, http://www.casa.org, discussion thread: "How Much Production Is Too Much?" (accessed October 5, 2005).

22. For example, see Carl Belz, *The Story of Rock,* 2nd ed. (New York: Oxford University Press, 1972), viii; Reebee Garofalo, "Understanding Mega-Events," in Reebee Garofalo, ed., *Rockin' the Boat: Mass Music and Mass Movements* (Boston: South End Press, 1992), 24; and Albin Zak, *The Poetics of Rock: Cutting Tracks, Making Records* (Berkeley: University of California Press, 2001), 12, 14. In contrast, David R. Shumway claims that, "although recordings have aural priority because they are the means by which any rock 'n' roll song is likely to be first and most often heard, live performance continues to be an aesthetic ideal by which recordings themselves are judged" ("Performance," in *Key Terms in Popular Music and Culture,* ed. Bruce Horner and Thomas Swiss [Malden, MA: Blackwell, 1999], 193). The debate has also surfaced in the realm of classical music recording. See Timothy Day, *A Century of Recorded Music: Listening to Musical History* (New Haven: Yale University Press, 2000).

23. Theodore Gracyk, *Rhythm and Noise: An Aesthetics of Rock* (Durham: Duke University Press, 1996), 1, 38.

24. For a critique of "overproduction," see Dylan Bell, "Dylan Bell Blog: Shiny, Happy Robots," posted on the CASA website, June 11, 2010, http://www.casa.org (accessed June 12, 2010).

25. See Joshua S. Duchan, "Collegiate A Cappella: Emulation and Originality," *American Music* 25, no. 4 (winter 2007): 477–506.

26. Matt Revely [Stixnstr], posted on the RARB forum, March 2, 2005, http://forum.rarb.org/forum/viewtopic.php?t=1402 (accessed March 13, 2005).

27. Paul D. Greene, "Introduction: Wired Sound and Sonic Cultures," in *Wired for Sound: Engineering and Technologies in Sonic Cultures,* ed. Paul D. Greene and Thomas Porcello (Middletown, CT: Wesleyan University Press, 2005), 10.

28. Rapkin, *Pitch Perfect,* 36.

29. Bill Hare, posted on the RARB forum, March 2, 2005, http://forum.rarb.org/forum/viewtopic.php?t=1402 (accessed March 13, 2005).

30. Ed Boyer, posted on the RARB forum, March 4, 2005, http://forum.rarb.org/forum/viewtopic.php?t=1402 (accessed March 13, 2005).

31. John Sullivan [jpchip], posted on the RARB forum, March 2, 2005, http://forum.rarb.org/forum/viewtopic.php?t=1402 (accessed March 28, 2006).

32. Dave Trendler, posted on the RARB forum, March 12, 2006, http://forum.rarb.org/forum/viewtopic.php?t=2218 (accessed March 28, 2006).

33. Bill Hare, posted on the RARB forum, March 2, 2005, http://forum.rarb.org/

forum/viewtopic.php?t=1402 (accessed March 13, 2005): "Last week, I mixed [the Beelzebubs'] new album [*Shedding*]. After the hubbub over *Code Red*, they were noticeably more gun[-]shy this time, to the point of using very few effects." See also Rapkin, *Pitch Perfect*, 36–40, 128.

34. Bill Hare, posted on the RARB forum, May 23, 2005, http://forum.rarb.org/forum/viewtopic.php?t=1627 (accessed May 31, 2005).

35. Dave Trendler, RARB review of University of Pennsylvania Off the Beat, *More Screaming* (2003), November 17, 2003, http://www.rarb.org/reviews/426.html (accessed January 9, 2007).

36. *Dark Side of the Moon A Cappella* (Vocomotion Records, 2005) re-creates the original Pink Floyd album with near perfect timing (the a cappella version is described as "Wizard of Oz compatible"). It was arranged by Jon Krivitzky and produced by Freddie Feldman. The singers appearing on the album—several of whom are collegiate a cappella alumni—were assembled specifically for the project (although they gave one complete live performance of the work in 2004). See http://www.darksidevoices.com (accessed July 15, 2008).

37. MattRyd, posted on the RARB forum, May 25, 2005, http://forum.rarb.org/forum/viewtopic.php?t=1627 (accessed May 31, 2005). EQ refers to equalization, a process by means of which particular frequencies are made louder or quieter.

38. Robert B. Ray, "Tracking," in *Present Tense: Rock and Roll and Culture,* ed. Anthony DeCurtis (Durham: Duke University Press, 1992), 140.

39. See Walter Everett, *The Beatles as Musicians:* Revolver *through the* Anthology (New York: Oxford University Press, 1999), 30–31, 69–71, 99–100.

40. Zak, *The Poetics of Rock,* 12. Gracyk notes that some art music composers saw similar creative possibilities in sound-recording technology, particularly those who wrote musique concrète (*Rhythm and Noise,* 42; see also 1–8).

41. Deke Sharon, posted on the RARB forum, November 21, 2007, http://forum.rarb.org/forum/viewtopic.php?t=3976 (accessed November 26, 2007).

42. Bill Hare, posted on the RARB forum, December 15, 2004, http://forum.rarb.org/forum/viewtopic.php?t=1161 (accessed December 21, 2004).

43. See Mark Lewisohn, *The Beatles: Recording Sessions* (New York: Harmony, 1988); and George Martin, with William Pearson, *With a Little Help from My Friends* (Boston: Little, Brown, 1994).

44. MattRyd, posted on the RARB forum, May 24, 2005, http://forum.rarb.org/forum/viewtopic.php?t=1627 (accessed May 31, 2005).

45. Following the struggles between music publishers and broadcasters in the 1940s and 1950s, Phillip Ennis argues, an increased emphasis was placed on new songs, which resulted in two rules for pop music producers: either create new songs that sound as similar as possible to last week's hits or create new songs that sound as different as possible from them (*The Seventh Stream: The Emergence of Rocknroll in American Popular Music* [Hanover, NH: Wesleyan University Press, 1992], 33).

46. See Zak, *The Poetics of Rock,* 70. Zak cites Peter Guralnick, *Last Train to Memphis: The Rise of Elvis Presley* (Boston: Little, Brown, 1994), 235–39.

47. H. F., posted on the CASA website, July 22, 2005, http://www.casa.org, discussion thread: "How Much Production Is Too Much?" (accessed October 5, 2005).

48. Thomas King writes in his RARB review of the University of Pennsylvania Penny Loafers' album, *Prophets & Pawns* (2007), "[B]ecause of the *higher quality of recordings overall,* the group is going to have to incorporate some stronger attention to musicality to make them stand out from the crowd" (May 14, 2008, http://www.rarb.org/reviews/801.html, accessed May 14, 2008, emphasis added). And Elie Landau writes in a RARB review of the Brandeis University Starving Artists' *Midnight Snack* (2008), "What [RARB reviewer] Mark Manley called 'mediocre from start to finish' [in his review of Starving Artists' album, *Honestly*] in 2004 is just plain poor in this day and age as the bar moves every higher for what can be considered average, let alone good or excellent collegiate a cappella (or contemporary a cappella in general for that matter)" (July 15, 2008, http://www.rarb.org/reviews/840.html, accessed July 15, 2008). Note that the perception of changing standards in recorded music not only has arisen in a cappella—or popular music in general—but has also been a feature of classical music. See Day, *A Century of Recorded Music,* 156–99.

49. Elie Landau, RARB review of the University of North Carolina Loreleis, *Take a Big Whiff* (2004), January 25, 2005, http://www.rarb.org/reviews/479.html (accessed January 9, 2007).

50. Matt Cohen, RARB review of the University of Pennsylvania Counterparts, *Afterglow* (1999), February 25, 2000, http://www.rarb.org/reviews/124.html (accessed January 9, 2007).

51. Jevan Soo, RARB review of the University of Pennsylvania Off the Beat, *Burn Like a Roman Candle* (2004), February 6, 2005, http://www.rarb.org/reviews/513.html (accessed January 9, 2007): "I have a lot of respect for Ethan Fixell '04, who I understand has shaped the musical direction of OTB quite a bit over the past few years. But keep in mind this respect is tempered by the fact that I don't actually like said direction so much. This reviewer (and the listening world more broadly) will wait with interest to see where OTB heads next."

52. I was assigned to judge the Male Collegiate, Female Collegiate, High School, and Jazz categories; I was not assigned to the Mixed Collegiate category, I suspect, due to my past and continuing performing experience with such ensembles.

53. James F. English, *The Economy of Prestige: Prizes, Awards, and the Circulation of Cultural Value* (Cambridge: Harvard University Press, 2005), 187–96.

54. Sharon is closely associated with (and an alumnus of) the Tufts University Beelzebubs, which has been selected for *BOCA* repeatedly, and occasionally serves as producer for other groups' recording projects. However, he routinely recuses himself from *BOCA* deliberations on any track that he helped to produce (such as the Beelzebubs' "The Trail," on *BOCA 2002,* and Colorado College Back Row's "Peaches" in 2007) (personal communication, May 5, 2008).

55. Peter Hollens [PHollens], posted on the RARB forum, May 4, 2005, http://forum.rarb.org/forum/viewtopic.php?t=1578 (accessed May 13, 2005). The discussion continued through May 13, with others examining the numerical judging system and brainstorming possible improvements.

56. The National Championship of High School A Cappella was founded in 2004 by Mark Suprenant as an alternative to the International Championship of High School A Cappella, a venture by Varsity Vocals (the same company that owns and administers the ICCA tournament), and once established a similar college-level competition was planned. The 2004–5 season was a rocky one, however, ending with several host groups and producers unpaid. A 2006–7 season ended with the final round, which was to be held in Orlando, Florida, canceled. See RARB forum, discussion threads: "NCHSA Payments . . . Again," June–September 2005, http://forum.rarb.org/forum/viewtopic .php?t=1724 (accessed October 1, 2005); "NCHSA Payments . . . Who'd Have Guessed," October–November 2005, http://forum.rarb.org/forum/viewtopic.php?t=1908 (accessed December 2, 2005); and "NCHSA and High School Finals . . . What the Heck Is Going On?," March–April 2007, http://forum.rarb.org/forum/viewtopic.php?t=3376 (accessed February 3, 2010).

57. English, *The Economy of Prestige*, 105: "We should . . . see the various aberrational or eccentric manifestations of the contemporary prize frenzy . . . not as signs of exhaustion or saturation, but as a measure of the cultural prize's flexibility and of the resourcefulness of those who wield it as an instrument of distinction making."

58. This final remark rehashes the common trope in popular music discourse: money can buy commercial success but not guarantee artistic worth.

59. English, *The Economy of Prestige*, 215, 240–41.

60. Some members became interested in *BOCA* after a year of conversations with me. Emily, however, was aware of both *BOCA* and an equivalent compilation of high school recordings. Most group members, however, did not seek out more information on *BOCA*.

61. Dorothy Noyes, "Group," in *Eight Words for the Study of Expressive Culture*, ed. Burt Feintuch (Urbana: University of Illinois Press, 2003), 33.

62. See Pierre Bourdieu, *The Logic of Practice* (Stanford: Stanford University Press, 1990); and David Swartz, *Culture and Power: The Sociology of Pierre Bourdieu* (Chicago: University of Chicago Press, 1997), 78–82.

63. NasonW, posted on the RARB forum, October 22, 2006, http://forum.rarb.org/ forum/viewtopic.php?t=2818 (accessed January 3, 2007).

64. Daniel Herriges [dherriges], posted on the RARB forum, October 22, 2006, http://forum.rarb.org/forum/viewtopic.php?t=2818 (accessed January 3, 2007).

65. Box_Beatin_Lady, posted on the RARB forum, December 31, 2006, http:// forum.rarb.org/forum/viewtopic.php?t=2818 (accessed January 3, 2007).

Conclusion

1. Richard Crawford, *America's Musical Life: A History* (New York: W. W. Norton, 2001), x.

2. John Blacking, "Towards an Anthropology of the Body," in *The Anthropology of the Body*, ed. John Blacking (London: Academic Press, 1977), 7–9.

3. See Judah Cohen, "'Beautiful Stories, Told in Some Very Melodic Ways': An Ethnography of Under Construction, Harvard-Radcliffe's Christian A Cappella Singing Group," unpublished graduate paper, Harvard University, 1997.

4. Jimmy Leathers, posted on the RARB forum, November 20, 2006, http://forum .rarb.org/forum/viewtopic.php?t=3976 (accessed November 26, 2007).

5. Deke Sharon, posted on the RARB forum, July 18, 2003, http://forum.rarb.org/ forum/viewtopic.php?t=64 (accessed September 20, 2009).

6. Jonathan Minkoff, RARB review of Stanford University Fleet Street Singers, *Fleet Street* (2005), June 14, 2005, http://www.rarb.org/reviews/532.html (accessed September 14, 2009); Elie Landau, RARB review of Stanford University Fleet Street Singers, *Fleet Street* (2005), June 14, 2005, http://www.rarb.org/reviews/532.html (accessed September 14, 2009).

7. See the RARB discussion entitled "Selling Arrangements," January 2010, http:// forum.rarb.org/forum/viewtopic.php?t=5846 (accessed February 15, 2010).

8. See, for example, Amy Harmon, "261 Lawsuits Filed on Music Sharing: Industry Threatens Thousands of Cases against Web Users," *New York Times,* September 9, 2003, A1.

9. See "ASCAP Launches Infringement Actions against Establishments Performing Copyrighted Music without Permission," ASCAP news release, January 24, 2005, http://www.ascap.com/press/2005/infringement_012405.html (accessed February 15, 2010). The press release notes that ASCAP had "achieved a 100% success rate with its copyright infringement litigation, with all concluded cases resulting in either a cash settlement or a judgment in favor of ASCAP members," although it "only take[s] legal action when all other means of resolution have been exhausted."

10. See Jonathan Hawkins, "Collegiate A Cappella and Music Licensing in the 21st Century," unpublished paper, Northwestern University School of Law, 2009.

11. Mickey Rapkin, *Pitch Perfect: The Quest for Collegiate A Cappella Glory* (New York: Gotham, 2008); Ben Folds, *Ben Folds Presents: University A Cappella!,* Epic 88697473012, 2009; NBC, *The Sing-Off!,* television series, December 2009. Additionally, alumni of the men's group Straight No Chaser, from Indiana University, were awarded a record contract by Atlantic Records in 2008, suggesting that at least one record company may be aware of these issues. See Mickey Rapkin, "A Cappella Dreaming: 10 Voices, One Shot," *New York Times,* October 5, 2008.

12. It bears mentioning that this commentary does not constitute professional legal advice.

13. United States Code, Title 17, Chapter 1, § 107. The Chilling Effects Clearinghouse at the George Washington University Law School has an informative website regarding fair use: http://www.chillingeffects.org/fairuse (accessed February 15, 2010).

Bibliography

Works Cited

Abbott, Lynn. "'Play That Barber Shop Chord': A Case for the African-American Origin of Barbershop Harmony." *American Music* 10, no. 3 (1992): 289–325.

"A Cappella Frenzy." *Sunday Morning*, CBS News, January 11, 2004.

"A Cappella Group Wins Championship." *University Record* (University of Michigan), May 6, 2002.

Ahlquist, Karen, ed. "Introduction." In *Chorus and Community*. Urbana: University of Illinois Press, 2006.

Alén, Olavo. "Rhythm as Duration of Sounds in Tumba Francesa." *Ethnomusicology* 39, no. 1 (1995): 55–71.

al Faruqi, Lois. "Qur'an Reciters in Competition in Kuala Lumpur." *Ethnomusicology* 31, no. 2 (1987): 221–28.

Andersen. *1989–90 Fact Book on Higher Education*. New York: Macmillan, 1989.

Anderson, Benedict. *Imagined Communities: Reflections on the Origins and Spread of Nationalism*. London: Verso, 1993.

Appadurai, Arjun. *Modernity at Large: Cultural Dimensions of Globalization*. Minneapolis: University of Minnesota Press, 1996.

Arbus, Doon. "James Brown Is Out of Sight." *New York Herald Tribune*, March 20, 1966. Reprinted in *The James Brown Reader: Fifty Years of Writing about the Godfather of Soul*, ed. Nelson George and Alan Leeds (New York: Plume, 2008).

Arenson, Karen W. "Songsters off on a Spree: Campuses Echo with the Sound of Enthusiastic A Cappella Groups." *New York Times*, April 25, 2002, E1, 4.

Askew, Kelly. *Performing the Nation: Swahili Music and Cultural Politics in Tanzania*. Chicago: University of Chicago Press, 2002.

Averill, Gage. *Four Parts, No Waiting: A Social History of American Barbershop Harmony*. New York: Oxford University Press, 2003.

Baker, Rachel. "These Are the Biggest Studs on Campus?" *Boston*, February 2007.

Bartholomew, Marshall. "The 1st 100 Years, 1861–1961: A Short History of the Yale Glee

Club." Unpublished manuscript at the Irving S. Gilmore Music Library, Yale University, Marshall Bartholomew Papers, MSS 24, Box 3, Folder 1.

Bartholomew, Marshall. "Singing for the Fun of It." Typescript at the Irving S. Gilmore Music Library, Yale University, Marshall Bartholomew Papers, MSS 24, Box 3, Folder 1.

Bartholomew, Marshall. "The Whiffenpoofs." Unpublished typescript at the Irving S. Gilmore Music Library, Yale University, Marshall Bartholomew Papers, MSS 24, Box 4, Folder 1.

Bartholomew, Marshall, ed. *Songs of Yale*. New York: Miller Music, 1935.

Barz, Gregory. "'We Are from Different Ethnic Groups, but We Live Here as One Family': The Musical Performance of Community in a Tanzanian *Kwaya*." In *Chorus and Community*, ed. Karen Ahlquist, 19–44. Urbana: University of Illinois Press, 2006.

Barz, Gregory, and Timothy Cooley, eds. *Shadows in the Field: New Perspectives for Fieldwork in Ethnomusicology*. New York: Oxford University Press, 1997.

Bayton, Mavis. "Women and the Electric Guitar." In *Sexing the Groove: Popular Music and Gender,* ed. Sheila Whiteley, 37–49. New York: Routledge, 1997.

Becker, Judith. *Deep Listeners: Music, Emotion, and Trancing*. Bloomington: Indiana University Press, 2004.

Belz, Carl. *The Story of Rock*. 2nd ed. New York: Oxford University Press, 1972.

"Ben Folds Goes A Cappella, with Help." *All Things Considered,* National Public Radio, April 26, 2009.

Bennett, H. Stith. *On Becoming a Rock Musician*. Amherst: University of Massachusetts Press, 1980.

Blacking, John. "Towards an Anthropology of the Body." In *The Anthropology of the Body,* ed. John Blacking, 1–28. London: Academic Press, 1977.

Bourdieu, Pierre. *Distinction: A Social Critique of the Judgment of Taste*. Cambridge: Harvard University Press, 1984.

Bourdieu, Pierre. "The Forms of Capital." In *Handbook of Theory and Research for the Sociology of Education,* ed. John G. Richardson, 241–58. Westport, CT: Greenwood Press, 1986.

Bourdieu, Pierre. *The Logic of Practice*. Stanford: Stanford University Press, 1990.

Bourdieu, Pierre. *Outline of a Theory of Practice*. Trans. Richard Nice. New York: Cambridge University Press, 1977.

Bourdieu, Pierre, and Loïc J. D. Wacquant. *An Invitation to Reflexive Sociology*. Chicago: University of Chicago Press, 1992.

Bower, Adam. "Sons of Adam: An A Cappella Experience." Undergraduate thesis, Kalamazoo College, 1995.

Brackett, David. *Interpreting Popular Music*. Berkeley: University of California Press, 1995.

Brinner, Benjamin. *Knowing Music, Making Music: Javanese Gamelan and the Theory of Musical Competence and Interaction*. Chicago: University of Chicago Press, 1995.

Brown, Andrew R. *Computers in Music Education: Amplifying Musicality.* New York: Routledge, 2007.

Broyles, Michael. *"Music of the Highest Class": Elitism and Populism in Antebellum Boston.* New Haven: Yale University Press, 1992.

Brucher, Kate. "A Banda da Terra: Bandas Filarmónicas and the Performance of Place in Portugal." PhD diss., University of Michigan, 2005.

Buechner, Alan Clark. *Yankee Singing Schools and the Golden Age of Choral Music in New England, 1760–1800.* Boston: Boston University Scholarly Publications, 2003.

Burnett, Robert. *The Global Jukebox: The International Music Industry.* New York: Routledge, 1996.

Burnim, Mellonee V. "Religious Music." In *African American Music: An Introduction,* ed. Mellonee V. Burnim and Portia K. Maultsby, 51–78. New York: Routledge, 2006.

Burt, Ramsay. *The Male Dancer: Bodies, Spectacle, Sexualities.* London: Routledge, 1995.

Callahan, Anna. *Anna's Amazing A Cappella Arranging Advice: The Collegiate A Cappella Arranging Manual.* Southwest Harbor, ME: Contemporary A Cappella Publishing, 1995.

Chapple, Steve, and Reebee Garofalo. *Rock 'n' Roll Is Here to Pay.* Chicago: Nelson Hall, 1977.

Christiansen, F. Melius. *Choir Director's Guide.* Boston: Charles W. Homeyer, 1932; reprint, Minneapolis: Augsburg, 1940.

Chua, Jason. "Wolverine Vocals: Detailing the History, Function, and Racial Homogeneity of A Cappella Groups in the University of Michigan." Undergraduate musicology paper, University of Michigan, 2005.

Clague, Mark. "Choral Music." In *The Encyclopedia of Chicago,* ed. James R. Grossman, Ann Durkin Keating, and Janice L. Reiff, 159. Chicago: University of Chicago Press, 2004.

Clawson, Mary Ann. "Masculinity and Skill Acquisition in the Adolescent Rock Band." *Popular Music* 18, no. 1 (1999): 99–114.

Clifford, James, and George E. Marcus, eds. *Writing Culture: The Poetics and Politics of Ethnography.* Berkeley: University of California Press, 1986.

Cohen, Judah. " 'Beautiful Stories, Told in Some Very Melodic Ways': An Ethnography of Under Construction, Harvard-Radcliffe's Christian A Cappella Singing Group." Graduate ethnomusicology paper, Harvard University, 1997.

Cohen, Sara. "Identity, Place, and the 'Liverpool Sound.' " In *Ethnicity, Identity, and Music: The Musical Construction of Place,* ed. Martin Stokes, 117–34. Oxford: Oxford University Press, 1994.

Cohen, Sara. "Men Making a Scene: Rock Music and the Production of Gender." In *Sexing the Groove: Popular Music and Gender,* ed. Sheila Whiteley, 17–36. New York: Routledge, 1997.

Comber, Helen R. "We Are Still Singing: The Musical Backgrounds and Motivations of Participants in Collegiate A Cappella Groups at One University." Bachelor's thesis, Pennsylvania State University, 2008.

Connor-Simmons, Adam. "A Cappella Groups Have Gotten People's Ears with Many a Style." *Boston Globe,* April 26, 2009.

Contemporary A Cappella Newsletter 2, no. 2 (December 1991).

Contemporary A Cappella Newsletter 2, no. 4 (April 1992).

Coyle, Michael. "Hijacked Hits and Antic Authenticity: Cover Songs, Race, and Postwar Marketing." In *Rock over the Edge: Transformations in Popular Music Culture,* ed. Roger Beebe, Denise Fulbrook, and Ben Saunders, 133–57. Durham: Duke University Press, 2002.

Crawford, Richard. *America's Musical Life: A History.* New York: W. W. Norton, 2001.

Davison, Archibald T. *Choral Conducting.* Cambridge: Harvard University Press, 1940.

Day, Timothy. *A Century of Recorded Music: Listening to Musical History.* New Haven: Yale University Press, 2000.

Decker, Harold A., and Julius Herford. *Choral Conducting: A Symposium.* Englewood Cliffs, NJ: Prentice Hall, 1973.

Doane, Randal. "Digital Desire in the Daydream Machine." *Sociological Theory* 24, no. 2 (2006): 150–69.

Duchan, Joshua S. "Collegiate A Cappella: Emulation and Originality." *American Music* 25, no. 4 (winter 2007): 477–506.

Duchan, Joshua S. "'Hide and Seek': A Case of Collegiate A Cappella 'Microcovering.'" In *Play It Again: Cover Songs in Popular Music,* ed. George Plasketes, 191–204. Burlington, VT: Ashgate, 2010.

Dudley, Shannon. "Creativity and Control in Trinidad Carnival Competitions." *The World of Music* 45, no. 1 (2003): 11–34.

Durrant, Colin. *Choral Conducting: Philosophy and Practice.* New York: Routledge, 2003.

Eichewald, Kurt. "'Doo-Wop-a-Doo' Will No Longer Do." *New York Times,* June 22, 1997, B32.

Ekman, Paul. "Biological and Cultural Contributions to Body and Facial Movement." In *The Anthropology of the Body,* ed. John Blacking, 34–84. London: Academic Press, 1977.

English, James F. *The Economy of Prestige: Prizes, Awards, and the Circulation of Cultural Value.* Cambridge: Harvard University Press, 2005.

Ennis, Philip. *The Seventh Stream: The Emergence of Rocknroll in American Popular Music.* Hanover, NH: Wesleyan University Press, 1992.

Erlmann, Veit. *Nightsong: Performance, Power, and Practice in South Africa.* Chicago: University of Chicago Press, 1996.

Everett, Walter. *The Beatles as Musicians:* Revolver *through the* Anthology. New York: Oxford University Press, 1999.

Fabian, Johannes. *Power and Performance: Ethnographic Explorations through Proverbial Wisdom and Theater in Shaba, Zaire.* Madison: University of Wisconsin Press, 1990.

Farber, Jim. "A Cappella Poised for a Serious Makeover." *New York Daily News,* April 27, 2009.

Finnegan, Ruth. *The Hidden Musicians: Music-Making in an English Town.* Cambridge: Cambridge University Press, 1989.

Fox, Aaron. *Real Country: Music and Language in Working Class Culture.* Durham: Duke University Press, 2004.

Frith, Simon. "'The Magic That Can Set You Free': The Ideology of Folk and the Myth of the Rock Community." *Popular Music* 1 (1981): 159–68.

Frith, Simon. *Performing Rites: On the Value of Popular Music.* Cambridge: Harvard University Press, 1996.

Frith, Simon. *Sound Effects: Youth, Leisure and the Politics of Rock 'n' Roll.* London: Constable, 1983.

Frith, Simon. "Towards an Aesthetic of Popular Music." In *Music and Society: The Politics of Composition, Performance, and Reception,* ed. Richard Leppert and Susan McClary, 133–50. New York: Cambridge University Press, 1987.

Frith, Simon, and Angela McRobbie. "Rock and Sexuality." *Screen Education* 29 (1978): 3–19. Reprinted in *On Record: Rock, Pop, and the Written Word,* ed. Simon Frith and Andrew Goodwin, 371–89. New York: Pantheon, 1998.

Fuller, Albert. *Alice Tully: An Intimate Portrait.* Urbana: University of Illinois Press, 1999.

Gardner, Elysa. "'Pitch Perfect': Drama a Cappella." *USA Today.* June 19, 2008. D4.

Garnett, Liz. *The British Barbershopper: A Study in Socio-musical Values.* Burlington, VT: Ashgate, 2005.

Garnett, Liz. "Ethics and Aesthetics: The Social Theory of Barbershop Harmony." *Popular Music* 18, no. 1 (1999): 41–61.

Garofalo, Reebee. *Rockin' Out: Popular Music in the USA.* Boston: Allyn and Bacon, 1997.

Garofalo, Reebee. "Understanding Mega-Events." In *Rockin' the Boat: Mass Music and Mass Movements,* ed. Reebee Garofalo, 15–36. Boston: South End Press, 1992.

Garratt, Sheryl. "Teenage Dreams." In Sheryl Garratt and Sue Steward, *Signed, Sealed, and Delivered.* London: Pluto Press, 1984. Reprinted in *On Record: Rock, Pop, and the Written Word,* ed. Simon Frith and Andrew Goodwin, 399–409. New York: Routledge, 1997.

Garretson, Robert L. *Choral Music: History, Style, and Performance Practice.* Upper Saddle River, NJ: Prentice Hall, 1993.

Garretson, Robert L. *Conducting Choral Music.* Boston: Allyn and Bacon, 1961. Reprinted in 1965, 1970, 1975, and 1981. Reprinted by Prentice Hall in 1986, 1988, 1993, and 1998.

Gay, Leslie C. "Commitment, Cohesion, and Creative Process: A Study of New York City Rock Bands." PhD diss., Columbia University, 1991.

Giesley, Markus. "Cybernetic Gift Giving and Social Drama: A Netnography of the Napster File-Sharing Community." In *Cybersounds: Essays on Virtual Music Culture,* ed. Michael D. Ayers, 21–56. New York: Peter Lang Publishing, 2006.

Gilbert, Joanne. *Performing Marginality: Humor, Gender, and Cultural Critique.* Detroit: Wayne State University Press, 2004.

Gillett, Charlie. *Making Tracks: Atlantic Records and the Growth of a Multi-Billion-Dollar Industry.* New York: E. P. Dutton, 1974.

Gillett, Charlie. *The Sound of the City: The Rise of Rock and Roll.* New York: Da Capo, 1996.

Giddens, Anthony. *The Constitution of Society: Outline of the Theory of Structuration.* Cambridge: Polity, 1984.

Goertzen, Chris. "George Cecil McLeod, Mississippi's Fiddling Senator, and the Modern History of American Fiddling." *American Music* 22, no. 3 (2004): 339–79.

Goffman, Erving. *Frame Analysis: An Essay on the Organization of Experience.* Cambridge: Harvard University Press, 1974.

Goffman, Erving. *The Presentation of Self in Everyday Life.* Woodstock, NY: Overlook Press, 1973.

Goosman, Stuart L. "The Black Atlantic: Structure, Style, and Values in Group Harmony." *Black Music Research Journal* 17, no. 1 (1997): 81–99.

Gould, Richard Nash. *Yale, 1900–2001.* Vol. 2: *The Whiffenpoofs: Twentieth Century.* New York: Twentieth Century Project, 2004.

Gracyk, Theodore. *Rhythm and Noise: An Aesthetics of Rock.* Durham: Duke University Press, 1996.

Graham, Sandra J. "Reframing Negro Spirituals in the Nineteenth Century." In *Music, American Made: Essays in Honor of John Graziano,* ed. John Koegel. Warren, MI: Harmonie Park Press, 2011.

Greene, Paul D., and Thomas Porcello. *Wired for Sound: Engineering and Technologies in Sonic Cultures.* Middletown, CT: Wesleyan University Press, 2005.

Gribin, Anthony J., and Matthew M. Schiff. *Doo-Wop: The Forgotten Third of Rock 'n Roll.* Iola, WI: Krause, 1992.

Grier, Gene. "Choral Resources: A Heritage of Popular Styles." *Music Educators Journal* 77, no. 8 (1991): 25–39.

Groia, Philip. *They All Sang on the Corner: New York City's Rhythm and Blues Vocal Groups of the 1950's.* Setauket, NY: Edmond Publishing, 1974.

Gunderson, Frank. "Preface." *The World of Music* 45, no. 1 (2003): 7–10.

Gunderson, Frank, and Gregory Barz, eds. *Mashindano! Competitive Music Performance in Tanzania.* Dar es Salaam: Mkuki wa Nyota Press, 2000.

Harmon, Amy. "261 Lawsuits Filed on Music Sharing: Industry Threatens Thousands of Cases against Web Users." *New York Times,* September 9, 2003, A1.

Harvard University Fact Book, 2004–2005. Cambridge: Office of Budgets, Financial Planning, and Institutional Research, Harvard University, 2005.

Hawkins, Jonathan. "Collegiate A Cappella and Music Licensing in the 21st Century." Unpublished paper, Northwestern University School of Law, 2009.

Hebdige, Dick. *Cut 'n' Mix: Culture, Identity, and Caribbean Music.* New York: Methuen, 1987.

Hebdige, Dick. *Subculture: The Meaning of Style.* London: Methuen, 1979.

Herbert, Trevor. *Bands: the Brass Band Movement in the 19th and 20th Centuries.* Philadelphia: Open University Press, 1991.

The History of the University of Michigan Men's Glee Club. N.p., 2003. Available on the Glee Club website, http://www.umich.edu/~ummgc. Accessed November 11, 2005.

Hitchcock, H. Wiley. *Music in the United States: A Historical Introduction*. 3rd ed. Englewood Cliffs, NJ: Prentice Hall, 1988.

Holden, Stephen. "Neil Young and Billy Joel Revisit the Roots of Rock." *New York Times*, August 7, 1983. H19.

Holland, Dorothy C., and Margaret A. Eisenhart. *Educated in Romance: Women, Achievement, and College Culture*. Chicago: University of Chicago Press, 1990.

Holst, Imogen. *Conducting a Choir: A Guide for Amateurs*. New York: Oxford University Press, 1973. Reprinted in 1990, 1993, 1995, 2000, and 2002.

Horn, David. "Some Thoughts on the Work in Popular Music." In *The Musical Work: Reality or Invention?*, ed. Michael Talbot, 14–34. Liverpool: Liverpool University Press, 2000.

Horowitz, Helen Lefkowitz. *Alma Mater: Design and Experience in the Women's Colleges from Their Nineteenth-Century Beginnings to the 1930s*. New York: Alfred A. Knopf, 1984.

Horowitz, Helen Lefkowitz. *Campus Life: Undergraduate Cultures from the End of the Eighteenth Century to the Present*. New York: Alfred A. Knopf, 1987.

Horowitz, Joseph. *The Ivory Trade: Music and the Business of Music at the Van Cliburn International Piano Competition*. New York: Summit Books, 1990.

Housewright, Wiley L., Emmett R. Sarig, Thomas MacCluskey, and Allen Hughes. "Youth Music: A Special Report." *Music Educators Journal* 56, no. 3 (1969): 43–74.

Howard, James M. "An Authentic Account of the Founding of the Whiffenpoofs." In "A History of the Whiffenpoofs of Yale University and a Roster of the Membership: Prepared for the 85th Anniversary Celebration, April 29–May 1, 1994, New Haven, Connecticut." Manuscripts and Archives, Yale University. RU 156, Ascension 2000-A-044, Box 1. Reproduced on the Whiffenpoofs website, http://www.yale.edu/whiffenpoofs. Accessed October 3, 2005.

Hyde, Bob. "Compiler's Notes." Liner notes to *The Doo Wop Box: 101 Vocal Group Gems from the Golden Age of Rock 'n' Roll*. Rhino Records compact disc 71463, 1993.

Itkin, David. "Dissolving the Myths of the Show Choir." *Music Educators Journal* 72, no. 8 (1986): 39–41.

Jackson, Ben. "Vocal Percussion: A Phonetic Description." Bachelor's thesis, Harvard University, 2001.

Johnson, Harold Earle. *Hallelujah, Amen! The Story of the Handel and Haydn Society of Boston*. Reprint with introduction by Richard Crawford. New York: Da Capo, 1981.

Johnson, Harold Earle. *History of the Handel and Haydn Society of Boston, Massachusetts*. New York: Da Capo, 1977.

Johnson, Jenna. "The Nerd Turns: A Cappella Singers Suddenly the Popular Kids on Campus." *Washington Post*, October 18, 2010.

Jones, Aled. "The Choir: A Cappella USA." BBC Radio 3, April 27, 2008.

Jurgensen, John. "Harmony 101: A Pop Pianist Recruits College Singers for a New Album of A Cappella Songs." *Wall Street Journal*, April 24, 2009, W2.

Kaplan, E. Ann. *Rocking around the Clock: Music Television, Postmodernism, and Consumer Culture.* New York: Methuen, 1987.

Karp, David A., Lynda Lytle Holmstrom, and Paul S. Gray. "Leaving Home for College: Expectations for Selective Reconstruction of Self." *Symbolic Interaction* 21, no. 3 (1998): 253–76.

Katz, Mark. *Capturing Sound: How Technology Has Changed Music.* Berkeley: University of California Press, 2005.

Keene, James A. *A History of Music Education in the United States.* Hanover, NH: University Press of New England, 1982.

Kegerreis, Richard. "The Handel Society of Dartmouth." *American Music* 4, no. 2 (1986): 177–93.

Keil, Charles. "Participatory Discrepancies and the Power of Music." *Cultural Anthropology* 2, no. 3 (1987): 275–83.

Kenney, William Howland. *Recorded Music in American Life: The Phonograph and Popular Memory, 1890–1945.* New York: Oxford University Press, 1999.

Kiner, Larry F. *The Rudy Vallée Discography.* Westport, CT: Greenwood Press, 1985.

Kingsbury, Henry. *Music, Talent, and Performance: A Conservatory Cultural System.* Philadelphia: Temple University Press, 1988.

Kipling, Rudyard. *Rudyard Kipling's Verse: Definitive Edition.* London: Hodder and Stoughton, 1940.

Kliff, Sarah. "Songs in the Key of Cheese." *Newsweek,* May 26, 2008.

Kloer, Phil. "Who Needs a Band When College Students Discover the Power of the . . . Naked Voice." *Atlanta Journal-Constitution,* April 6, 2006, D1.

Knapp, J. Merrill. "Samuel Webbe and the Glee." *Music and Letters* 33, no. 4 (1952): 346–51.

Koskoff, Ellen. "Cognitive Strategies in Rehearsal." In *Selected Reports in Ethnomusicology,* vol. 7, 59–68. Los Angeles: Department of Ethnomusicology, University of California, Los Angeles, 1988..

Lacasse, Serge. "Intertextuality and Hypertextuality in Recorded Popular Music." In *The Musical Work: Reality or Invention?,* ed. Michael Talbot, 35–58. Liverpool: Liverpool University Press, 2000.

Levy, Barbara. *Ladies Laughing: Wit as Control in Contemporary American Women Writers.* Amsterdam: Gordon and Breach, 1997.

Lewisohn, Mark. *The Beatles: Recording Sessions.* New York: Harmony, 1988.

Linn, Karen. *That Half-Barbaric Twang: The Banjo in American Popular Culture.* Urbana: University of Illinois Press, 1991.

Lucas, Christopher J. *American Higher Education: A History.* New York: St. Martin's Press, 1994.

Lysloff, René T. A., and Leslie C. Gay Jr., eds. *Music and Technoculture.* Middletown, CT: Wesleyan University Press, 2003.

Manley, Mark. *"ROOM ZERO:* The Dialectical Worlds of Live Performance and the

Recording Studio in Collegiate A Cappella." Bachelor's thesis, University of Virginia, 2002.

Mark, Michael L., and Charles L. Gary. *A History of American Music Education*. New York: Schirmer, 1992.

Marsh, J. B. T. *The Story of the Jubilee Singers, with Their Songs*. Rev. ed. New York: Negro Universities Press, 1969. Originally published Boston: Houghton, Mifflin, 1881.

Martin, Claude Trimble "Deac." In *A Handbook for Adeline Addicts: A Starter for Cold Voices and a Survey of American Balladry*. Cleveland: Schonberg Press, 1932.

Martin, George, with William Pearson. *With a Little Help from My Friends*. Boston: Little, Brown, 1994.

Matier, Philip, and Andrew Ross. "Firestorm over Yale Attack." *San Francisco Chronicle*, January 14, 2007, A1.

Matier, Philip, and Andrew Ross. "New Year's Nightmare for Visiting Yale Singers." *San Francisco Chronicle*, January 10, 2007, B1.

Matthews, Anne. *Bright College Years: Inside the American Campus Today*. New York: Simon and Schuster, 1997.

McClary, Susan. *Feminine Endings: Music, Gender, and Sexuality*. Minneapolis: University of Minnesota Press, 1991.

McCracken, Allison. "'God's Gift to Us Girls': Crooning, Gender, and the Re-creation of American Popular Song, 1928–1933." *American Music* 17, no. 4 (1999): 365–95.

McIntosh, Jane Alexander. "In Harmony: A Look at the Growth of Collegiate A Cappella Groups and the Future of the Movement." Master's thesis, Teachers College, Columbia University, 1999.

McLuhan, Marshall. *Understanding Media: The Extensions of Man*. London: Sphere Books, 1964.

McRobbie, Angela. "Settling Accounts with Subcultures: A Feminist Critique." *Screen Education* 34 (1980): 111–23. Reprinted in *On Record: Rock, Pop, and the Written Word*, ed. Simon Frith and Andrew Goodwin, 66–80. New York: Pantheon, 1990.

Meintjes, Louise. *Sound of Africa! Making Music Zulu in a South African Studio*. Durham: Duke University Press, 2003.

Miller, Jim, ed. *The Rolling Stone Illustrated History of Rock and Roll*. New York: Random House and Rolling Stone Press, 1980.

Milne, Geoff. Liner notes to *The Mills Brothers: Chronological Volume 1*. London, JSP Records, compact disc JSPCD 301, 1988.

Moe, Daniel. *Basic Choral Concepts*. Minneapolis: Augsburg, 1972.

Moffatt, Michael. *Coming of Age in New Jersey: College and American Culture*. New Brunswick, NJ: Rutgers University Press, 1989.

Monson, Ingrid. *Saying Something: Jazz Improvisation and Interaction*. Chicago: University of Chicago Press, 1996.

Montgomery, Bruce. *Brothers, Sing On! My Half-Century around the World with the Penn Glee Club*. Philadelphia: University of Pennsylvania Press, 2005.

Mook, Richard. "The Sounds of Liberty: Nostalgia, Masculinity, and Whiteness in Philadelphia Barbershop, 1900–2003." PhD diss., University of Pennsylvania, 2004.

Moore, Allan F. *Rock: The Primary Text—Developing a Musicology of Rock.* 2nd ed. Burlington, VT: Ashgate, 2001.

Morrow, Mary Sue. "Somewhere between Beer and Wagner: The Cultural and Musical Impact of German Männerchöre in New York and New Orleans." In *Music and Culture in America, 1861–1918,* ed. Michael Saffle, 79–109. New York: Garland, 1998.

"Music: Russia's Songs in the Ukraine." *New York Times,* October 1, 1922, 91.

Nannyonga-Tamusuza, Sylvia. "Competitions in School Festivals: A Process of Reinventing *Baakisimba* Music and Dance of the Baganda (Uganda)." *The World of Music* 45, no. 1 (2003): 97–118.

Negus, Keith. *Producing Pop: Culture and Conflict in the Popular Music Industry.* New York: E. Arnold, 1992.

Neuen, Donald. *Choral Concepts.* Bellmont, CA: Wadsworth, 2002.

Noyes, Dorothy. "Group." In *Eight Words for the Study of Expressive Culture,* ed. Burt Feintuch, 7–41. Urbana: University of Illinois Press, 2003.

Plasketes, George. "Re-flections on the Cover Age: A Collage of Continuous Coverage in Popular Music." *Popular Music and Society* 28, no. 2 (2005): 137–62.

Porcello, Thomas. "Sonic Artistry: Music, Discourse, and Technology in the Sound Recording Studio." PhD diss., University of Texas at Austin, 1996.

Potter, John. *Vocal Authority: Singing Style and Ideology.* New York: Cambridge University Press, 1998.

Potter, John, ed. *The Cambridge Companion to Singing.* New York: Cambridge University Press, 2000.

"Profile: Yale's A Cappella Groups Rush Current Crop of Freshmen." *Morning Edition,* National Public Radio, September 9, 2002.

Prögler, J. A. "Searching for Swing: Participatory Discrepancies in the Jazz Rhythm Section." *Ethnomusicology* 39, no. 1 (1995): 21–54.

Pruter, Robert. *Doowop: The Chicago Scene.* Urbana: University of Illinois Press, 1996.

Rapkin, Mickey. "A Cappella Dreaming: 10 Voices, One Shot." *New York Times,* October 5, 2008.

Rapkin, Mickey. "Perfect Tone, in a Key That's Mostly Minor." *New York Times,* March 23, 2008.

Rapkin, Mickey. *Pitch Perfect: The Quest for Collegiate A Cappella Glory.* New York: Gotham, 2008.

Rasmussen, Anne K. "The Qur'an in Indonesian Daily Life: The Public Project of Musical Oratory." *Ethnomusicology* 45, no. 1 (2001): 30–57.

Ray, Robert B. "Tracking." In *Present Tense: Rock and Roll and Culture,* ed. Anthony DeCurtis, 135–48. Durham: Duke University Press, 1992.

Redhead, Steve, and John Street. "Have I the Right? Legitimacy, Authenticity, and Community in Folk's Politics." *Popular Music* 8, no. 2 (1989): 177–84.

Reed, Brian. "After 160 Years, Fabled Yale Club Shuts Doors." *Weekend Edition,* National Public Radio, January 11, 2009.

Reeves, Marcus. *Somebody Scream! Rap Music's Rise to Prominence in the Aftershock of Black Power.* New York: Faber and Faber, 2008.

Regev, Motti. "Israeli Rock, or a Study in the Politics of 'Local Authenticity.'" *Popular Music* 11, no. 1 (1992): 1–14.

Reiman, Rebecca. Untitled undergraduate anthropology paper, Brandeis University, 2005.

Rheingold, Howard. *The Virtual Community: Homesteading on the Electronic Frontier.* Reading, MA: Addison-Wesley, 1993.

Robertson, Carol E. "Power and Gender in the Musical Experiences of Women." In *Women and Music in Cross-Cultural Perspective,* ed. Ellen Koskoff, 225–44. Westport, CT: Greenwood Press, 1987.

Robinson, Veronica L. S. "University of Michigan A Cappella Group Pre-concert Traditions." Undergraduate folklore paper, University of Michigan, 2005.

"Rock Reverberations." *Music Educators Journal* 56, no. 6 (1970): 3–15.

Rosalsky, Mitch. *Encyclopedia of Rhythm and Blues and Doo-Wop Vocal Groups.* Lanham, MD: Scarecrow Press, 2000.

Rose, Tricia. *Black Noise: Rap Music and Black Culture in Contemporary America.* Hanover, NH: Wesleyan University Press, 1994.

Rubin, Emmanuel. *The English Glee in the Reign of George III: Participatory Art Music for an Urban Society.* Warren, MI: Harmonie Park Press, 2003.

Russell, Melinda. "Putting Decatur on the Map: Choral Music and Community in an Illinois City." In *Chorus and Community,* ed. Karen Ahlquish, 45–69. Urbana: University of Illinois Press, 2006.

Sandman, Victor. "Boy Bands over Bach." *American Music Teacher* 54, no. 5 (2005): 40–41.

Sanjek, Roger, ed. *Fieldnotes: The Makings of Anthropology.* Ithaca, NY: Cornell University Press, 1990.

Schechner, Richard. "Toward a Poetics of Performance." In *Performance Theory.* Rev. and expanded ed., 147–78. New York: Routledge, 1988.

Shackley, George. *Close Harmony: Male Quartets, Ballads, and Funnies with Barber Shop Chords.* New York: Pioneer Music, 1925.

Shank, Barry. *Dissonant Identities: The Rock 'n' Roll Scene in Austin, Texas.* Hanover, NH: Wesleyan University Press, 1994.

Sharar, Tim J. "Eyes of the Beholder." *Music Educators Journal* 73, no. 1 (1986): 16–17.

Sharon, Deke. "Contemporary A Cappella Arranging in 10 Steps." N.p., 2000.

Shelemay, Kay Kaufman. "The Ethnomusicologist, Ethnographic Method, and the Transmission of Tradition." In *Shadows in the Field: New Perspectives for Fieldwork in Ethnomusicology,* ed. Gregory F. Barz and Timothy J. Cooley, 189–204. New York: Oxford University Press, 1997.

Shuker, Roy. *Understanding Popular Music.* 2nd ed. New York: Routledge, 2001.

Shumway, David R. "Performance." In *Key Terms in Popular Music and Culture,* ed. Bruce Horner and Thomas Swiss, 188–98. Malden, MA: Blackwell, 1999.

Slobin, Mark. *Subcultural Sounds: Micromusics of the West.* Middletown, CT: Wesleyan University Press, 1993.

Smith, Brenda, and Robert T. Sataloff. *Choral Pedagogy.* San Diego: Singular, 1999. Reprint, San Diego: Plural, 2006.

Snyder, Suzanne G. "The Indianapolis Männerchör: Contributions to a New Musicality in Midwestern Life." In *Music and Culture in America, 1861–1918,* ed. Michael Saffle, 111–40. New York: Garland, 1998.

Snyder, Thomas D. *Digest of Educational Statistics, 1993.* Washington, DC: National Center for Educational Statistics, 1993.

Solis, Ted, ed. *Performing Ethnomusicology: Teaching and Representation in World Music Ensembles.* Berkeley: University of California Press, 2004.

Solomon, Barbara Miller. *In the Company of Educated Women: A History of Women and Higher Education in America.* New Haven: Yale University Press, 1985.

Southern, Eileen. *The Music of Black Americans: A History.* 3rd ed. New York: W. W. Norton, 1997.

Spaeth, Sigmund. *Barbershop Ballads and How to Sing Them.* New York: Prentice Hall, 1940.

Spaeth, Sigmund. *A History of Popular Music in America.* New York: Random House, 1948.

Spaeth, Sigmund, ed. *Barbershop Ballads.* New York: Simon and Schuster, 1925.

Spalding, Walter Raymond. *Music at Harvard: A Historical Review of Men and Events.* New York: Coward-McCann, 1935.

SPEBSQSA, Inc. *Barbershop Arranging Manual.* Kenosha, WI: SPEBSQSA, 1980.

Stebbins, Robert A. *The Barbershop Singer: Inside the Social World of a Musical Hobby.* Toronto: University of Toronto Press, 1996.

Steward, Sue, and Sheryl Garratt. *Signed, Sealed, Delivered: True Life Stories of Women in Pop.* Boston: South End Press, 1984.

Stone, James C., and Donald P. DeNevi, eds. *Portraits of the American University, 1890 to 1910.* San Francisco: Jossey-Bass, 1971.

Stowell, Dan, and Mark D. Plumbley. "Characteristics of the Beatboxing Vocal Style." Queen Mary, University of London, Department of Electronic Engineering, Centre for Digital Music, Technical Report C4DM-TR-08-01, February 19, 2008.

Straw, Will. "Authorship." In *Key Terms in Popular Music and Culture,* ed. Bruce Horner and Thomas Swiss, 199–208. Malden, MA: Blackwell, 1999.

Street, Stacey. "Voices of Womanhood: Gender Ideology and Musical Practice in American Women's Vocal Groups." Bachelor's thesis, Harvard University, 1990.

Swartz, David. *Culture and Power: The Sociology of Pierre Bourdieu.* Chicago: University of Chicago Press, 1997.

Tannen, Deborah. *You Just Don't Understand: Women and Men in Conversation.* New York: William Morrow, 1990.

Taylor, Timothy D. *Global Pop: World Music, World Markets.* New York: Routledge, 1997.

Taylor, Timothy D. *Strange Sounds: Music, Technology, and Culture.* New York: Routledge, 2001.

Théberge, Paul. "The 'Sound' of Music: Technological Rationalization and the Production of Popular Music." *New Formations* 8 (summer 1989): 99–112.

Thelin, John R. *A History of American Higher Education.* Baltimore: Johns Hopkins University Press, 2004.

Tirrell, Meg. "A Cappella in the Digital Age." Medill Reports, Medill School of Journalism, Northwestern University, February 15, 2007.

Toop, David. *The Rap Attack: African Jive to New York Hip Hop.* London: Pluto Press, 1984.

Toynbee, Jason. *Making Popular Music: Musicians, Creativity, and Institutions.* London: Arnold, 2000.

Tucker, Sherrie. "The Prairie View Co-Eds: Black College Women Musicians and Class on the Road during World War II." *Black Music Research Journal* 19, no. 1 (1999): 93–126.

Turner, Victor. *The Ritual Process: Structure and Anti-Structure.* Chicago: Aldine, 1969.

Ulrich, Homer. *A Survey of Choral Music.* New York: Harcourt Brace Jovanovich, 1973.

Vaill, George D. *Mory's: A Brief History.* New Haven: Mory's Association, 1977.

Van Camp, Leonard. "The Rise of American Choral Music and the A Cappella 'Bandwagon.'" *Music Educators Journal* 67, no. 3 (1980): 36–40.

Vinson, Duncan. "An Ethnomusicological Study of the Chorus of Westerly, an Amateur/Volunteer Chorus in Rhode Island." PhD diss., Brown University, 2004.

Vinson, Duncan. "Liberal Religion, Artistic Autonomy, and the Culture of Secular Choral Societies." *Journal of the Society for American Music* 4, no. 3 (2010): 339–68.

Visweswaran, Kamala. *Fictions of Feminist Ethnography.* Minneapolis: University of Minnesota Press, 1994.

Waleson, Heidi. "College A Cappella!" *The Voice of Chorus America* 27, no. 4 (summer 2004): 1, 16.

Ward, Andrew. *Dark Midnight When I Rise: The Story of the Jubilee Singers, Who Introduced the World to the Music of Black America.* New York: Farrar, Straus and Giroux, 2000.

Waters, Edward. *Victor Herbert: A Life in Music.* New York: Macmillan, 1995.

Weinstein, Deena. "The History of Rock's Pasts through Rock Covers." In *Mapping the Beat: Popular Music and Contemporary Theory,* ed. Thomas Swiss, John Sloop, and Andrew Herman, 137–52. Malden, MA: Blackwell, 1998.

Whitehead, John, ed. *The Barrack-Room Ballads of Rudyard Kipling.* Shropshire: Hearthstone, 1995.

Whiteley, Sheila. *Women and Popular Music: Sexuality, Identity, and Subjectivity.* London: Routledge, 2000.

Whitson, David. "Sport and the Social Construction of Masculinity." In *Sport, Men, and the Gender Order: Critical Feminist Perspectives,* ed. Michael A. Messner and Donald F. Sabo, 19–29. Champaign, IL: Human Kinetics Books, 1990.

Who Needs a Band? NECN television network, March 15, 2010.

Wicke, Peter. *Rock Music: Culture, Aesthetics, and Sociology.* Trans. Rachel Fogg. New York: Cambridge University Press, 1987.

Williams, Sean. "Competing against 'Tradition' in the Sudanese Performing Arts." *The World of Music* 45, no. 1 (2003): 79–96.

Wodell, Frederick William. *Choir and Chorus Conducting: A Treatise on the Organization, Management, Training, and Conducting of Choirs, Choral Societies, and Other Vocal Ensembles.* Philadelphia: Theodore Presser, 1901. Reprinted in 1905, 1909, 1919, and 1931.

Wong, Deborah. *Speak It Louder: Asian Americans Making Music.* New York: Routledge, 2004.

Wrong, Charles J. "The Officiers de Fortune in the French Infantry." *French Historical Studies* 9, no. 3 (1976): 400–431.

Young, Percy. *The Choral Tradition.* Rev. ed. New York: W. W. Norton, 1962. Reprinted in 1981.

Zak, Albin. *The Poetics of Rock: Cutting Tracks, Making Records.* Berkeley: University of California Press, 2001.

Zanes, R. J. Warren. "A Fan's Notes: Identification, Desire, and the Haunted Sound Barrier." In *Rock over the Edge: Transformations in Popular Music Culture,* ed. Roger Beebe, Denise Fulbrook, and Ben Saunders, 291–310. Durham: Duke University Press, 2002.

Interviews and Correspondence

Barnathan, Julia, and Lianna Levine. Personal interview, October 3, 2004.

Callahan, Anna. Personal interview, November 12, 2004.

Cohen, Drew. Personal communication, April 11, 2007.

Cohen, Drew. Personal interview, October 5, 2004.

Cohen, Jake. Personal interview, January 13, 2005.

Curtiss, Caroline. Personal interview, December 28, 2004.

"Danielle." Personal interview, July 21, 2006.

Firestone, Ashley. Personal interview, April 13, 2005.

Fox, Laura. Personal interview, January 8, 2010.

Gooding, Don. Personal communications, January 30, 2006; July 14, 2008.

Hare, Bill. Personal communications, February 14, 2007; February 17, 2010.

Hare, Bill. Personal interviews, August 10, 2005; August 11, 2005.

Harrington, James. Personal interview, March 23, 2005.

Hsiung, Debra. Personal interview, November 12, 2004.

Kalu, Chimnomnso. Personal interview, May 27, 2005.

Kemper, Charlotte. Personal interview, May 27, 2005.

Kovac, Andrea. Personal interview, January 21, 2005.

Kraut, Larry. Personal interview, April 3, 2005.

Lesser, Kira. Personal interview, August 10, 2006.

Macholan, Christina. Personal interview, August 10, 2006.

Manley, Mark. Personal interview, March 23, 2005.

Newman, Amanda. Personal interview, July 21, 2006.

Ransom, Dave. Personal interview, February 9, 2005.

Reiman, Rebecca. Personal interview, April 13, 2005.

Rifken, Jennifer. Personal interview, November 12, 2004.

"Susan." Personal interview, February 15, 2005.

Schneider, Eli. Personal interview, September 28, 2004.

Schwartz, Mike. Personal interview, March 29, 2005.

Sharon, Deke. Personal communications, January 30, 2006; February 19, 2006; February 20, 2007; July 14, 2008; February 26, 2010.

Sharon, Deke. Personal interview, August 9, 2005.

Stone, Bill. Personal interview, March 29, 2005.

Toms, Paul. Personal interview, March 30, 2005.

Torgrimson, Emily. Personal interview, December 6, 2004.

Van Lanen, Roel. Personal interview, March 27, 2003.

Waters, Anne. Personal communication, February 15, 2007.

Waters, Anne. Personal interview, May 27, 2005.

Weinstein, Jon. Personal interview, September 23, 2004.

Zalta, Alyson. Personal interview, March 28, 2005.

Internet Sources

A-Cappella.com. "A Century of A Cappella." http://www.a-cappella.com/category/century_of_acappella. N.d. Accessed September 30, 2009.

The A Cappella Blog. http://www.acappellablog.com. Accessed February 1, 2010.

AcaTunes. http://www.acatunes.com. Accessed December 28, 2009.

Adune. Posted on the RARB forum. April 19, 2009. http://forum.rarb.org/forum/view topic.php?t=5285. Accessed April 19, 2009.

Alliance for A Cappella Initiatives. http://www.allforacappella.org. Accessed December 30, 2009.

"ASCAP Launches Infringement Actions against Establishments Performing Copyrighted Music without Permission." ASCAP news release. January 24, 2005. http://www.ascap.com/press/2005/infringement_012405.html. Accessed February 15, 2010.

Barbershop Harmony Society. http://www.barbershop.org. Accessed June 16, 2009.

Bell, Dylan. "Dylan Bell Blog: Shiny, Happy Robots." Posted on the CASA website. June 11, 2010. http://www.casa.org. Accessed June 12, 2010.

Bill Hare Productions website. http://www.dyz.com/bhp/awards.html. Accessed July 8, 2008.

Box_Beatin_Lady. Posted on the RARB forum. December 31, 2006. http://forum .rarb.org/forum/viewtopic.php?t=2818. Accessed January 3, 2007.

Boyer, Ed. Posted on the RARB forum. March 4, 2005. http://forum.rarb.org/forum/ viewtopic.php?t=1402. Accessed March 13, 2005.

Brown University Chattertocks. http://www.brown.edu/Students/Chattertocks. Accessed July 24, 2009.

bsw24. Posted on the RARB forum. April 19, 2009. http://forum.rarb.org/forum/view topic.php?t=5285. Accessed April 19, 2009.

Cannon, James. Posted on the RARB forum. April 18, 2008. http://forum.rarb.org/ forum/viewtopic.php?t=4455. Accessed December 30, 2009.

Carroll, Wes. "Can Women Do Mouthdrumming?" Posted on the Contemporary A Cappella Society website. May 19, 2005. http://www.casa.org. Accessed May 19, 2005.

Cerulo, Cooper. Posted on the RARB forum. December 10, 2005. http://forum.rarb.org/ forum/viewtopic.php?t=2038. Accessed December 30, 2009.

Chilling Effects Clearinghouse, George Washington University Law School. http:// www.chillingeffects.org/fairuse. Accessed February 15, 2010.

Chin, Mike. "Friday Factoid: The Site of the First Collegiate A Cappella Show." Posted on The A Cappella Blog. February 12, 2010. http://www.acappellablog.com/2010/02/12. Accessed February 16, 2010.

The College Board. http://www.collegeboard.com. Accessed January 8, 2010.

Cohen, Matt. RARB review of the University of Pennsylvania Counterparts, *Afterglow* (1999), February 25, 2000. http://www.rarb.org/reviews/124.html. Accessed January 9, 2007.

Cohen, Matt. RARB review of the University of Pennsylvania Counterparts, *Ten* (2001). December 14, 2001. http://www.rarb.org/reviews/268.html. Accessed December 31, 2009.

Colton, John. Posted on the RARB forum. August 29, 2009. http://forum.rarb.org/ forum/viewtopic.php?t=5523. Accessed September 2, 2009.

Contemporary A Cappella Society [of America]. http://www.casa.org. Accessed August 13, 2010.

CuriousGeorge. Posted on the RARB forum. February 24, 2004. http://forum.rarb.org/ forum/viewtopic.php?t=513. Accessed November 17, 2004.

davidcharliebrown. "The Yale Whiffenpoofs, the first collegiate a cappella group, were formed in 1909. Modern a cappella is 100 years old!" Posted on the CASA website. January 28, 2009. http://www.casa.org/node/1571. Accessed August 13, 2010.

Davidfourshadow. Posted on the CASA forum. July 29, 2005. Discussion thread: "How Much Production Is Too Much?" http://www.casa.org. Accessed October 5, 2005.

DeLaura, Mike [Doc]. Posted on RARB forum. April 16, 2006. http://forum.rarb.org/ viewtopic.php?t=2373. Accessed April 20, 2006.

Diego, Jim. "To showchoir . . . or not to showchoir. Well, a cappella ain't showchoir . . .

K?" Posted on the CASA website. April 15, 2010. http://www.casa.org. Accessed June 1, 2010.

"Early Repertoire." Yale Whiffenpoofs Alumni website. http://www.whiffalumni.com/early_repertoire. Accessed February 16, 2010.

eksingpuccusser. Posted on the RARB forum. June 10, 2005. http://forum.rarb.org/forum/viewtopic.php?t=1639. Accessed February 1, 2010.

Feldman, Michael. Posted on the RARB forum. May 30, 2005. http://forum.rarb.org/forum/viewtopic.php?t=1639. Accessed February 1, 2010.

Ferguson, Ben. Posted on the RARB forum. April 12, 2005. http://forum.rarb.org/viewtopic.php?t=1517. Accessed April 13, 2005.

GangstaisCold. Posted on the RARB forum. April 16, 2006. http://forum.rarb.org/viewtopic.php?t=2373. Accessed April 20, 2006.

Grossman, Dave. Posted on the RARB forum. April 19, 2009. http://forum.rarb.org/forum/viewtopic.php?t=5285. Accessed April 19, 2009.

H. F. Posted on the CASA forum. July 22, 2005. Discussion thread: "How Much Production Is Too Much?" http://www.casa.org. Accessed October 5, 2005.

Hare, Bill. Posted on the RARB forum. April 30, 2004. http://forum.rarb.org/forum/viewtopic.php?t=697. Accessed December 30, 2009.

Hare, Bill. Posted on the RARB forum. December 15, 2004. http://forum.rarb.org/forum/viewtopic.php?t=1161. Accessed December 21, 2004.

Hare, Bill. Posted on the RARB forum. March 2, 2005. http://forum.rarb.org/forum/viewtopic.php?t=1402. Accessed March 13, 2005.

Hare, Bill. Posted on the RARB forum. May 23, 2005. http://forum.rarb.org/forum/viewtopic.php?t=1627. Accessed May 31, 2005.

Hare, Bill. Posted on the RARB forum. October 16, 2005. http://forum.rarb.org/viewtopic.php?t=1891. Accessed January 27, 2006.

Hare, Bill. Posted on the RARB forum. April 16, 2006. http://forum.rarb.org/viewtopic.php?t=2373. Accessed April 20, 2006.

Hare, Bill. Posted on the RARB. December 29, 2009. http://forum.rarb.org/forum/viewtopic.php?t=5831. Accessed December 30, 2009.

Hare, Bill. "Recording VP? You'll Be Sorry You Asked!" Posted on the CASA website. December 12, 2005. http://www.casa.org. Accessed December 28, 2006.

Harrington, James. Posted on the RARB forum. September 27, 2004. http://forum.rarb.org/forum/viewtopic.php?t=954. Accessed January 29, 2010.

Herriges, Daniel. Posted on the RARB forum. June 4, 2006. http://forum.rarb.org/forum/viewtopic.php?t=2519. Accessed December 30, 2009.

Herriges, Daniel. Posted on the RARB forum. October 22, 2006. http://forum.rarb.org/forum/viewtopic.php?t=2818. Accessed January 3, 2007.

Herriges, Daniel. Posted on the RARB forum. August 13, 2009. http://forum.rarb.org/forum/viewtopic.php?t=5511. Accessed December 30, 2009.

Hollens, Peter [PHollens]. Posted on the RARB forum. May 4, 2005. http://forum.rarb.org/forum/viewtopic.php?t=1578. Accessed May 13, 2005.

Howard, James. "An Authentic Account of the Founding of the Whiffenpoofs." The Whiffenpoofs of Yale, Inc., website. http://www.yale.edu/whiffenpoofs. Accessed October 3, 2005.

Hyperdel. Posted on the RARB forum. May 22, 2005. http://forum.rarb.org/forum/view topic.php?t=1627. Accessed May 31, 2005.

Jennings, Brendan. Posted on RARB forum. February 1, 2005. http://forum.rarb.org/ forum/viewtopic.php?t=1282. Accessed February 1, 2005.

King, Thomas. RARB review of the University of Pennsylvania Penny Loafers, *Prophets & Pawns* (2007). May 14, 2008. http://www.rarb.org/reviews/801.html. Accessed May 14, 2008.

Landau, Elie. RARB review of the Brandeis University Starving Artists, *Midnight Snack* (2008). July 15, 2008. http://www.rarb.org/reviews/840.html. Accessed July 15, 2008.

Landau, Elie. RARB review of Stanford University Fleet Street Singers, *Fleet Street* (2005). June 14, 2005. http://www.rarb.org/reviews/532.html. Accessed September 14, 2009.

Landau, Elie. RARB review of the University of North Carolina Loreleis, *Take a Big Whiff* (2004). January 25, 2005. http://www.rarb.org/reviews/479.html. Accessed January 9, 2007.

Leathers, Jimmy. Posted on the RARB forum. November 20, 2006. http://forum .rarb.org/forum/viewtopic.php?t=3976. Accessed November 26, 2007.

LilVPboy. Posted on the Contemporary A Cappella Society forum. Topic: "Vocal Percussion"–"Naïve Question." September 26, 2005. http://www.casa.org. Accessed September 26, 2005.

Mahka. Posted on the RARB forum. January 17, 2005. http://forum.rarb.org/forum/ viewtopic.php?t=1241. Accessed December 30, 2009.

Manley, Mark. RARB review of Brandeis University Starving Artists, *Honestly* (2004). October 26, 2004. http://www.rarb.org/reviews/487.html. Accessed January 9, 2007.

MattRyd. Posted on the RARB forum. May 25, 2005. http://forum.rarb.org/forum/view topic.php?t=1627. Accessed May 31, 2005.

Miller, Michael R. Posted on the RARB forum. August 29, 2009. http://forum.rarb.org/ forum/viewtopic.php?t=5523. Accessed September 2, 2009.

Minkoff, Jonathan. RARB review of Stanford University Fleet Street Singers, *Fleet Street* (2005). June 14, 2005. http://www.rarb.org/reviews/532.html. Accessed September 14, 2009.

Moffitt, Julie. "Competition Ethics (What We Can Learn from Pick-Up Artists)." Posted on the CASA website. July 12, 2006. http://www.casa.org. Accessed July 13, 2006.

NasonW. Posted on the RARB forum. October 22, 2006. http://forum.rarb.org/forum/ viewtopic.php?t=2818. Accessed January 3, 2007.

Ng, Chris. Posted on the RARB forum. January 25, 2008. http://forum.rarb.org/ forum/viewtopic.php?t=4181. Accessed December 30, 2009.

"Origins." Yale Whiffenpoofs Alumni website. http://www.whiffalumni.com/origins. Accessed February 16, 2010.

Poe, Andy. "Amazin' Blue history." http://euclid.nmu.edu/~apoe/acappella/Amazin Blue/index.html. Accessed August 26, 2009.

RARB. "BOCA 2006 Thoughts?" October–November 2005. http://forum.rarb.org/forum/viewtopic.php?t=1925. Accessed February 3, 2010.

RARB. "BOCA 2006 Thoughts?" January–March 2006. http://forum.rarb.org/forum/viewtopic.php?t=2140. Accessed February 3, 2010.

RARB. "BOCA '07?" October–November 2006. http://forum.rarb.org/forum/viewtopic.php?t=2777. Accessed February 3, 2010.

RARB. "BOCA 07—Reactions?" January–February 2007. http://forum.rarb.org/forum/viewtopic.php?t=3123. Accessed February 3, 2010.

RARB. "BOCA 2008 Submissions." September–November, 2007. http://forum.rarb.org/forum/viewtopic.php?t=3829. Accessed February 3, 2010.

RARB. "BOCA 2008 Tracklist." November 2007–January 2008. http://forum.rarb.org/forum/viewtopic.php?t=3957. Accessed February 3, 2010.

RARB. "CARA's, BOCA, etc. . ." May 2008. http://forum.rarb.org/forum/viewtopic.php?t=4532. Accessed February 3, 2010.

RARB. "ICCA Tournament Pool." January 2004. http://forum.rarb.org/forum/viewtopic.php?t=426. Accessed February 3, 2010.

RARB. "NCHSA and High School Finals . . . What the Heck Is Going On?" March–April 2007. http://forum.rarb.org/forum/viewtopic.php?t=3376. Accessed February 3, 2010.

RARB. "NCHSA Payments . . . Again." June–September 2005. http://forum.rarb.org/forum/viewtopic.php?t=1724. Accessed October 1, 2005.

RARB. "NCHSA Payments . . . Who'd Have Guessed." October–November 2005. http://forum.rarb.org/forum/viewtopic.php?t=1908. Accessed December 2, 2005.

RARB. "Selling Arrangements." January 2010. http://forum.rarb.org/forum/viewtopic.php?t=5846. Accessed February 15, 2010.

RARB. "Speculation on CARA Winners Anyone??" March 2008. http://forum.rarb.org/forum/viewtopic.php?t=4383. Accessed February 3, 2010.

Recorded A Cappella Review Board (RARB). Information page. http://www.rarb.org/what_is_rarb.html. Accessed January 30, 2006.

Revely, Matt [Stixnstr]. Posted on the RARB forum. March 2, 2005. http://forum.rarb.org/forum/viewtopic.php?t=1402. Accessed March 13, 2005.

Sahjahpah. Posted on the RARB forum. July 28, 2005. http://forum.rarb.org/forum/viewtopic.php?t=1789. Accessed December 30, 2009.

saveit. Posted on the RARB forum. January 30, 2005. http://forum.rarb.org/forum/viewtopic.php?t=1282. Accessed February 1, 2005.

Sharon, Deke. Posted on the RARB forum. July 18, 2003. http://forum.rarb.org/forum/viewtopic.php?t=64. Accessed September 20, 2009.

Sharon, Deke. Posted on the RARB forum. November 28, 2003. http://forum.rarb.org/forum/viewtopic.php?t=321. Accessed February 3, 2010.

Sharon, Deke. Posted on the RARB forum. March 1, 2004. http://forum.rarb.org/forum/viewtopic.php?t=513. Accessed November 17, 2004.

Sharon, Deke. Posted on RARB forum. November 16, 2004. http://forum.rarb.org/forum/viewtopic.php?t=1091. Accessed March 1, 2005.

Sharon, Deke. Posted on the RARB forum. April 29, 2006. http://forum.rarb.org/viewtopic.php?t=2393. Accessed February 3, 2010.

Sharon, Deke. Posted on the RARB forum. November 8, 2006. http://forum.rarb.org/forum/viewtopic.php?t=2777. Accessed February 3, 2010.

Sharon, Deke. Posted on the RARB forum. November 21, 2007. http://forum.rarb.org/forum/viewtopic.php?t=3976. Accessed November 26, 2007.

Sharon, Deke. Posted on the RARB forum. May 15, 2008. http://forum.rarb.org/forum/viewtopic.php?t=4532. Accessed February 3, 2010.

Soo, Jevan. RARB review of the University of Pennsylvania Off the Beat, *Burn Like a Roman Candle* (2004). February 6, 2005. http://www.rarb.org/reviews/513.html. Accessed January 9, 2007.

Stevens, Benjamin. Posted on the RARB forum. April 19, 2009. http://forum.rarb.org/forum/viewtopic.php?t=5285. Accessed April 19, 2009.

Sullivan, John [jpchip]. Posted on the RARB forum. March 2, 2005. http://forum.rarb.org/forum/viewtopic.php?t=1402. Accessed March 28, 2006.

Trendler, Dave. Posted on the RARB forum. March 12, 2006. http://forum.rarb.org/forum/viewtopic.php?t=2218. Accessed March 28, 2006.

Trendler, Dave. RARB review of University of Pennsylvania Off the Beat, *More Screaming* (2003). November 17, 2003. http://www.rarb.org/reviews/426.html. Accessed January 9, 2007.

Trendler, Dave. RARB review of the University of Pennsylvania Penny Loafers, *Prophets & Pawns* (2007). May 14, 2008. http://www.rarb.org/reviews/801.html. Accessed May 14, 2008.

Trendler, Dave. RARB review of University of Wisconsin–Madison MadHatters, *Friday After Class* (2005). September 10, 2005. http://www.rarb.org/reviews/563.html. Accessed January 25, 2007.

Tufts University Beelzebubs website. http://www.bubs.com. Accessed February 16, 2010.

TyTe and Definicial. "The Real History of Beatboxing, Part 1: The Prehistory of Beatboxing." http://www.humanbeatbox.com/history. Accessed July 17, 2009.

TyTe and White Noise. "The Real History of Beatboxing, Part 2: The Old Skool." http://www.humanbeatbox.com. Accessed July 17, 2009.

VocalSource. Posted on the RARB forum. November 23, 2009. http://forum.rarb.org/viewtopic.php?t=5723. Accessed December 30, 2009.

Voices Only A Cappella. http://www.voicesonlyacappella.com. Accessed December 30, 2009.

Walker, Kurt [playdeep]. Posted on the RARB forum. November 16, 2005. http://forum.rarb.org/forum/viewtopic.php?t=1634. Accessed May 25, 2005.

WareHauser. Posted on RARB forum. April 16, 2006. http://forum.rarb.org/viewtopic.php?t=2373. Accessed April 20, 2006.

Yale University Whiffenpoofs website. http://www.whiffenpoofs.com. Accessed February 14, 2010.

Yale University Whim 'N Rhythm website. http://www.yale.edu/whim/about.html. Accessed July 9, 2009.

Songs, Scores, Discography, and Videography

Abromeit, Kathleen A. *An Index to African American Spirituals for the Solo Voice.* Westport, CT: Greenwood, 1999.

"Addicted." By Kelly Clarkson, David Hodges, and Ben Moody. Originally recorded by Kelly Clarkson. From *Breakaway.* RCA compact disc 64491, 2004. As performed by the University of Michigan Gimble.

"All I Have To Do Is Dream." By Boudleaux Bryant and Felice Bryant. Originally recorded by the Everly Brothers. Priority 9710, 1953. As performed by Brandeis University VoiceMale.

American Idol. Fox network. Television series. 2002–.

Animal House. By Douglas Kenney, Chris Miller, and Harold Ramis. Directed by John Landis. 109 min. Film. Universal City, CA, 1978.

"Are You Happy Now?" By Michelle Branch and John Shanks. Originally performed by Michelle Branch. From *Are You Happy Now?* Maverick compact disc 9362426402, 2003. As performed by Elon University Twisted Measure.

Armstrong, M. F., Helen W. Ludlow, and Thomas P. Fenner. *Hampton and Its Students, by Two of Its Teachers, Mrs. M. F. Armstrong and Helen W. Ludlow, with Fifty Cabin and Plantation Songs, Arranged by Thomas P. Fenner.* New York: G. P. Putnam's Sons, 1874.

"Band of Gold." By Ronald Dunbar and Edyth Wayne. Originally recorded by Frieda Payne. Invictus ST-7301, 1970. As performed by the Harvard Fallen Angels.

The Beatles. *Sgt. Pepper's Lonely Hearts Club Band.* Parlophone LP 46442, 1967.

Beat Street. By Steven Hager, Andrew Davis, David Gilbert, and Paul Golding. Directed by Stan Lathan. 105 min. Film. Santa Monica, MGM, 1984.

"Beautiful." By Tony Rabalao. Originally recorded by Joydrop. From *Metasexual.* Tommy Boy 1237, 1998. As performed by the University of California Sirens.

The Big Broadcast. By William Ford Manley and George Marion Jr. Directed by Frank Tuttle. 80 min. Film. Hollywood, Paramount Pictures, 1932.

"Big Girls Don't Cry." By Frankie Valli and the Four Seasons. From *Big Girls Don't Cry and Twelve Others.* Vee-Jay 1056, 1962.

Boston University Treblemakers. . . . *And We're Back.* 2002.

Boston University Treblemakers. *Not Gonna Lie . . .* 2007.

"Boy From New York City." By George Davis and John T. Taylor. Originally performed by The Manhattan Transfer. From *Mecca for Moderns.* Atlantic 16036, 1981.

Boyz II Men. *Cooleyhighharmony.* Motown 6320, 1991.

Brandeis University Starving Artists. *Honestly.* 2004.

Brandeis University VoiceMale. *Propeller.* 2003.

Carroll, Wes. *Mouthdrumming.* Vol. 1: *Introduction to Vocal Percussion.* Videocassette and DVD, Southwest Harbor, ME, Mainely A Cappella, 1988.

"Chattanooga Choo Choo." By Mack Gordon and Harry Warren. As performed by the University of North Carolina Clef Hangers.

"Comrades In Arms." By Thomas Adams (1785–1858).

"Daddy's All Gone." By James Taylor. From *In the Pocket.* Warner Bros. 2912, 1976. As performed by the University of Pennsylvania Counterparts.

"December 1963 (Oh What A Night)." By Bob Gaudio and Judy Parker. Originally performed by Franki Valli and the Four Seasons. From *Who Loves You.* Curb Records 77713, 1975. As performed by the University of Michigan Amazin' Blue.

"Don't Worry, Be Happy." By Bobby McFerrin. From *Simple Pleasures.* EMI compact disc 48059, 1988.

"An Englishman In New York." By Sting. From *Ten Summoner's Tales.* A&M compact disc 540070, 1993. As performed by the University of Michigan Amazin' Blue.

"Everything She Wants." By George Michael. Originally performed by Wham! From *Make It Big.* Columbia CK-39595, 1984. As performed by the Wesleyan University Spirits.

"Falling Over You." By Sean Altman and Billy Straus. Recorded by Rockapella. From *Primer* (1995). Later released on *Rockapella* (For Life compact disc 3503, 1999). As performed by Brandeis University VoiceMale.

Folds, Ben. *Ben Folds Presents: University A Cappella!* Epic compact disc 88697473012, 2009.

"The Girl from Ipanema." By Vinicius de Moraes, Norman Gimbel, and Antonio Carlos Jobim. From *The Composer Desafinado, Plays.* Verve V6-8547, 1963. As performed by the Yale University Whiffenpoofs.

Glee. Fox network. Television series. 2009–.

"Harder to Breathe." By Jesse Carmichael and Adam Levine. Originally recorded by Maroon 5. From *Songs About Jane.* Octone 50001, 2002. As performed by the Boston University Dear Abbeys.

"Helter Skelter." By John Lennon and Paul McCartney. Originally recorded by the Beatles. From *The Beatles.* Capitol 000131, 1968. Recorded by the Bobs on *The Bobs.* Kaleidoscope F-18, 1983.

"Hey You." By Roger Waters. Originally recorded by Pink Floyd. From *The Wall.* Columbia H2C-46183, 1983. As performed by the Tufts University Beelzebubs.

"How Sweet It Is (To Be Loved By You)." By Lamont Dozier and Brian Holland. Originally recorded by Marvin Gaye. Motown 11004, 1964. As performed by the University of Michigan Amazin' Blue.

"Human Nature." By Steven Porcaro and John Bettis. Originally recorded by Michael Jackson. From *Thriller.* Epic QE-38112, 1982. Also recorded by Boyz II Men on

Throwback (Koch/MSM Music Group compact disc 5735, 2004). As performed by Brandeis University VoiceMale.

"I Don't Know Where I Stand." By Joni Mitchell. From *Clouds*. Reprise 6341, 1969. As performed by the Yale University Whiffenpoofs.

"If I Ever Lose My Faith In You." By Sting. From *Ten Summoner's Tales*. A&M 540070, 1993. As performed by the University of Michigan Amazin' Blue.

"Insomniac." By Kristian Bush. Originally recorded by Billy Pilgrim. From *Billy Pilgrim*. Atlantic 82515-2, 1994. As performed by the University of Virginia Gentlemen.

"Instant Pleasure." By Seth Swirsky. Originally recorded by Rufus Wainwright. From the *Big Daddy* soundtrack. Sony 69949, 1999. As performed by the Boston University Treblemakers.

"In the Still of the Nite." By Fred Parris. Originally recorded by the Five Satins. Ember 1005, 1956. Later recorded by Dion DiMucci on *Wish Upon a Star* (Laurie P-2006, 1959), the Crests on *The Crests Sing All Biggies* (CoEd 901, 1960), the Del Vikings on *Come Go With Me* (Dot DP-35695, 1966), and Paul Anka on *Goodnight My Love* (RCA 4142, 1969).

"It's So Hard To Say Goodbye To Yesterday." By Freddie Perren and Christine Yarian. Originally recorded by Boyz II Men. From *Cooleyhighharmony*. Motown 6320, 1991.

"I've Been a-List'ning All de Night Long." Spiritual. First published: T. F. Seward. *Jubilee Songs*. Chicago: Bigelow and Main, 1872.

"I've Got a Right." By Oleta Adams. From *Circle of One*. Fontana 846346-2, 1989. As performed by the University of Pennsylvania Counterparts.

"I Want You Back." by Berry Gordy Jr., Alphonso Mizell, Freddie Perren, and Deke Richards. Originally recorded by the Jackson 5. Motown 715, 1963. As performed by the Yale University Duke's Men.

"Kiss Him Goodbye." By Gary DeCarlo, Dale Frashuer, and Paul Leka. Originally recorded by Steam on *Happy Together*. Windham Hill 306, 1987. As recorded by the Nylons.

"Kyrie." By Steve George, John Lang, and Martin Page. Originally recorded by Mr. Mister. From *Welcome To the Real World*. RCA 89647, 1985. As performed by the University of Michigan Amazin' Blue.

"The Last Cigar." Poem by Joseph Warren Fabens. Published in *"The Last Cigar" and Other Poems*, 9–10. New York: M. L. Holbrook, 1887. Musical setting published in the *Yale Song Book: Compiled from Yale Songs, Yale Glees, and Yale Melodies*. New York: G. Shirmer, 1906.

"Let It Be." By John Lennon and Paul McCartney. Originally performed by the Beatles. From *Let It Be*. Parlophone 7464472, 1970. As performed by the Yale University Whiffenpoofs.

"Let Me Entertain You." By Guy Chambers and Robbie Williams. Originally recorded by Robbie Williams. From *Life Thru a Lens*. Chrysalis compact disc 6127, 1997. As performed by Brandeis University VoiceMale.

"The Longest Time." By Billy Joel. From *An Innocent Man.* Columbia HC-48837, 1983.

"Magic Carpet Ride." By John Kay and Rushton Moreve. Originally recorded by Steppenwolf. From *Steppenwolf the Second.* Dunhill DS-50037, 1968. As performed by Brandeis University VoiceMale.

Manhattan Transfer. *Mecca for Moderns.* Atlantic 16036, 1981.

"Mavourneen." Adapted from "Barney O'Flynn." From *Babes in Toyland* (1903). Music by Victor Herbert. Lyrics by Glen MacDonough.

McFerrin, Bobby. *Simple Pleasures.* EMI 48059, 1988.

McFerrin, Bobby. *The Voice.* Elektra 60366, 1984.

Mean Girls. By Tina Fey. Directed by Mark Waters. 96 min. Film. Hollywood, Paramount Pictures, 2004.

"Midnight Train to Georgia." By Jim Weatherly. Originally performed by Gladys Knight and the Pips. From *Imagination.* Buddah 5141, 1973. As performed by the Yale University Whiffenpoofs.

"Mr. Roboto." By Dennis DeYoung. Originally recorded by Styx. From *Kilroy Was Here.* A&M 75021-3734-2, 1983. As performed by the Tufts University Beelzebubs.

"My Evalyne." By Mae Auwerda Sloane. 1901.

"My Sharona." By Berton Averre and Doug Fieger. Originally recorded by the Knack. From *Get the Knack.* Capitol C4-91848, 1979. As performed by the Boston University Treblemakers.

Napoleon Dynamite. By Jared and Jerusha Hess. Directed by Jared Hess. 95 min. Film. Beverly Hills, Twentieth Century-Fox, 2004.

"Only You." By Vince Clarke. Originally recorded by Yaz. From *Upstairs at Eric's.* Sire 2-23737, 1987.

"The Owl and the Pussy Cat." By Reginald DeKoven. Musical score. New York: Schirmer MV-0140, 1889.

"Pehchaan." By Penn Masala. Originally recorded on *Pehchaan.* 2008.

"Raindrops Keep Fallin' On My Head." By Burt Bacharach and Hal David. Originally performed by B. J. Thomas. From *The Sound of Bacharach.* Westside Records 894, 1965. As performed by the Yale University Whiffenpoofs.

Raugh, Anne, and Deke Sharon. *Contemporary A Cappella Songbook.* 2 vols. Milwaukee, WI: Hal Leonard, 1995.

"Renegade." By Tommy Shaw. Originally recorded by Styx. From *Pieces of Eight.* A&M 4724, 1978. As performed by the Boston University Dear Abbeys.

Rockapella. *Primer.* 1995.

Rundgren, Todd. *A Capella.* Warner Bros. 9251281, 1985.

Seward, T. F. *Jubilee Songs.* Chicago: Bigelow and Main, 1872.

"Shall I, Wasting in Despair." By George Wither and George A. Barker. 1861.

"Sherry." By Frankie Valli and the Four Seasons. From *Sherry and 11 Others.* Vee-Jay 1053, 1962.

"She Will Be Loved." By A. Levine and J. Valentine. Originally recorded by Maroon 5. From *Songs About Jane*. Octone compact disc 50001, 2002. As performed by the Boston University Treblemakers.

"The Show." By Doug E. Fresh. From *Oh My God!* Reality Entertainment LP F-9649, 1986.

Simon, Paul. *Graceland*. Warner Bros. compact disc 46430-2, 1986.

The Sing-Off. NBC network. Television series. 2009–.

"Sixty Minute Man." Originally recorded by the Dominoes. Federal 12022, 1951.

"Slumber." By Gabriel Mann. Originally performed by Gabriel Mann. From *Tug of War*. BigHelium Records compact disc 691045924224, 2002. Recorded by the University of Southern California SoCal VoCals on *The SoCal VoCals* (2004). Also featured on *BOCA 2004* (2004).

Spike & Co.: Do It A Cappella. By Spike Lee and Debbie Allen. 86 min. Video. Electra Video, New York, 1990.

Stanford University Fleet Street Singers. *Fleet Street*. 2005.

Stanford University Talisman. *Passage*. 2004.

"Things I'll Never Say." By Avril Lavigne and Matrix. Originally recorded by Avril Lavigne. From *Let Go*. Arista compact disc 14740, 2002. As performed by the Harvard University Fallen Angels.

"Tiger Rag." By Harry DaCosta, Eddie Edwards, James LaRocca, Henry Ragas, Tony Sbarbaro, and Larry Shields. Recorded by the Mills Brothers, 1931 and 1932. Recordings appear on *The Mills Brothers: Chronological, Vol. 1*. Storyville compact disc 3011, 2000.

Tufts University Beelzebubs. *Code Red*. 2003.

Tufts University Beelzebubs. *Foster Street*. 1991.

Tufts University Beelzebubs. *Pandæmonium*. 2007.

Tufts University Beelzebubs. *Shedding*. 2005.

"Turn the Beat Around." By Pete Jackson and Gerald Jackson. Originally performed by Gloria Estefan. From *Hold Me, Thrill Me, Kiss Me*. Epic compact disc 66205, 1994.

University of Michigan Amazin' Blue. *Amazin' Blue's Compact Disc*. 1992.

University of Michigan Amazin' Blue. *Lost In Sound*. 2008.

University of North Carolina Clef Hangers. *Safari*. 1992.

University of Pennsylvania Counterparts. *Afterglow*. CP0008, 1999.

University of Pennsylvania Counterparts. *Ten*. CP010, 2001.

University of Pennsylvania Off the Beat. *Burn Like a Roman Candle*. 2004.

Various artists. *Best of College A Cappella I*. Mainely A Cappella compact disc, 1995.

Various artists. *Best of College A Cappella II*. Mainely A Cappella compact disc, 1996.

Various artists. *Best of College A Cappella 2K*. Varsity Vocals compact disc MAC1801, 2000.

Various artists. *Best of College A Cappella 2002*. Varsity Vocals compact disc MAC1806, 2002.

Various artists. *Best of College A Cappella 2003.* Varsity Vocals compact disc VV1807, 2003.

Various artists. *Best of College A Cappella 2004.* Varsity Vocals compact disc VV1808, 2004.

Various artists. *Best of College A Cappella 2005.* Varsity Vocals compact disc VV1809 2005.

Various artists. *Best of College A Cappella 2006.* Varsity Vocals compact disc VV1811, 2006.

Various artists. *Best of College A Cappella 2008.* Varsity Vocals compact disc VV1813, 2008.

Various artists. *Dark Side of the Moon A Cappella.* Vocomotion Records compact disc, 2005.

"Velia." By Franz Lehar. English translation by Adrian Ross. From *The Merry Widow.* 1905. Also known as "The Vilja Song."

"Waiting In Vain." By Bob Marley. From *Exodus.* Tuff Gong 9498, 1977. As performed by the Yale University Whiffenpoofs.

"Waiting In Vain." By Bob Marley. As performed by Annie Lennox. From *Medusa.* Arista compact disc 25717, 1995. As performed by the Yale University Whiffenpoofs.

"The Wanderer." By M. Broussard and M. Altman. From *Carencro.* Island Records compact disc B0002938-02, 2004. As performed by the University of Michigan Amazin' Blue.

"(We're Gonna) Rock Around the Clock." By Max Freedman and James E. Myers [as Jimmy DeKnight]. Originally performed by Bill Haley and His Comets. Decca, 1954.

West Side Story. By Leonard Bernstein. Book by Arthur Laurents. Lyrics by Stephen Sondheim. New York: Random House, 1958.

"What a Good Boy." By Steven Page and Ed Robertson. Originally recorded by Barenaked Ladies. From *Gordon.* Reprise compact disc 26956, 1992. As performed by the Yale University Duke's Men.

"When It Don't Come Easy." By Patty Griffin. From *Impossible Dream.* Ato 21520, 2004. As performed by the Boston University Treblemakers.

"Where in the World Is Carmen Sandiego?" By Sean Altman and David Yazbek. Originally recorded by Rockappella. From *Where in the World Is Carmen Sandiego?* Zoom Express compact disc 30018, 1992.

The "Whiffenpoof Song." Based on the poem "Gentlemen-Rankers," by Rudyard Kipling (1892). Music by Tod Galloway and Guy H. Scull (?). Words by Meade Minnegerode and George S. Pomeroy. Originally published New York: Miller Music, 1936. Later published in Marshall Bartholomew, *Songs of Yale,* 16th ed., 50–52. New York: G. Schirmer, 1953. As performed by the Yale University Whiffenpoofs.

"Work With Me Annie." Originally recorded by the Midnighters. Federal 12169, 1953.

Yale Song Book: Compiled from Yale Songs, Yale Glees, and Yale Melodies. New York: G. Shirmer, 1906. Earlier copyright dates: 1882, 1885, 1889, 1893, 1903.

Yale University Whiffenpoofs. *The Whiffenpoofs of 1958.* LP, 1958.

"Yeah!" By Chris Bridges, Sean Garrett, LaMarquis Mark Jefferson, Robert "Rob" McDowell, James Phillips, Jonathan Smith, and Smith Patrick J. Que. Originally recorded by Usher on *Confessions*. Arista compact disc, 52141, 2004. As performed by the University of Oregon Divisi.

"Your Smiling Face." By James Taylor. From *JT*. Columbia 69801, 1977. As performed by the Tufts University Beelzebubs.

Zoolander. By John Hamburg, Drake Sather, and Ben Stiller. Directed by Ben Stiller. 89 min. Film. Hollywood, Paramount, 2001.

Index

Note: Collegiate a cappella groups are listed by their name, followed by the name of their college or university in parentheses. Albums are listed by title, followed by the name of the performing group in parentheses. Songs are listed by title, followed by the principal performers discussed in the text in parentheses (if applicable).

Made in United States
North Haven, CT
30 August 2022

23471014R00161